ARBITRARY JUSTICE

ARBITRARY JUSTICE

THE POWER OF
THE AMERICAN PROSECUTOR

ANGELA J. DAVIS

OXFORD
UNIVERSITY PRESS

2007

OXFORD
UNIVERSITY PRESS

Oxford University Press, Inc., publishes works that further
Oxford University's objective of excellence
in research, scholarship, and education.

Oxford   New York
Auckland   Cape Town   Dar es Salaam   Hong Kong   Karachi
Kuala Lumpur   Madrid   Melbourne   Mexico City   Nairobi
New Delhi   Shanghai   Taipei   Toronto

With offices in
Argentina   Austria   Brazil   Chile   Czech Republic   France   Greece
Guatemala   Hungary   Italy   Japan   Poland   Portugal   Singapore
South Korea   Switzerland   Thailand   Turkey   Ukraine   Vietnam

Copyright © 2007 by Oxford University Press, Inc.

Published by Oxford University Press, Inc.
198 Madison Avenue, New York, New York 10016

www.oup.com

Oxford is a registered trademark of Oxford University Press

Library of Congress Cataloging-in-Publication Data
Davis, Angela J., 1956–
Arbitrary justice : the power of the American prosecutor / Angela J. Davis.
p. cm.
Includes bibliographical references and index.
ISBN 978-0-19-517736-7
1. Public prosecutors—United States.   2. Prosecution—Decision making—United States.
I. Title.
KF9640.D38 2007
345.73'01—dc22   2006026096

3 5 7 9 8 6 4

Printed in the United States of America
on acid-free paper

To Howard Davis, my husband and the love of my life

ACKNOWLEDGMENTS

I grew up in the segregated South and learned about injustice at a very early age. I guess I've spent most of my life being angry about one injustice or another. Many people along the way have been instrumental in showing me how to fight injustice and supporting me in the fight. My brilliant and beautiful sisters Jackie Jordan Irvine, Jennifer Jordan, and Patricia Jordan Van Dyke figure most prominently. They were students at Howard University during the 60s when I was growing up in Phenix City, Alabama, and were the greatest influence on my thinking and development when I was a child. They still are.

I was the only African American in my high school graduating class at Brookstone School in Columbus, Georgia, and my high school teachers Nan Rainwater and Dale Smith inspired, encouraged, and protected me through some difficult times. At Howard University, my professors Adolph Reed, Ronald Walters, Sharon Banks, and Jennifer Jordan (my sister), significantly shaped my thinking and writing. At Harvard Law School, Professor Derrick Bell kept my spirit alive.

My years at the Public Defender Service for the District of Columbia (PDS) were perhaps the most formative in my development as a lawyer and advocate for the disadvantaged. The work I did there was the most important work I have ever done or will ever do, and I am forever grateful to all of the lawyers and clients with whom I worked. I especially thank Charles Ogletree, Frank Carter, Michele Roberts, Rhonda Reid Winston, Kim Taylor-Thompson, and James McComas for teaching me how to try a case and James Berry, Cynthia Lester, and the late Deborah Creek for their support and guidance during my years at PDS. I thank all the lawyers and support staff who have ever worked at PDS and those who continue to fight the good fight.

I could not have written this book without the help of many people. I am grateful to them all. I thank the following people who either read early drafts of chapters, participated in interviews, answered questions, and/or provided advice: Norman Bay, Barbara Bergman, Elizabeth Branda, Stephen Bright, Paul Butler, Susan Carle, Julian Cook, Richard Dieter, Peter Gilchrist, Bernie Grimm, Julie Grahofsky, Vanita Gupta, Laura Hankins, Lenese Herbert, Elizabeth Herman, H. Marshall Jarrett, Tim Junkin, George Kendall, James Klein, Niki Kuckes, Ellen Kreitzberg, Milton C. Lee, Julia Leighton, Sandra Levick, Michael McCann, James McComas, Gwendolyn McDowell, Wayne McKenzie, Robert Morin, Olinda Moyd, Ellen Podgor, Michele Roberts, Stephen Saltzburg, Tim Silard, Santha Sonenberg, Kim Taylor-Thompson, Anthony Thompson, and Gladys Weatherspoon. I also thank the many dean's fellows who provided excellent research assistance over the years, including Aku Aghazu, Kelly Barrett, Ebise Bayisa, Duane Blackman, Joseph Caleb, Jesse Campbell, Timothy Curry, Jennifer Davis, Melissa Davis, Jennifer Farer, Lauryn Fraas, Kate Goldstein, Nicholas Hankey, Timothy Harris, Molly Hostetler, Elizabeth Janelle, and Tara Kelly. My gratitude goes to David Cole, Congressman Jesse Jackson, Jr., Michael McCann, Charles Ogletree, Barry Scheck, and Frank Watkins for their kind words and encouragement; to Marc Mauer, Tracey Meares, Spencer Overton, and Katheryn Russell-Brown for providing invaluable advice during the book-writing process; to Althea Mundle and Kathy Perkins Scott for keeping me together; and to Hilary Schwab for her amazing photographic skills.

I am grateful to all of my colleagues at the Washington College of Law and to Dean Claudio Grossman, for his support, financial and otherwise, throughout this process. James May, Mark Niles, Michael Tigar, and Tony Varona gave me great advice and encouragement, and the strength to make a number of important decisions about the book along the way. Jeff Barsky, Walter Crawford, Mark Burrowes, and Elma Gates provided great administrative and technical support. I especially thank Mark for finding my book in a crashed laptop and introducing me to flashdrives! I would not have survived the process without the Jet Historical Society (you know who you are), especially Trishana Bowden, Brenda Smith, Sherry Weaver, and Barbara Williams. Jamin Raskin, as always, was one of my greatest inspirations and provided wonderful advice and support from day one. A special debt of gratitude is owed to my dear friend and colleague, Cynthia Jones, who with her brilliance, expansive knowledge, and incredible sense of humor, advised and inspired me daily and helped me conceptualize so many of the ideas in this book.

I thank the Open Society Institute, not only for the financial support, but for continued support throughout the process. I also thank my editors at Oxford University Press, James Cook and Dedi Felman, for their great advice, assistance, and support. I am the most grateful to Carol Steiker, who took time from her own important work, to push me to write a better book. She forced me to calm down and take a deep breath and provided critical guidance and very clear direction. I will remain forever appreciative to Carol for the advice I took and the advice I didn't take but probably should have.

Last but not least, I thank my incredible family: my wonderful husband Howard who never complained when I spent countless days and evenings in front of my laptop; my talented and creative daughter Zahra Davis, who is a much better writer than I am; my stepdaughters Erica and Aasha Davis; my son-in-law Jesse Pforzheimer; my aforementioned sisters Jackie, Jennifer, and Pat; my niece Kelli Neptune, a PDS alumnus and brilliant trial lawyer who provided invaluable information for the book; my nephew, Lionel Neptune, who promoted the book in so many important ways from the very beginning; all of my wonderful nieces and nephews; and my parents Eddie Jordan and the late Sarah Harris Jordan, who both still watch over me.

For the sake of privacy, the names of the prosecutors, lawyers, judges, clients, and others in the stories and cases I discuss in this book are pseudonyms unless they were reported in published cases or widely reported in the media.

CONTENTS

ARBITRARY JUSTICE

ONE

Prosecutorial Discretion:
Power and Privilege

Delma Banks was convicted of capital murder in Texas and sentenced to death. Just ten minutes before he was scheduled to die, the United States Supreme Court stopped his execution and a year later reversed his sentence. The Court found that the prosecutors in his case withheld crucial exculpatory evidence.

Dwayne Washington was charged with assault with intent to kill and armed burglary in the juvenile court of Washington, D.C. Two adults were arrested with Dwayne and prosecuted in adult court. The prosecutors in the adult cases threatened to charge Dwayne as an adult if he refused to testify against the adults. When Dwayne said he could not testify against them because he didn't know anything about the crime, the prosecutors charged him as an adult, and he faced charges that carried a maximum sentence of life in an adult prison.

Andrew Klepper lived in Montgomery County, a suburb of Washington, D.C. He was arrested for attacking a woman with a baseball bat, sodomizing her at knifepoint with the same bat, and stealing over $2,000 from her. The prosecutors in his case agreed to a plea bargain in which Andrew would plead guilty to reduced charges. As part of the agreement, Andrew would be placed on probation and sent to an out-of-state facility for severely troubled youth, where he would be in a locked facility for six to eight weeks, followed by intensive group therapy in an outdoor setting. Andrew's parents—a lawyer and a school guidance counselor—agreed to foot the bill. Andrew's two accomplices—whose involvement in the crime was much less serious than Andrew's—each served time in jail.

All three of these cases illustrate the wide-ranging power and discretion of the American prosecutor. In each case, the prosecutor's actions profoundly affected the lives of the accused. Mr. Banks was almost executed by the state of Texas before the Supreme Court reversed his conviction. When Dwayne Washington told prosecutors he couldn't help them, they followed through on their threat to charge him as an adult and he faced charges that carried a life sentence in adult prison. The favorable treatment afforded Andrew Klepper allowed him to avoid prison after committing a violent sex offense—a rare occurrence in these types of cases.

The Supreme Court ultimately found that the prosecutors in Mr. Banks's case engaged in misconduct by failing to turn over exculpatory evidence, but the prosecutors were neither punished nor reprimanded. A trial judge found the prosecutor's behavior in Dwayne Washington's case to be vindictive and dismissed the charges against him. The prosecutor's decision in Andrew Klepper's case was never challenged; in fact, there was no legal basis for doing so.

I was a public defender at the Public Defender Service for the District of Columbia (PDS) for twelve years.[1] It was then that I learned of the formidable power and vast discretion of prosecutors. During my years at PDS, I noticed that prosecutors held almost all of the cards, and that they seemed to deal them as they saw fit. Although some saw themselves as ministers of justice and measured their decisions carefully, very few were humbled by the power they held. Most wanted to win every case, and winning meant getting a conviction. In one of its more famous criminal cases,[2] the U.S. Supreme Court, quoting a former solicitor general, stated that "the Government wins its point when justice is done in its courts."[3] A paraphrased version of this quotation is inscribed on the walls of the U.S. Department of Justice: "The United States wins its point whenever justice is done its citizens in the courts."[4] Yet most prosecutors with whom I had experience seemed to focus almost exclusively on securing convictions, without consideration of whether a conviction would result in the fairest or most satisfactory result for the accused or even the victim.

During my years as a public defender, I saw disparities in the way prosecutors handled individual cases. Cases involving educated, well-to-do victims were frequently prosecuted more vigorously than cases involving poor, uneducated victims. The very few white defendants represented by my office sometimes appeared to receive preferential treatment from prosecutors. Although I saw no evidence of intentional discrimination based on race or class, the consideration of class- and race-neutral factors in the prosecutorial process often produced disparate results along class and race lines.

Sometimes neither race nor class defined the disparate treatment. At times it simply appeared that two similarly situated people were treated differently. Why did the prosecutor choose to give a plea bargain to one defendant and not another charged with the same offense? If there were a difference in prior criminal history or some other relevant factor, the disparate treatment would be explainable. But without a difference in the legitimate factors that prosecutors are permitted to consider in making these decisions, the disparities seemed unfair. Yet I saw such disparities all the time.

Prosecutors are the most powerful officials in the criminal justice system.[5] Their routine, everyday decisions control the direction and outcome of criminal cases and have greater impact and more serious consequences than those of any other criminal justice official. The most remarkable feature of these important, sometimes life-and-death decisions is that they are totally discretionary and virtually unreviewable. Prosecutors make the most important of these discretionary decisions behind closed doors and answer only to other prosecutors. Even elected prosecutors, who presumably answer to the electorate, escape accountability, in part because their most important responsibilities— particularly the charging and plea bargaining decisions—are shielded from public view.

When prosecutors engage in misconduct, as in the cases of Delma Banks and Dwayne Washington, they rarely face consequences for their actions. Delma Banks almost lost his life, and Dwayne Washington lost his liberty and suffered the many other damaging effects of criminal prosecution, but their prosecutors just moved on to the next case. As for Andrew Klepper, perhaps he should have been afforded the opportunity to receive treatment and rehabilitation, but fairness demands that other similarly situated youth receive the same or similar opportunities. Current laws and policies do not require equitable treatment.

DISCRETION—A NECESSARY EVIL

Prosecutors certainly are not the only criminal justice officials who make important, discretionary decisions. Discretion is a hallmark of the criminal justice system, and officials at almost every stage of the process exercise discretion in the performance of their duties and responsibilities. In fact, without such discretion, there would be many more unjust decisions at every stage of the criminal process. A system without discretion, in which police, judges, and prosecutors were not permitted to take into account the individual facts, circumstances, and characteristics of each case, would undoubtedly produce unjust results.

Police officers, for example, who are most often at the front line of the criminal process, routinely exercise discretion when making decisions about whether to stop, search, or arrest a suspect. Although they are permitted to arrest an individual upon a showing of probable cause to believe he or she has committed a crime, they are not required to do so, and frequently do not. A police officer may observe two individuals involved in a fistfight. Such an observation provides probable cause to arrest the individuals. Yet the officer has the discretion to break up the fight, resolve the conflict between the individuals, and send them on their way without making an arrest. Such an exercise of discretion may well be in the interest of justice for all involved and would save the valuable resources of the court system for other, more serious offenses.

Traffic stops are among the most common of discretionary police decisions. There are hundreds of potential traffic violations, and every motorist commits at least a few each time he or she drives. Failing to come to a complete stop at a stop sign, driving over the speed limit, and changing lanes without signaling are just a few of the most common traffic violations for which police officers may issue tickets. They also are permitted to arrest drivers for some traffic violations,[6] but are rarely required to do so. Few people would support a law that required police officers to stop and issue a ticket to every person who committed a traffic violation or to arrest every person who committed an arrestable traffic violation. In addition to the unpopularity of such a law, most would agree that the limited resources of most criminal justice systems should be preserved for more serious offenses.

Although discretion in the exercise of the police function appears necessary and desirable, the discretionary nature of police stops and arrests sometimes produces unjust, discriminatory results. When police officers exercise their discretion to stop or arrest blacks or Latinos but not whites who are engaging in the same behavior, they are engaging in racial profiling—a practice that has been widely criticized[7] and even outlawed[8] in some jurisdictions.[9] Thus, the discretion granted to police officers to make reasonable decisions in individual cases also sometimes produces unfair disparities along racial lines. Although the laws and policies passed to eliminate racial profiling may not totally control police discretion, they demonstrate society's recognition that such discretion must be scrutinized to assure fairness in our criminal justice system.

Judges exercise discretion in the criminal justice system as well. It is the role of the judge to make decisions in individual cases about everything from whether a particular defendant should be detained before his trial to what sentence he should receive if he is convicted of a crime. Judges who preside over trials must make decisions throughout the trial about numerous issues, including whether particular pieces of evidence should be admitted and whether to sustain or overrule objections. Although there are laws and rules that govern many of these decisions, most of them involve the exercise of judicial discretion. In fact, the standard appellate courts often use when reviewing a decision of a trial judge is whether her decision was "an abuse of discretion."[10]

Judges, however, like police officers, have been criticized widely for their discretionary decisions. If a judge releases a defendant pending his trial date and he is arrested for another crime, the judge is criticized for exercising discretion poorly.[11] Judges have received the most criticism for their sentencing decisions, primarily from individuals who have complained that a judge's sentence was not harsh enough in a particular case. In fact, widespread criticism of the exercise of judicial discretion resulted in the institution of mandatory minimum and sentencing guideline schemes in the federal government and many states. Like police officers, judges were accused of treating similarly situated defendants differently. Proponents of mandatory minimum sentencing laws and sentencing guidelines argued that all defendants who committed certain offenses should be sentenced to the same period of incarceration, regardless of other factors such as their socioeconomic background, education or lack thereof, or other factors that are unrelated to the offense. These laws severely curtailed, and in some instances, entirely eliminated, judicial discretion.[12]

Discretionary parole and pardon decisions also have been the object of harsh criticism. Highly publicized cases of individuals committing violent crimes after parole boards made discretionary release decisions[13] were partially responsible for the elimination of parole in the federal system and in many states.[14] Governors and the president may exercise their discretion to pardon individuals who have been convicted of crimes. However, several presidents in recent history were severely criticized for exercising this discretionary power.[15]

Just about every official who exercises power and discretion in the criminal justice system has been criticized, held accountable, and, in some instances, stripped of some of his or her power and discretion for making discretionary decisions that produce disparate or unfair results, with one exception—the prosecutor. Although numerous scholars in the legal academy have criticized the unchecked exercise of prosecutorial discretion,[16] with a few exceptions,[17] public criticism of prosecutors has been almost entirely absent. The U.S. Supreme Court consistently has deferred to and affirmed prosecutorial discretion.[18] The legislative branch has acted accordingly. Most of the criminal laws passed by state legislatures and the U.S. Congress have served to increase rather than reduce prosecutorial power.[19]

If prosecutors always made decisions that were legal, fair, and equitable, their power and discretion would be less problematic. But, as has been demonstrated with police officers, judges, parole officers, and presidents, the exercise of discretion often leads to dissimilar treatment of similarly situated people. This is no less true for prosecutors than for any other government agent or official. In fact, since prosecutors are widely recognized as the most powerful officials in the criminal justice system, arguably they should be held more accountable than other officials, not less. However, for reasons that are not entirely clear, the judiciary, the legislature, and the general public have given prosecutors a pass. Prosecutors' power and discretion have not been reduced, even when their decisions have produced grave injustices in the criminal justice system, and the mechanisms of accountability that purport to hold them accountable have proven largely ineffective.[20] An examination of the history of the American prosecutor offers insight into how prosecutorial power developed and expanded but provides no support or justification for how it became so entrenched and accepted over time.

A BRIEF HISTORY OF THE AMERICAN
PROSECUTOR

In the early Middle Ages, when no formal system of criminal justice existed in England, the crime victim acted as police, prosecutor, and judge.[21] The victim and the victim's family tracked down the alleged criminal, decided on the appropriate punishment, and implemented it themselves.[22] Such punishment included physical punishment, restitution, or both.[23] The victim of a crime or the victim's family brought all criminal prosecutions in English common law.[24] This model reflected the philosophical view that a crime involved a wrong against an individual rather than against society as a whole.[25] As the legal system became more complex, individuals and their families hired private barristers to prosecute cases.[26] Obviously, this system provided no legal redress for poor and uneducated victims of crime who could neither navigate the legal system nor hire legal assistance.[27] The only public prosecutor in English common law was the king's attorney, whose sole responsibility was to prosecute violations of the king's rights.[28]

Reformists such as Jeremy Bentham and Sir Robert Peel argued that the English private prosecution system promoted abusive practices, such as arrangements between private attorneys and police to secure prosecutions, prosecutions initiated out of personal animosity or vengeance, and abandonment of prosecutions after corrupt financial settlements between the criminal defendant and the private prosecutor.[29] Reform efforts were met with great opposition from those who profited most from the private system—the rich and the legal profession.[30] In 1879, Parliament passed the Prosecutions of Offenses Act, which conferred limited prosecutorial powers on the director of public prosecutions.[31] The Act did not eliminate private prosecutions entirely, but the involvement of the victim in the initiation of English prosecutions decreased significantly due to the development of modern police departments in the late nineteenth and early twentieth centuries.[32]

Criminal prosecutions in colonial America mirrored the early English experience. Before the American Revolution, the crime victim maintained sole responsibility for apprehending and prosecuting the criminal suspect.[33] The victim conducted the investigation and acted as prosecutor if the case went to trial. Alternately, the victim hired a detective and a private lawyer to perform these functions.[34] If

convicted, the court frequently ordered the suspect to pay restitution
to the victim.[35] Poor criminal defendants paid for their crimes by
working for the victim as a servant or having their services sold for the
financial benefit of the victim.[36] If the victim did not want these
services or was unable to sell them, the law mandated that the victim
pay the jailer for maintaining custody of the prisoner.[37]

After the commercial revolution of the eighteenth century, the population in colonial America grew. Large urban areas began to develop,
and the crime rate increased.[38] The private mode of prosecution could
no longer maintain order in the rapidly growing colonies. Some victims
negotiated private settlements with their offenders, resulting in spo-
radic, unequal applications of the law, as well as abuses similar to those
that brought about the reform movement in England.[39]

The colonies began to develop a system of public prosecution to
combat the "chaos and inefficiency" of private prosecutions in a rapidly industrializing society.[40] This development occurred not only as a
remedy for the problems and abuses of private prosecution but also as a
result of the shift in philosophical view of crime and society. European
scholars such as Cesare Beccaria argued that crime should be viewed as
a societal problem, not simply as a wrong against an individual victim.[41]
Thus, several colonies adopted a system of public prosecution that
sought to manage the crime problem in a manner that best served the
interests of society as a whole.

In 1643, Virginia became the first colony to appoint a public
prosecutor—the attorney general.[42] Virginia modeled its system on
the early English one. Other colonies' systems of public prosecution
mirrored those of the native European countries of their early settlers.[43]
Either the court or the governor appointed these first public prosecutors.[44] Such prosecutors had little independence or discretion. Their
mandate involved consulting with the court or governor before making
decisions.[45]

The precursor to today's elected prosecutor emerged during the
rise of Jacksonian democracy in the 1820s, coinciding with the country's move toward a system of popularly elected officials.[46] This period marked the first effort to hold prosecutors directly accountable to
the people they served through the democratic process. Mississippi was
the first state to hold public elections for district attorneys. By 1912,
almost every state had followed this trend.[47] Today, only the District

of Columbia[48] and four states—Delaware, New Jersey, Rhode Island, and Connecticut—maintain a system of appointed prosecutors.[49]

Although popular elections intuitively seemed to operate as a check on prosecutorial power and an effective mechanism of accountability, the popular election of the prosecutor actually established and reinforced his power, independence, and discretion. No longer beholden to the governor or the court, the prosecutor was now accountable to the amorphous body called "the people." However, since the actions and decisions of the prosecutor were not generally a matter of public record, the people could not actually hold the prosecutor accountable. Nonetheless, the ballot box was seen as the most democratic mechanism of accountability.[50]

The early system of federal prosecution began with the Judiciary Act of 1789.[51] This Act created the office of the attorney general, whose only duties were representing the United States in cases before the Supreme Court and providing legal advice to the president and heads of departments.[52] The same Act created district attorneys to prosecute suits for the United States in the district courts, but until 1861, the attorney general did not supervise the district attorneys.[53] In fact, it appears that no entity supervised these district attorneys from 1789 to 1820, when they were placed under the supervision of the secretary of the treasury (until 1861).[54] There was no clear organizational structure or chain of command, with federal prosecutors either operating independently or receiving instructions from several different federal agencies.[55] State officials and private citizens even conducted some federal prosecutions.[56]

In the 1920s, a number of states formed crime commissions to examine both the status of the criminal justice system and its ability to manage the post–World War I rise in crime.[57] Their findings about the role of the prosecutor and the extent of his power and discretion shocked most of these commissions. A report by the National Commission on Law Observance and Enforcement (NCLOE) noted: "In every way the Prosecutor has more power over the administration of justice than the judges, with much less public appreciation of his power. We have been jealous of the power of the trial judge, but careless of the continual growth of the power of the prosecuting attorney."[58] Commissions formed in California, Georgia, Illinois, Minnesota, New York, and Pennsylvania made similar observations about the power of the prosecutor.[59]

The most well-known crime commission of this era was the Wickersham Commission, a national body "formed to study the status of the criminal justice system."[60] Like virtually all of the state crime commissions, the Wickersham Commission criticized the role of the prosecutor, particularly the absence of a meaningful check on prosecutorial power and discretion.[61] It noted that the popular election of prosecutors provided neither an adequate check on this power nor the best qualified candidates for the position.[62] The Commission also recognized abuses in the plea bargaining power of prosecutors.[63] It recommended a number of reforms, including the establishment of a state director of public prosecutions with secure tenure to control the prosecutorial process in a systemized fashion.[64] Despite the findings and recommendations of the Wickersham Commission, other commissions, and legal scholars of the 1920s, there has been no significant reform of the prosecutorial process. In fact, today prosecutors retain even more power, independence, and discretion than they did in the early nineteenth century.[65]

THE IMPORTANCE OF PROSECUTORIAL DISCRETION

Prosecutorial discretion is essential to the operation of our criminal justice system, despite the potential for abuse. Society, through the legislature, criminalizes certain behaviors and provides a process for holding people accountable when they commit crimes. The prosecutor's duty is to use discretion in making the all-important decision of whether an individual should be charged, which charges to bring, and whether and how to plea bargain. If the accused chooses to exercise his constitutional right to a trial, the prosecutor represents the state in that trial.

The criminal justice system is adversarial by design. Ideally, a capable and zealous defense attorney represents the accused, and a similarly capable prosecutor represents the state. If both sides have sufficient resources and follow the rules, the criminal process should work fairly and produce a fair result. But the process is not that simple, nor is the theory always realized in practice. Most people charged with crimes are represented by public defenders or court-appointed attorneys who do not have sufficient resources to provide an adequate defense. Some prosecutors don't always follow the rules, and some defense attorneys don't work hard enough for their clients. To complicate matters even more, prosecutors have a special, very different role in the criminal process. Their duty is not to simply represent the state in the pursuit of a conviction but to pursue justice. "Doing justice" sometimes involves seeking a conviction and incarceration, but at other times, it might involve dismissing a criminal case or forgoing a prosecution. These decisions, however, are left to the prosecutor's discretion. Without enforceable laws or policies to guide that discretion, all too often it is exercised haphazardly at worst and arbitrarily at best, resulting in inequitable treatment of both victims and defendants.

Discretion is as necessary to the prosecution function as it is to the police and judicial functions. It is difficult to imagine a fair and workable system that does not include some level of measured discretion in the prosecutorial process. As a part of the executive branch of government, it is the prosecutor's duty to enforce the laws, and it would be virtually impossible for her to perform this essential function without exercising discretion.

One of the reasons prosecutorial discretion is so essential to the criminal justice system is the proliferation of criminal statutes in all fifty states and the federal government.[66] Legislatures pass laws criminalizing a vast array of behaviors, and some of these laws, such as fornication and adultery, for example, stay on the books long after social mores about these behaviors have changed. In addition, some offenses warrant prosecution in some instances but not others. For example, it may be reasonable to bring a prosecution in a jurisdiction that criminalizes gambling for someone engaged in a large-scale operation but not for individuals placing small bets during a Saturday night poker game in a private home. In addition, in some cases, the evidence may not be sufficient to meet the government's heavy burden of proving guilt beyond a reasonable doubt. Without discretion, prosecutors might be required to bring criminal charges in cases that most people would view as frivolous and in cases where the evidence is weak or lacking in credibility.

Other closely related reasons why prosecutorial discretion is so essential are the limitation on resources and the need for individualized justice.[67] There are not enough resources in any local criminal justice system to prosecute every alleged criminal offense. Of course with every prosecution comes the corresponding need for defense attorneys, judges, and other court personnel, and if there is a conviction, possibly prison facilities. Some entity must decide which offenses should be prosecuted, and prosecutors are presumably best suited to make these judgments. Most would agree that the state's limited resources should be used to prosecute serious and/or strong cases, while minor or weak cases should be dismissed or resolved short of prosecution.

Just prosecutions require a consideration of the individual facts and circumstances of each case. All defendants and crime victims are not the same. Similarly, there are significant differences between perpetrators and victims of particular types of crimes. For example, some robbers have long criminal histories while others are first offenders or provide minor assistance to more serious offenders. Some assault victims are totally innocent of wrongdoing while others may have provoked their assailants with their own criminal behavior. These examples illustrate just a few of the many factors that should be considered in deciding whether, and to what extent, a case should be prosecuted.

Despite the obvious need for the exercise of discretion at this stage of the criminal process, one might question why we delegate this important function to prosecutors and why we don't provide more oversight by the judiciary or some other entity. The most common answer has to do with the separation of powers. As part of the executive branch of government, prosecutors have been granted the power and responsibility to enforce the laws.[68] Courts have consistently deferred to the expertise of prosecutors in declining to question their motives for charging and other important prosecutorial decisions. The Supreme Court explains this deference as follows:

> This broad discretion rests largely on the recognition that the decision to prosecute is particularly ill-suited to judicial review. Such factors as the strength of the case, the prosecution's general deterrence value, the Government's enforcement priorities, and the case's relationship to the Government's overall enforcement plan are not readily susceptible to the kind of analysis the courts are competent to undertake. Judicial supervision in this area, moreover, entails systemic costs of particular concern. Examining the basis of a prosecution delays the criminal proceeding, threatens to chill law enforcement by subjecting the prosecutor's motives and decisionmaking to

outside inquiry, and may undermine prosecutorial effectiveness by revealing the Government's enforcement policy.[69]

The Court is concerned that too much interference with the prosecutor's responsibilities might interfere with the enforcement of the
criminal laws, either because prosecutors might decline some prosecutions for fear of judicial reprisal or because judicial review or requiring prosecutors to explain their decisions to some other entity
might result in law enforcement secrets being revealed to criminals.

THE DILEMMA OF PROSECUTORIAL DISCRETION

All of the reasons in support of prosecutorial discretion explain why it is
so essential, but they do not address the problems that have resulted from
the failure to monitor how that discretion is exercised. In their effort
to give prosecutors the freedom and independence to enforce the law,
the judicial and legislative branches of government have failed to perform the kind of checks and balances essential to a fair and effective democracy. Consequently, prosecutors, unlike judges, parole boards, and
even other entities within the executive branch such as police, presidents, and governors, have escaped the kind of scrutiny and accountability that we demand of public officials in a democratic society. Prosecutors have been left to regulate themselves, and, not surprisingly, such
self-regulation has been either nonexistent or woefully inadequate.
    There have been some efforts to promote the fair and equitable
exercise of prosecutorial discretion, but these efforts have been minimal and largely ineffective. For example, the Criminal Justice Section
of the American Bar Association (ABA) promulgates standards of
practice for judges, defense attorneys, and prosecutors. The standards
for prosecutors address how prosecutors should perform their most
important responsibilities, with the goal of assuring that prosecutors
exercise their discretion fairly and in a way that will promote the
administration of justice. However, these standards are aspirational.
No prosecutor is required to follow or even consider them. The
Justice Department also sets standards and guidelines for federal prosecutors in its U.S. attorney's manual. However, like the ABA standards, the extent to which individual prosecutors follow these guidelines is left to the U.S. attorneys in each district or, in some instances,

to the attorney general of the United States. There is no legal requirement that federal prosecutors act in accordance with the U.S. attorney's manual, nor are they accountable to anyone outside the Department of Justice if and when they fail to follow their own rules. Similarly, individual state and local prosecutors may establish policies and standards of practice in their offices, but they are not required to do so, and most don't. Although a few states have passed laws that establish standards for prosecutors,[70] there is virtually no public accountability when the standards are not followed.

Proponents of the current system of prosecution argue that prosecutors are held accountable to the people through the electoral system. They maintain that if prosecutors do not perform their duties and responsibilities fairly and effectively, they will be voted out of office. However, for reasons that will be discussed in detail in chapter 9, the electoral system and other mechanisms of accountability have proven to be ineffective.

The lack of enforceable standards and effective accountability to the public has resulted in decision-making that often appears arbitrary, especially during the critical charging and plea bargaining stages of the process. These decisions result in tremendous disparities among similarly situated people, sometimes along race and/or class lines. The rich and white, if they are charged at all, are less likely to go to prison than the poor and black or brown—even when the evidence of criminal behavior is equally present or absent. Although prosecutors certainly are not the only criminal justice officials whose discretionary decisions contribute to unfair disparities, their decisions carry greater consequences and are most difficult to challenge, as the following chapters will demonstrate.

Most prosecutors join the profession with the goal of doing justice and serving their communities, and most work hard to perform their responsibilities fairly, without bias or favoritism. But even well-meaning prosecutors often fail because they exercise discretion arbitrarily and without guidance or standards, under the daily pressures of overwhelming caseloads in a system with inadequate representation for most defendants, and judges who are more interested in efficiency than justice. The absence of meaningful standards and effective methods of accountability has resulted in widely accepted prosecutorial practices that play a significant role in producing many of the injustices in the criminal justice system.

It is important that prosecutors make charging and plea bargaining decisions on the basis of the facts and circumstances of individual cases to achieve individualized justice. But when they do so without meaningful guidance, standards, or supervision, their decisions become more arbitrary than individualized, and deep-seated, unconscious views about race and class are more likely to affect the decision-making process. It is not enough for prosecutors to base their decisions on the malleable standard of "doing justice" because such a standard is subjective and ultimately produces unexplainable and unjustifiable disparities. The goal should be to establish practices that promote the goals of individualized justice without producing unfair disparities among similarly situated defendants and victims of crime. So far, despite the worthy intentions of many hard-working prosecutors, frequently that goal is not being met.

This book will focus on how the everyday, legal exercise of prosecutorial discretion is largely responsible for the tremendous injustices in our criminal justice system. It does not focus on the intentional, illegal practices that some prosecutors engage in—fabricating evidence, coercing and threatening witnesses, and hiding exculpatory evidence. Only one chapter is devoted to these horrendous cases; others have written about them extensively. Most of the chapters will demonstrate that, despite their intent to justly enforce the laws, prosecutors engage in widely accepted practices that produce unfair results for victims, criminal defendants, and the entire justice system. This book does not tell the story of the good deeds prosecutors do. That story is told every day in the countless television dramas and news stories about prosecutors and how effectively they fight crime.[71] Instead, this book will tell the story that is almost never told: that even well-meaning prosecutors routinely engage in practices that produce unfair results—practices that are hidden from the public, and even when revealed, are somehow accepted as legitimate.

Chapters 2 through 5 discuss prosecutorial discretion in the context of issues and practices that apply to both state and federal prosecutors— charging, plea bargaining, victim issues, and the death penalty. Chapter 6 focuses on federal prosecutions and the unique issues and problems they present. Chapter 7 discusses prosecutorial misconduct, and chapter 8 explores how the rules of professional conduct for lawyers have failed to monitor and give guidance to prosecutors. Chapter 9 attempts to explain how and why the existing mechanisms of prosecutorial accountability have failed to prevent the unfair practices and results described in the previous chapters. Finally, chapter 10 discusses prospects for reform of the prosecution function.

The criminal justice system is important to all of us. Some of us and members of our families will have the unfortunate experience of being crime victims or criminal defendants. Most will be fortunate enough to avoid personal involvement with the system. But everyone has an interest in assuring the fair and just operation of a system with the power to deprive liberty and life. Everyone who believes in democracy has a vested interest in assuring that no one individual or institution exercises power without accountability to the people. This book will demonstrate that for some reason, we have given prosecutors a pass—allowing them to circumvent the scrutiny and accountability that we ordinarily require of those to whom we grant power and privilege while affording them more power than any other government official. It will show that we have become complacent, affording trust without requiring responsibility. The time has come to focus on prosecutors, require information, and, most important, institute fundamental reforms that will result in more fairness in the performance of the prosecution function.

TWO

The Power to Charge

It was one of the happiest days of David McKnight's life. That evening, he went to a bar in Washington, D.C., to celebrate. He bought a bottle of Dom Perignon and popped it open ceremoniously. "Drinks for everybody—my treat!" he announced. "What are we celebrating?" someone asked. "I killed someone and got away with it!" replied McKnight. He had just learned that a District of Columbia grand jury had voted not to indict him for the murder of John Nguyen.[1]

The year was 1987. I was a staff attorney at PDS. Marcia Ross, the chief of our trial division, and Bob Gordon, a staff attorney, were appointed to represent McKnight. The case was one of the most peculiar I had observed in my dozen years as a public defender in the nation's capital. Two factors were noteworthy. First, someone had been brutally killed, and the grand jury, with a silent and consenting prosecuting attorney, decided that the killer should go free. Second, the accused killer was white. The way the case was handled convinced me that the two factors were related.

David McKnight was a twenty-five-year-old white Georgetown University student who worked as a bartender in a restaurant in Washington, D.C. He lived in a small, one-bedroom apartment that he shared with John Nguyen, a fifty-five-year-old Vietnamese immigrant who worked as a cook in the restaurant. Nguyen paid McKnight rent to sleep in the walk-in closet of the apartment, a space barely large enough for a small bed.

One Saturday evening, McKnight hosted a party at his apartment. Nguyen was at the apartment during the party, and McKnight asked him to leave. The two men began to argue, and the argument escalated into a fight after the guests left. McKnight attacked Nguyen with a large machete. McKnight was much taller and heavier than Nguyen, who was just over five feet tall. Nguyen was able to escape into the bathroom, but McKnight hacked the bathroom door open with the machete. He then "almost sliced [Nguyen] in half."[2] Nguyen managed to stagger out of the apartment and into the street. Both men were covered with Nguyen's blood. Ironically, the first ambulance on the scene picked up McKnight, leaving Nguyen to die. A second ambulance came for Nguyen and took him to the hospital. Nguyen died later that night.

The case never went to trial. The prosecutor, who was white, called Ross and Gordon within a day or two and invited them to identify witnesses who might testify before the grand jury on behalf of McKnight. The prosecutor suggested that McKnight might have a good claim of self-defense and thought there might be witnesses who could testify about Nguyen's reputation for violence and McKnight's peaceful reputation. Ross was stunned. She had been a trial lawyer at PDS for seven years and had probably tried more homicide cases than any other lawyer in the office. As the chief of the Trial Division for the office, she had supervised most of the homicide cases handled by PDS. Ross had never before received or heard of such an offer by a prosecutor to assist a criminal defendant, especially one who may have been guilty of murder.

Ross and Gordon identified witnesses willing to testify on behalf of McKnight. Although defense attorneys are not allowed to be present during grand jury hearings, the witnesses indicated that they would testify about McKnight's good character. Several weeks later, the prosecutor informed Ross that the grand jury had voted not to indict McKnight. All charges were dismissed.

Contrast McKnight's case with that of Daniel Ware, a thirty-three-year-old African American man who lived in an impoverished neighborhood in the District of Columbia. He was a high school graduate, employed periodically doing house painting and other manual labor. He got into an argument with Darryl Brown, a young gangster in the neighborhood who was known to carry guns. Brown had done time for armed robbery and weapons offenses and had a well-known reputation for violence.

The argument stemmed from Brown's alleged threats against Ware's younger brother. Ware approached Brown and told him to stay away from his brother, and the two men began to argue. The argument ended when they heard a police car approaching, but Brown made it clear that he was going to punish Ware for challenging him.

Ware heard that Brown was looking for him, so he began to carry a knife when he walked through the neighborhood. Three days after the argument, Brown approached Ware in an alley as Ware was going to the neighborhood corner store. Brown threatened Ware and reached inside his jacket. Ware then pulled out his knife and stabbed Brown once in his chest. Brown died later that evening.

Jim Morris was appointed to represent Ware, and I served as his co-counsel. Our investigator spoke to numerous residents of the neighborhood who recounted incidents demonstrating Brown's reputation for violence. He also found eyewitnesses who confirmed Ware's version of the incident—that Brown was the aggressor and that Ware had acted in self-defense. One witness claimed to have seen someone remove a gun from the inside pocket of Brown's jacket before the ambulance and police arrived on the scene.

The prosecutor in Ware's case, at a minimum, was aware of Mr. Brown's criminal record and violent reputation. Most likely he was aware of the witness accounts confirming Ware's claim of self-defense. The prosecutor never offered to present exculpatory evidence to the grand jury on Ware's behalf. Ware was indicted for first-degree murder.

The same prosecutor's office charged both David McKnight and Daniel Ware. Both cases were homicides involving a decedent with a reputation for violence and a defendant who claimed that he acted in self-defense. Yet the cases were prosecuted differently, with no apparent justification for the difference in treatment. It was difficult not to attribute McKnight's favorable treatment to his status as a white student at a prestigious university.

Although race and class appear to have played a part in the decision in McKnight's case, there was no evidence that the prosecutor took either race or class into account in making his decision. In fact, it is very unlikely that he consciously decided to give favorable treatment to McKnight because he was white. However, the prosecutor, who was white, may very well have unconsciously empathized with McKnight as a young college student with a future, while simultaneously feeling no such empathy for Nguyen, a poor Vietnamese immigrant whose future extended no further than the kitchen of the restaurant where he worked. The fact that Nguyen had no family or anyone else demanding that McKnight be punished made the decision even easier.

Other factors may have affected the decision as well. The prosecutor had a good relationship with Bob Gordon, one of McKnight's attorneys. The ever-present desire to dispose of the constantly growing number of criminal cases as expeditiously as possible undoubtedly played a part as well.

Although it is clear that some or all of these factors may have played a part in the prosecutor's decision, it is not clear whether any of them were consciously considered. Does the arbitrary exercise of prosecutorial discretion lead to arbitrary justice—one outcome in one case and a very different outcome in another very similar case? The prosecutor in McKnight's case definitely did not invite exculpatory witnesses to testify in all, or even most, of his cases. Nor was this practice used by other prosecutors, as is illustrated by Ware's case.

Although the prosecutor in Ware's case handled homicide cases in the same office, his approach was entirely different and much more typical. There was at least as much evidence of self-defense in Ware's case as in McKnight's case, yet the prosecutor never considered presenting this evidence to the grand jury. It is doubtful that race or class played a conscious role in his decision-making process, but dismissing the charges against Ware was never a consideration. The different approaches resulted in very different outcomes for reasons that may not be justifiable. This chapter examines whether these different outcomes can be traced to the way prosecutors exercise discretion during the charging process.

HOW THE CHARGING PROCESS WORKS

The charging decision is the most important prosecutorial power and the strongest example of the influence and reach of prosecutorial discretion. When the prosecutor makes the decision to charge an individual, she pulls that person into the criminal justice system, firmly entrenches him there, and maintains control over crucial decisions that will determine his fate. Police officers exercise expansive discretionary power as well, and the arrest power can have a monumental effect on a person's life. But without the prosecutor's charging power, the arrest takes the individual no further than the police station.

After the police officer makes the arrest, it is the prosecutor who decides whether that individual should face the criminal charges that lead to imprisonment. There is no law that requires an individual to be charged if he commits a crime. That all-important decision is left in the hands of the prosecutor. If the prosecutor decides to bring charges, the person faces imprisonment. If she decides to forgo charges, the person is free to go.

Prosecutors exercise discretion in a variety of ways. Sometimes, whether to charge and what to charge are fairly straightforward decisions. The police officer arrests the suspect when there is probable cause to believe he has committed a crime. Frequently the officer will recommend charges to the prosecutor. If there is probable cause and supporting evidence, the prosecutor follows the recommendation by filing a charging document or seeking an indictment through the grand jury process.

Although prosecutors sometimes follow the recommendation of the arresting officer, they frequently exercise other charging options. They may decline to bring charges, bring only charges that they believe they can prove, or "inflate" the charges by convincing a grand jury to indict a defendant for more and greater charges than they can prove beyond a reasonable doubt at the trial stage of the process. The decision to forgo charges may be based on practical considerations such as the triviality of the offense and/or the victim's lack of interest in prosecution. The decision may also be based on considerations of fairness and justice in a particular case. For example, some jurisdictions offer alternative dispositions such as diversion programs for certain minor offenses. On the other hand, a prosecutor's conscious or unconscious bias toward or against a particular defendant or victim may influence the decision either to forgo or bring charges.

At any rate, all of these decisions are entirely within the prosecutor's discretion, and there is frequently no readily discernible explanation for why one decision is made over another. Very few offices have manuals with guidelines or policies on how to make charging decisions. Offices that do have such guidelines or policies rarely enforce them.

Prosecutors use a variety of procedures for filing charges against criminal defendants. There is no constitutionally required procedure for either state or federal prosecutions, and the process varies from jurisdiction to jurisdiction. There are also different procedures depending on the seriousness of the offense. However, some version of the following process is generally used in most jurisdictions.

When an individual is arrested, within forty-eight hours he must be brought before a magistrate or judge who determines whether he will be released or detained prior to his trial date.[3] In some jurisdictions, the prosecutor will file charges at this hearing, especially if the offense is a misdemeanor. The process is fairly straightforward for misdemeanor charges. Most misdemeanors involve an uncomplicated set of facts. For example, if a person is in possession of a small quantity of marijuana, the only possible charge is possession of marijuana. If an individual hits someone without using a weapon, the charge is simple assault.

Even for misdemeanors, a prosecutor frequently has a variety of options at the charging stage of the process. First, she must decide whether to bring charges at all. If the charge is very minor, and the arrestee has no criminal record, the prosecutor may decide to forgo charges altogether. Some jurisdictions have diversion programs in which the prosecutor agrees to abandon the prosecution if the defendant completes a program of community service or pays restitution to the victim. The prosecutor may simply choose to charge the defendant with the offense recommended by the arresting police officer. All of these decisions are discretionary and are made unilaterally by the prosecutor.

In jurisdictions that do not use the grand jury process, prosecutors charge felonies through the same basic process. The prosecutor reviews the police reports and files a charging document based on the offenses in the state criminal statute. As with misdemeanors, a prosecutor has the same option of forgoing criminal charges when she sees fit. There is no requirement that this decision be justified or explained, and it is a unilateral decision.

Prosecutors will sometimes consult with crime victims before making a charging decision. If charges are filed at the initial hearing, crime victims may not be available to consult with the prosecutor. Often charges are filed at the initial hearing, and prosecutors dismiss them at a later date after consulting with the victim. If the victim is not interested in supporting a prosecution, the prosecutor may take this factor into account when making the charging decision. Though it is far more difficult to prosecute a defendant successfully without the active participation of the crime victim, the prosecutor may pursue the prosecution without the victim's support.[4]

THE GRAND JURY

Many jurisdictions use the grand jury process for charging felony offenses. This process is more far-reaching and time-consuming than the prosecutor simply filing a charging document on her own. However, because the prosecutor maintains unilateral control over the grand jury, in most cases the grand jury is simply a tool of the prosecutor and no more democratic than the prosecutor acting independently.

The grand jury is a group of citizens (usually between five and twenty-three) whose responsibility is to determine whether there is probable cause to believe an individual committed a crime, whether he or she should be charged, and what charges to bring.[5] The Fifth Amendment to the U.S. Constitution requires the grand jury process for all felonies in federal court, but grand juries are not a constitutional requirement for the states.[6] Nonetheless, the constitutions or statutes of approximately one-half of all states require a grand jury process for serious crimes.[7]

Although police officers determine whether there is probable cause to believe a crime has been committed when they make an arrest, the purpose of the grand jury is to serve as a democratic and more thorough check on this decision. Police officers must often make the probable cause decision on the spur of the moment under stressful circumstances. Grand jurors are provided with more information and time to make this determination and are able to do so in a more thoughtful way. The prosecutor subpoenas and presents witnesses to the alleged crime, and the grand jurors are permitted to question the witnesses. Grand jurors may also require prosecutors to subpoena additional witnesses they deem necessary. The prosecutor provides the jurors with the applicable laws and advises them on the appropriate charges.

After hearing from all of the witnesses, the grand jurors determine if there is probable cause to believe the defendant committed the offense. If they decide that there is not probable cause, they do not bring charges, and the defendant is freed from the system. If the grand jurors do find probable cause, they determine which charges to bring, and those charges are set forth in a formal charging document called an indictment. The defendant is served with a copy of the indictment at a brief court hearing, and pretrial hearings and a trial date are scheduled.

Grand jurors rarely have difficulty concluding that there is probable cause to believe the defendant committed the offense. Probable cause is the lowest legal standard on the legal spectrum and far from the high standard of proof beyond a reasonable doubt that prosecutors must meet before a defendant is convicted of a crime. Probable cause may be proven if it is more probable than not that the defendant committed the crime.[8] Although the probable cause standard is easy to meet, the grand jurors are expected to make the decision, not the prosecutor. Yet grand jurors rarely act independently of the prosecutor.

Why doesn't the grand jury work as a check on the power and discretion of the prosecutor? As with many criminal justice institutions, the theory sounds better than the actual practice. Grand jurors are ordinary citizens without legal training. The prosecutor controls the grand jury process, deciding which witnesses to call and which questions to ask. Although grand jurors may theoretically subpoena witnesses, they don't usually know enough about the case to know which witnesses to call. They may ask questions of witnesses, and frequently they do, but they are almost always brief, follow-up questions after the prosecutor has concluded her questioning. Grand jurors don't know the criminal statutes or how to apply them, so they must rely on the prosecutor, who interprets and explains the law to the grand jurors, suggesting the appropriate charges.

Neither the defendant nor the defense attorney is allowed to be present during the process. Thus, the witnesses are not subject to cross-examination, which could potentially expose weaknesses in their testimony. The defense may not present exculpatory evidence to the jury unless the prosecutor agrees, and if she does, the defense attorney may not be present during the witnesses' testimony. In federal prosecutions and in most states, prosecutors are not required to present exculpatory evidence to a grand jury, and they rarely do.[9] With only one side of the story being told, it's very easy for the prosecutor to convince the grand jurors that the relatively low standard of probable cause has been met. In essence, the grand jury is a very one-sided process entirely controlled by the prosecutor.[10] As a result of this *pro forma* process, grand jurors rarely decline to return an indictment.[11]

All jurisdictions have rules that require the grand jury to act within a certain period of time if the defendant is detained.[12] These rules are designed to protect the defendant's right to a speedy trial by preventing the prosecutor from delaying the grand jury process. For example, in the District of Columbia, if the defendant is detained, the prosecutor must return an indictment within nine months.[13] If the indictment is not produced within that time period, the complaint is dismissed, and the defendant is released. Of course, the dismissal of the complaint does nothing more than temporarily free the defendant from the criminal justice system. In most cases, the prosecutor is free to continue the grand jury investigation, but no restrictions may be imposed on the defendant during this process. If an indictment is returned at a later date, the defendant will receive a summons to appear in court to face charges rather than facing rearrest on the same charges.

Despite these rules, prosecutors maintain the power to delay the grand jury process. If a prosecutor has nine months to produce an indictment, she may legally produce the indictment eight months and twenty days later, even if he could have easily indicted the case in two weeks. Such unnecessary delay violates an individual's right to a speedy trial, especially for an innocent defendant who is detained in jail pending the outcome of his case. However, since the grand jury process is secret and thus inaccessible to the defense attorney, there is no way to easily discover whether prosecutors are intentionally causing delay. Even if the process were more open, it would be difficult to prove intentional abuse because there are so many legitimate reasons why an indictment might be delayed, such as difficulty locating witnesses, high prosecutorial caseloads, and so on.

Trevor Davis's case provides an example of how a prosecutor may easily abuse the grand jury process without consequences. He was arrested for the rape of a young woman who lived in his neighborhood, and I was appointed to represent him. He was a Jamaican immigrant who had recently moved to the United States with his mother. He was a very slight man—about 5'2" and barely 120 pounds. He had no prior convictions, but because of the seriousness of the offense and his lack of substantial ties to the community, the judge set a high money bond, which Davis was unable to post. His mother was devastated by the charges. She insisted that her son would never rape anyone, and she tried desperately to raise the money to post bond for him. Unfortunately, her housekeeper's salary barely paid her bills. She called me frequently, tearfully begging me to get her son out of jail.

Davis was adamant that he was innocent of the charges. He told me that he knew the young lady and that she had consented to having sex with him. He also informed me that she was totally deaf. He stated that she couldn't speak but that she had communicated her consent to sexual intercourse through her body language. I assured him that I would investigate the case thoroughly and prepare to present a consent defense at trial.

I sent my investigator to take a written statement from the complainant—a standard procedure and very important part of the investigative process. In the District of Columbia, prosecutors are not required to provide any information about the case to the defense team before the case is indicted. Even after indictment, the discovery rules do not require prosecutors to provide complainant or witness statements to the defense. These statements must only be turned over after the complainant or witness testifies in court. In most cases, such testimony would only occur at the time of trial. In order to advise the client and prepare for trial, competent defense attorneys conduct thorough investigations in each case as soon as possible after arrest. These investigations include finding witnesses and taking statements from them when possible.

In this case, getting a statement from the complainant was complicated by the fact that she was deaf. I hired a sign language interpreter to accompany my investigator to the complainant's home and translate her statement. The interpreter planned to communicate with the complainant directly, explain their purpose, and translate the investigator's questions and the complainant's answers. The investigator would write down the statement as interpreted. At the end of the statement, the interpreter would "sign" the written statement to the complainant and obtain her signature.

The statement was never taken. When the investigator and interpreter arrived at the complainant's home, her mother came to the door and informed them that her daughter would not be giving any statements to any member of the defense team. Complainants and witnesses are not required to give statements—written or oral—to defense counsel or their investigators. Some choose to give statements and some don't. Prosecutors are not legally permitted to dissuade witnesses from talking to members of the defense team, although some strongly suggest that witnesses would be better off if they didn't cooperate with the defense. My investigator never had the opportunity to communicate with the complainant directly.

I later went to speak with the complainant's mother to attempt to explain why I had sent my investigator and the interpreter to her home. I learned that communication with the complainant would have been impossible. During my conversation with the complainant's mother, she told me that her daughter wouldn't be able to give a statement because she didn't know sign language. When I asked her how her daughter ordinarily communicated, she said that her daughter only was able to communicate with her and that they had their own special language. I learned that her daughter had never been subpoenaed to the grand jury and that the prosecutor was aware of her inability to understand standard sign language.

If the complainant didn't understand sign language, how would the prosecutor ever be able to present her testimony to a grand jury or to a jury at trial? Hearsay evidence is permitted in the grand jury, so he might be able to persuade a grand jury to indict based on the testimony of the arresting officer.[14] However, it is highly unlikely that any court would allow anyone else to present the complainant's testimony at a trial, and only certified sign language interpreters with no interest in or connection to the case were permitted to translate in court. Certainly no judge would allow the complainant's mother to translate her testimony, not only because of the impossibility of verifying the accuracy and credibility of her translation but also because of her obvious bias toward her daughter. Would the prosecutor be able to convince a jury to convict my client of rape without the testimony of the complainant? I knew of cases where prosecutors had obtained convictions without putting the alleged victim on the stand, but there had always been other witnesses to the crime who could testify about what they had observed. There were no such witnesses in Davis's case. I didn't believe the prosecutor could ever prove my client's guilt. I wanted him to own up to that fact, so my client could be released from jail.

It soon became obvious that the prosecutor was ignoring my attempts at communication. I left dozens of phone messages and sent a letter requesting a meeting; I received no responses. When I finally reached the prosecutor and expressed my concerns, I told him that I was aware of the complainant's inability to understand standard American Sign Language and asked him how he planned to present evidence of a rape without her testimony. The prosecutor gave very evasive answers to my questions, insisting that he would be able to make his case. He reminded me that he had nine months within which to indict Davis. Although I suspected that the prosecutor knew that he would not be able to prove my client's guilt, I had no proof that he was abusing the grand jury process, nor did I have the right to demand proof that he wasn't. The rules permitted nine months to indict, and the time period had not expired.

Ultimately, my suspicions were proven correct. When I received notice that the case would not be indicted, I called the prosecutor. In a rare moment of candor, he said, "I know your client is guilty. At least he did nine months in jail." I was stunned. When this prosecutor was unable to prove my client's guilt legally, he took it upon himself to act as jury and judge—single-handedly finding him guilty and "sentencing" him to nine months in jail.

The prosecutor's actions certainly conflicted with the American Bar Association's standards for the prosecution function. These standards state that a prosecutor should only bring charges that she believes she can prove beyond a reasonable doubt.[15] Even if a jury ultimately found the defendant not guilty, the defendant would bear the emotional—and perhaps financial—burden of defending against the charges. Furthermore, the defendant might labor under the shadow of suspicion that often lingers even after charges are dismissed or not proven. Despite strong language that condemns the prosecutor's actions, the American Bar Association standards were useless. Prosecutors suffer no penalty for failure to follow these standards. In fact, they are not even required to consider them before making important prosecutorial decisions.

Other than his statement to me over the phone, I had no proof that the prosecutor had abused the process. Even if I had been able to produce better proof, action at this point seemed futile. Ordinarily, I would file a motion to dismiss the indictment for prosecutorial misconduct. But now that the case was dismissed and my client was free, that remedy was not available or necessary. The only apparent alternative appeared to be a referral to the local bar counsel on a claim of unethical behavior—an option that probably would have been futile and definitely would have caused difficulty for future clients that I represented.[16] Davis had his freedom and was not interested in supporting any action against the prosecutor. I decided to take no action.

OVERCHARGING

Prosecutors routinely engage in overcharging, a practice that involves "tacking on" additional charges that they know they cannot prove beyond a reasonable doubt or that they can technically prove but are inconsistent with the legislative intent or otherwise inappropriate. Prosecutors overcharge in the grand jury where they are the final arbiters and interpreters of the law and in jurisdictions that do not employ the grand jury process. The practice serves two purposes: (1) It gives the prosecutor a greater advantage in the plea bargaining process by providing him with more charges with which to bargain,[17] and (2) It gives him an advantage at trial because the additional charge or charges act as a "backup" in case the jury fails to convict on the more relevant charges.

The first purpose, discussed more thoroughly in chapter 3, is the most common, since most cases are resolved through the plea bargaining process. If the prosecutor charges five offenses instead of two, he may get the defendant to agree to plead guilty to three charges in exchange for his agreement to dismiss two, even if he would have a difficult time proving the two charges before a judge or jury. On the other hand, if the prosecutor only charges the three offenses for which he has solid proof beyond a reasonable doubt, he will have less with which to bargain and will probably secure a guilty plea to only one offense in exchange for his promise to dismiss two. Overcharging gives the prosecutor more "bang for the buck."

The second purpose of overcharging is fulfilled less frequently, primarily because most cases are resolved with a guilty plea. If a case does proceed to trial, the prosecutor has a psychological advantage if a jury is presented with a long list of charges to consider. A long list of charges makes the defendant look "guiltier" and provides subconscious pressure to find the defendant guilty of at least one or two charges. The juror thinks "with all of these charges, he must be guilty of something." Since jurors have a tendency to compromise when there is disagreement on the final verdict, it's more likely that at least one conviction will be secured.[18]

It is relatively easy for prosecutors to engage in overcharging because of the proliferation of criminal offenses in the United States. One criminal act can be charged as a number of different offenses, each with its own penalty. Although these offenses sometimes merge at the sentencing stage of the process,[19] jurors are permitted to find the defendant guilty of a number of offenses for commission of a single act.

How does the practice of overcharging lead to unjust results? The case of Marcus Dixon provides a stark example. Dixon was a football star and honor student at Pepperell High School in Rome, Georgia. He had a 3.96 GPA, scored over 1,200 on his SAT exam, and earned a full scholarship to Vanderbilt University. His dreams of going to college were dashed when he was charged with numerous sexual offenses as a result of a single sexual encounter with a fellow student. Marcus claimed he had had consensual sex with the fifteen-year-old girl, and she claimed he had raped her. Marcus was eighteen years old at the time of the incident.

Police and prosecutors believed the girl, and Marcus was charged with rape, sexual battery, aggravated assault, false imprisonment, statutory rape, and aggravated child molestation. All of these charges stemmed from a single act. The jury acquitted Marcus of rape, sexual battery, aggravated assault, and false imprisonment after only fifteen to twenty minutes of deliberation.[20] They convicted him of statutory rape, which consists of sexual intercourse with a minor, whether or not the minor consents. According to juror Kathy Tibitz, "We had no choice with that."[21] The jury had the most difficulty with the last charge. The Georgia statute defined aggravated child molestation as sex with a minor that causes injury. Because the girl was a virgin at the time of the incident, there was some vaginal injury, so the jury found Marcus guilty of this charge as well.

The penalty for aggravated child molestation in the state of Georgia was a mandatory minimum sentence of ten years in prison with no possibility of parole. The judge had no discretion to impose a lesser sentence. When juror Kathy Tibitz heard about the sentence, she was devastated. She later stated that if she had known the sentence was so harsh, she never would have convicted him of the crime.[22] Representative Tyrone Brooks, one of the state legislators who had passed the aggravated child molestation law, spoke out in Marcus's defense. According to Brooks, "the intent of the law is very clear—to protect children from predators. Marcus Dixon is not a predator."[23] Brooks introduced legislation to change the law, but his efforts came too late to help Marcus Dixon.

Marcus Dixon's case garnered much local and national attention. Marcus is African American and the adopted son of white parents. The alleged victim is white. Members of the African American community held rallies and otherwise advocated for Marcus's release, alleging that the prosecution was racially motivated.

Assistant district attorney John McClellen prosecuted the case. In a television interview, he admitted that the aggravated child molestation charge was used as a "backstop" in case Marcus was acquitted on the rape charge.[24] McClellan's remarkable candor underscores the extent to which prosecutors openly engage in practices that are clearly inconsistent with American Bar Association standards and their duty to seek justice in every case. This openness undoubtedly stems from their awareness that there is no effective system in place to hold them accountable for questionable practices and policies.

The Supreme Court of Georgia reversed Marcus Dixon's conviction for aggravated child molestation on May 3, 2004, on the ground that the state legislature did not intend that the statute be used in cases involving nonforced sex between teenagers less than three years apart in age.[25] The court presented a detailed explanation of the legislative history of the statutory rape and child molestation statutes and concluded that there was "a clear legislative intent to prosecute the conduct that the jury determined to have occurred in this case as misdemeanor statutory rape."[26] It concluded by urging the legislature to reexamine the statutes and make a clearer distinction between statutory rape, child molestation, and the other sex crimes.

The reversal of Marcus Dixon's conviction for child molestation is noteworthy from several perspectives. First, a reversal in any criminal case is a rare phenomenon. Second, the issue the court addressed—charging the same behavior under several statutes—is a common practice that courts have long upheld.[27] Third, although the court's opinion clearly dealt with prosecutorial discretion in charging, it does not directly address the issue. Instead, the court focused on the legislature's failure to clarify the laws, providing yet another example of the judiciary deferring to prosecutorial discretion.

DISCRETION IN THE CHARGING PROCESS

We have seen how prosecutors single-handedly control the charging process. This power is problematic because frequently it is exercised inequitably. Even when prosecutors intend to perform their duties responsibly and without bias or favoritism, as most do, they often fail. Is this failure largely the result of the arbitrary nature of the exercise of prosecutorial discretion and the relative absence of efforts to standardize or regulate charging practices?

Prosecutor offices handle the exercise of discretion in individual cases in different ways. Much depends on the practice of the chief prosecutor of a particular office. In most state and local jurisdictions, the chief prosecutor is called the district attorney or state's attorney and is an elected official. She hires assistant district or state's attorneys to work in her office and has the power to supervise, promote, and fire them. The chief prosecutor may grant total discretion to individual prosecutors to handle cases as they see fit. This practice obviously leads to dissimilar results in similar cases in a single office. At a minimum, even a chief prosecutor who seeks to grant maximum independence and freedom to her assistants tends to inform them of her general philosophy regarding the prosecution of certain cases. Prosecutors who want to be promoted or at least stay in favor with their boss would be inclined to follow that philosophy.

For example, if a district attorney ran for office on the promise of prosecuting drug offenses zealously to get drugs off the streets, she would want her assistant prosecutors to help her fulfill that promise. The assistant prosecutor who regularly declined to bring charges in these cases would probably face a reprimand and certainly would not be promoted or otherwise advance in that office. The district attorney with a more laissez-faire philosophy might not promulgate specific charging policies and require her assistants to follow them, but she would certainly give them general guidance.

Other district attorneys may establish specific charging policies for certain types of crimes. For example, a number of prosecution offices have established strict charging policies for firearms offenses, requiring that every person caught in possession of an illegal firearm be charged under the relevant statute, regardless of the circumstances. Others require assistants who wish to make an exception to the policy to seek permission from a supervisor or even from the district attorney herself.

Many chief prosecutors grant their assistants broad discretion to make decisions about individual cases. There are no prosecution offices that have mandatory charging policies for all offenses, and very few offices that have such policies for any offense. The combination of vast discretion and inconsistent charging decisions inevitably results in

THE POWER TO CHARGE

the disparity in charging illustrated by the treatment of McKnight and Ware described at the beginning of this chapter.

The arbitrariness of discretionary charging decisions sometimes results in race or class disparities, but not always. Sometimes the disparities seem unfair simply because there is dissimilar treatment of similarly situated people, regardless of their race or socioeconomic status. The vast majority of my clients at PDS were young, poor, African American men with limited formal education and no job skills. Yet there were vast disparities in how they were treated, even when significant factors like their criminal history and the nature of the offense were taken into account. The differences in treatment certainly varied from prosecutor to prosecutor, but even individual prosecutors were not consistent in their own charging policies. A great many unpredictable factors came into play, such as the recommendations of the arresting officer, the interest of the victim in prosecution, and the prosecutor's own caseload, to name a few. Although all of these factors are considered to be legitimate considerations,[28] their application creates disparate and often unfair results, even in the charging practices of a single prosecutor.[29]

A busy prosecutor with a large caseload has a limited amount of time to work on each case, so she prioritizes. As McKnight's case illustrates, there are even disparities in the treatment of very serious cases. However, for the most part, prosecutors will almost always devote the most attention to the most serious cases—homicides, rapes, serious assault, and other cases involving violent or otherwise dangerous offenses.

The prosecution of other, less serious cases depends on a variety of unpredictable factors. For example, if a prosecutor has a number of household burglaries among his pending cases, his consideration of a legitimate factor like the victim's interest in prosecution may produce disparities. Consider Burglary A committed in a poor, high-crime section of town. The police arrest Defendant A, who lives in the same neighborhood as the victim. The evidence is pretty strong. The police discover the defendant's fingerprints on various items in Victim A's apartment and proceeds of the burglary, including a radio and some costume jewelry, in the defendant's home. The defendant is arrested, and the prosecutor must make the charging decision.

First, the prosecutor notices the victim's address. She lives in a very rundown apartment building in a neighborhood known for drug dealing and other crimes. He decides to call the victim to ascertain her interest in prosecution, but he soon notices that she has no phone. At this point, the prosecutor is seriously considering dismissing the case altogether. He's been down this road before. With no means of contacting Victim A by phone, it is highly unlikely that she will show up for witness conferences, the grand jury, or the trial. Frequently, residents in Victim A's building never receive their mail because it is often stolen from the lobby because of broken mailbox locks. Even if by some miracle the victim receives the prosecutor's mailed notices of witness conferences, if she has a job, she probably won't show up because these conferences are scheduled during work hours. In addition, police officers are often unsuccessful when they attempt to serve subpoenas in that area because people in that building rarely open their doors for the police voluntarily.

The prosecutor looks at Defendant A's criminal record. He has a couple of misdemeanor arrests, but no convictions. Prosecution doesn't seem worth the trouble in this case. He dismisses the case, and Defendant A is free to go. The prosecutor is sure he won't receive complaints from Victim A, and he doesn't. She doesn't have a phone, and she doesn't know who to call.

The same prosecutor considers Burglary B. Victim B lives in a single-family home in an upper-middle-class neighborhood. Defendant B, like Defendant A, lives in the same neighborhood as the victim. The evidence is equally strong—a stolen portable CD player and gold necklace are found in Defendant B's possession, and his fingerprints are lifted from various items in Victim B's home. The prosecutor is quite familiar with Victim B's neighborhood. Its residents are professionals—primarily lawyers, doctors, and business owners— and they report very few crimes. The prosecutor notices that the victim is a college professor. He calls the first of the three phone numbers listed for her and is pleased to reach her instantly. Victim B is upset and angry. Defendant B is a neighbor's son whom she has known since his birth, and she is outraged that he would break into her home and steal her belongings. When Victim B found her home trashed and her personal belongings strewn throughout her home, she never dreamed that Defendant B was responsible. When she finds out, Victim B wants Defendant B prosecuted to the maximum extent of the law. Before the burglary, she had seen him smoking marijuana on her neighbor's porch and reported the incident to his parents. Victim B is confident that the burglary and particularly vicious trashing of her home was "payback."

The prosecutor checks Defendant B's criminal record. It's clean— no convictions or arrests. He is a college-bound high school senior. Ordinarily, the prosecutor would give someone like Defendant B a break, but he doesn't think he has much choice in this case. He has to prosecute. This victim would undoubtedly call his supervisor and make trouble for him if he didn't. Besides, the prosecution is likely to be easy. The victim will probably appear for every conference and court appearance and will make a great witness—articulate, sympathetic, and very appealing to a jury.

The victims and defendants in cases A and B were very similar in every way that should be relevant to a criminal prosecution. The victims suffered similar harms, and the defendants were very similarly situated—their actions were virtually identical, and neither had a criminal record. The prosecutor, victims, and defendants were all African American, so race wasn't an issue. Class seemed to play a role, but not in a clear and consistent way. Victim A may have been as interested in prosecution as Victim B, but because she didn't have a phone and lived in a depressed neighborhood, the prosecutor decided that the costs of prosecution outweighed the benefits. Victim B's middle-class status certainly affected the prosecutor's decision as he thought about her appeal as a witness, but it was probably her strong interest in prosecution that swayed him most. Had the prosecutor made an effort to communicate with Victim A, he might have learned that she was equally committed to prosecution. Defendant B's status as a middle-class college-bound student didn't help him at all in this case. The prosecutor might have given him a break if Victim B had not been so insistent on prosecution.

Neither race nor class was a conscious consideration of the prosecutor in cases A and B, but either factor may have had an unconscious effect on the prosecutor's decisions. The decisions on the surface appear to be driven by expediency: Victim B's case posed fewer demands on the prosecutor's already busy schedule. But should expediency carry greater weight than other factors in making the charging decision? Furthermore, the claim of expediency may mask deeper, unacknowledged attitudes influenced by class. Might the prosecutor have been more comfortable meeting with the college professor—an articulate, professional woman with whom he could empathize? Perhaps both expediency and class attitudes played a larger role in the decision-making process than other legitimate considerations.

Some of the factors that appear to be legitimate considerations in the charging decision may not be so legitimate when examined closely. For example, the victim's interest in prosecution, the criminal history of the defendant, and the strength of the government's case all appear to be valid factors at first blush, but the effect of other issues on these factors may lessen their validity. Cases A and B illustrate how the victim's interest in prosecution may be misconstrued and the role that class may play in making that determination. The prosecutor made assumptions about Victim A's interest in prosecution on the basis of where she lived and his prior experience with other victims in that neighborhood. He felt so comfortable with his unsubstantiated assumptions that he didn't even bother to try to contact her to ascertain her interest in prosecution.

The criminal history of the defendant seems to be a neutral and fair consideration. The defendant without a criminal record may be more deserving of less serious charges or a more favorable plea bargain than one who is a repeat offender. On the other hand, criminal records may be deceiving, especially arrest records. Blacks and Latinos are stopped, searched, and arrested more frequently, so they are more likely to have an arrest record, even if they are no more involved in criminal activity than their similarly situated white counterparts.[30]

The strength of the government's case must be considered in determining whether there is sufficient evidence to secure a conviction. A weak government case may be an indication that the defendant is not guilty, or at least that the case is not worthy of prosecution. For example, if a case depends on a weak eyewitness identification or minimal circumstantial evidence, the prosecutor would be wise to forgo prosecution. On the other hand, a case with a confession corroborated by solid physical evidence like fingerprints or DNA may be worthy of prosecution. However, prosecutors sometimes consider unreliable factors in assessing the strength of their cases. For example, the victim's interest in prosecution and her jury appeal are often considered in determining the strength of the case. Because prosecutors often miscalculate these factors or consider them unfairly, their importance may be either overstated or inappropriately considered. Prosecutors must certainly consider whether a witness is able to communicate with the jury effectively, but if such a problem exists, it is the prosecutor's job to work with the witness and prepare her to testify. Some witnesses need more help than others, but that factor should not determine whether their cases should be prosecuted, nor should it result in an arbitrary windfall for the accused.

WILLFUL BLINDNESS

The prosecutorial practices described in this chapter frequently produce uneven and unjust results, but they are common, legal practices. The U.S. Supreme Court has endorsed and protected prosecutorial discretion in its jurisprudence, even making it difficult to mount legal challenges to practices that appear to clearly violate the constitutional rights of the accused and/or the crime victim.[31] These clear cases of prosecutorial misconduct that involve intentional violations of the law will be discussed in detail in chapter 7.

In many ways, the legal exercise of prosecutorial discretion is more troubling than some of the cases involving the intentional prosecutorial misconduct that courts have found to be illegal and impermissible. Because these practices occur at a stage of the process that is hidden from public view, they are difficult to address. If the public were aware of the uneven exercise of power and discretion behind the scenes, it might choose to hold prosecutors accountable through the electoral process, but, as will be explained in chapter 9, this process has proven to be largely ineffective.

Prosecutors become so accustomed to the arbitrary exercise of their power and discretion at the charging stage that they, at best, honestly believe they are making evenhanded decisions, and, at worst, engage in willful blindness. When there is no effective system of public accountability, it is difficult to engage in honest and meaningful self-critique. It's a lot easier to simply forgo prosecution in a case where the victim is difficult to locate, inarticulate, and needy than to take the time to address those needs. It's harder to explain a decision to forgo charges in a case involving a first-time offender to an obstinate victim bent on prosecution than it is to go along with her wishes. Has willful blindness become the norm?

Sometimes prosecutors engage in willful blindness at the charging stage when it comes to police practices. When prosecutors review cases, they have a responsibility to ensure that the police investigative practices were lawful and constitutional. If the police engaged in an illegal arrest or search or used illegal practices to extract a confession from a suspect, prosecutors should reevaluate their desire to prosecute.[32] Yet some prosecutors don't even question police about these issues. It's easier to simply go forward with the prosecution than engage in the thorny exercise of confronting the very police officers on whom they rely to successfully prosecute their cases.

To what extent is the prosecutor liable for the behavior of a police officer when she goes forward in a case where the officer has broken the law? By engaging in a "don't ask, don't tell" policy, prosecutors may claim ignorance if it is discovered that the police acted illegally. Prosecutors should be held responsible for their failure to take affirmative steps to ensure that the evidence they sponsor in court is obtained legally.

The Tulia, Texas, cases provide a stark example of willful blindness gone awry.[33] In 1999, a police officer named Tom Coleman arrested forty-six individuals, thirty-nine of them African Americans, on alleged drug distribution charges in the tiny town of Tulia, Texas. Although the arrests and subsequent convictions were based solely on Coleman's word with almost no corroborating evidence, the prosecutor, Terry McEachern, secured convictions in thirty-eight cases. The defendants received lengthy sentences, some as long as ninety years. In 2003, a judge overturned all of the convictions because Coleman's testimony was not credible. The governor signed thirty-five executive pardons to free the wrongfully convicted residents of Tulia, Texas.

It is difficult to fathom how McEachern secured convictions in these cases. There was little to no physical evidence in any of the cases—no wiretaps, videotape, fingerprints, or marked money, and no other witnesses. When asked how he kept records of all of the alleged undercover drug buys, Coleman claimed to have written the date, time, and other information on his leg. Instead of questioning Coleman about the lack of corroborating evidence and investigating the arrests further, McEachern chose to march forward, knowing he would likely secure convictions from an all-white jury, despite the weakness of the cases.

The Tulia cases received widespread national attention, and the injustices were ultimately corrected after many of the residents spent years in prison. Tom Coleman has been prosecuted for perjury, and

McEachern was referred to the state bar disciplinary authorities for his failure to provide exculpatory information to the defense. The bar association found that he had violated a number of disciplinary rules and suspended his bar license for two years.[34]

The Tulia cases raise important questions about the extent to which willful blindness by prosecutors at the charging stage of the process can result in serious injustices. If Tulia had not been exposed in the national press, it is highly unlikely that McEachern would have been referred to the state bar for misconduct.[35] Some form of what happened in Tulia has likely happened before, in Texas and elsewhere, and likely continues to occur in prosecutor offices across the nation. When prosecutors have no affirmative duty to ensure the credibility of the evidence on which they rely to obtain convictions and are permitted to turn a blind eye to clear warnings of wrongdoing, results like those in Tulia should be expected.

Prosecutors can and should exercise their discretion at the charging stage of the process to ensure that similarly situated victims and defendants are treated evenhandedly and to ensure outcomes that are consistent with the fair, effective, and efficient administration of justice. They should consider the principles of punishment, including notions of rehabilitation and mercy, and they must also consider practical issues such as caseloads, resources, and particular, unpredictable issues that may arise in individual cases. In chapter 10, I will discuss specific approaches that prosecutors may use to reform the current system. It is clear that continuing the same approach to prosecution without consideration of broader notions of fairness will continue to produce the same results—inequitable treatment of victims and defendants in the criminal justice system.

THREE

Let's Make a Deal: The Power
of the Plea Bargain

The term "plea bargaining" usually evokes negative reactions from individuals who are not directly involved in the criminal justice system. It conjures up images of lawyers cutting deals in back rooms and criminals getting undeserved breaks. Despite the public's general disapproval, plea bargaining is one of the most pervasive practices in the criminal justice system. Almost all criminal cases are resolved with a guilty plea by the defendant.[1] Many believe that the entire system would come to a crashing halt if the practice were abolished.

Plea bargaining is the term that describes the process of prosecutors negotiating with criminal defendants to secure a guilty plea. Specifically, it consists of a bargain between the defendant and the prosecutor, with the defendant agreeing to forgo his constitutional right to a trial and plead guilty to one or more charges in exchange for one or more promises by the prosecutor, usually a promise to dismiss other charges and/or advocate for a favorable sentence. Like the charging decision, plea bargaining is controlled entirely by the prosecutor. The defendant may express a desire to plead guilty to certain charges in an indictment but not others. However, if the prosecutor does not agree to dismiss the other charges in exchange for the guilty plea, neither the defendant nor the judge has the power to compel her to do so.

Both the prosecutor and the defendant reap benefits from plea bargaining. Without it, prosecutors would be forced to conduct trials in every case they prosecute. The defendant has a constitutional right to a trial in every case, and the prosecutor has the burden of proving every element of each offense beyond a reasonable doubt before a judge or a jury.[2] Trying cases is hard work and very time-consuming. The prosecutor must subpoena the witnesses, prepare them to testify, and prepare witness questions, the opening statement, and the closing argument. Trials can be slow and protracted, with frequent interruptions. Depending on the type of case, they can last days, weeks, or even months. If prosecutors had to try every case they charged, they would not have time to fulfill their other prosecutorial duties and responsibilities. In addition, prosecutors may be reluctant to try a case where they may not be able to prove the offenses beyond a reasonable doubt. Thus, they have a strong incentive to offer plea bargains to defendants that will encourage them to give up their right to trial.

Defendants also benefit from plea bargaining. The constitutional rights to a trial and proof beyond a reasonable doubt are lofty, fundamental, and very important privileges that one should not readily surrender. As significant as these rights are, however, it is frequently in the defendant's best interest to give them up and plead guilty. The government's burden of proof in a criminal case sounds like a heavy one, but if there is strong evidence of guilt, the burden is easily met. When the exercise of one's constitutional rights will result in a long prison term, these rights begin to sound a lot less attractive.

At first glance, plea bargaining appears to be a great deal for both sides. The prosecution and the defense enter into an agreement with each other to further their respective interests and goals. Ideally, they come to the table on equal footing, with both sides experiencing some losses and some gains. However, in reality, the prosecutor always has the upper hand because of her control over the process. Does the arbitrary exercise of discretion during the plea bargaining process produce and perpetuate uneven results in the criminal process? This chapter will attempt to shed light on this issue.

HOW THE PROCESS WORKS

Plea bargaining is usually a very informal process. It can occur at any point after the charging decision has been made, or even before formal charges are brought. However, prosecutors are not required to offer a plea bargain in every case. As in the case of the charging decision, the prosecutor decides whether to offer a plea bargain and what that offer should be. She does not have to justify her decision to offer or decline a plea bargain to the judge, defense attorney, or anyone other than possibly the supervising prosecutor in her office.

In most cases, prosecutors make the plea bargaining decision early in the process. At some point after the defendant is presented with a copy of the charges, the prosecutor will let the defendant know whether there is a plea offer and whether the defendant must accept the offer by a certain date. The prosecutor may make a plea offer in open court during a hearing or by communicating the offer to the defense attorney outside of court. Typically, the judge will schedule a status hearing at some point before the trial date, primarily for the purpose of determining whether the defendant will plead guilty or exercise his right to a trial. Frequently, the prosecutor will have communicated the plea offer to the defendant before the status hearing. If the defendant accepts the offer, he may plead guilty at the status hearing, and the judge will either sentence him at that time or, in more serious cases, schedule a sentencing hearing for a later date.[3]

Although most plea offers are made early in the process, they can be made at any time, even during a trial or after a trial while the jury is still deliberating. If the trial didn't go as well as the prosecutor expected and she fears that the defendant may be acquitted of all charges, she may make a plea offer even at this late stage of the process. Because no one can be certain of how a jury will decide a case, the defendant may decide to play it safe and accept the offer.

Sometimes plea bargaining involves negotiating between the prosecutor and the defense attorney, with offers, counter-offers, and discussion about the relative strengths and weaknesses of the prosecutor's case. This informal negotiation always occurs outside the courtroom. The prosecutor will offer to dismiss one or more charges in exchange for the defendant's guilty plea to other charges. The defense attorney may make a counter-offer that would produce a more favorable result for her client. The prosecutor may not accept the counter-offer, but may respond with an offer that is more attractive to the defendant than her original offer. If the parties reach an agreement, they inform the judge, and the guilty plea is entered at the next court hearing.

A typical burglary case illustrates the process. If the defendant is arrested for breaking into a private home and stealing a number of items, he may be charged with several offenses. They may include

first-degree burglary, first-degree theft, and destruction of property. If
the prosecutor decides to make a plea offer, she has total discretion to
decide what the offer should be. There are no laws or rules that dictate
or even guide her decision.[4] A typical plea offer in such a case might be
a guilty plea to second-degree burglary (a less serious type of burglary
that carries a lighter penalty than first-degree burglary) in exchange for
the prosecutor's agreement to dismiss the other charges. If the defendant was not detained after his arrest, the prosecutor also might agree
not to oppose him staying in the community after his guilty plea,[5] or
even to support a sentence of probation at the sentencing hearing.

A different plea offer in the same case might involve a more favorable result for the defendant than a plea to second-degree burglary.
For example, the prosecutor might offer a plea to attempted burglary,
which is a misdemeanor with a penalty of a year or less in jail. The
prosecutor might also offer a deal less attractive to the defendant—for
example, a plea to the first-degree burglary. Any of these offers might
be sweetened by the prosecutor's agreement to support the defendant's
release at the time of the plea or to support probation or a reduced
penalty at the sentencing hearing.

The defense attorney may always try to encourage the prosecutor to offer a better deal for her client, and often she is successful,
depending on a variety of different factors. If the defense attorney has
investigated the facts of the case, she may discover weaknesses in the
government's evidence. For example, she may discover that there are
eyewitnesses who failed to identify the defendant or that her client's
fingerprints were not found on the scene. During plea negotiations,
the defense attorney might point out these weaknesses in an attempt
to broker a more favorable deal for her client. If the defendant has no
prior criminal record, this factor may also persuade the prosecutor to
reduce the stakes.

With so many options and no limits or guidelines, how does the
prosecutor make the decision? The answer is as simple as it is fright-
ening: any way she likes. Arbitrary decision-making is as likely in the
plea bargaining process as in the charging process. There are a number of
legitimate factors that prosecutors may consider in deciding whether
to plea bargain with the defendant. However, as with charging, there is
no requirement that they take these factors into account as they make
the plea bargaining decision. One of the most significant factors is the
prosecutor's caseload. Most prosecutors have very heavy caseloads[6]

and must make plea offers in the majority of their cases because they simply do not have the time and resources to go to trial in all of them. Another factor is the victim's interest in prosecution. As with the charging decision, the prosecutor is not required to consult with the victim, but the victim's interest in participating in a trial, his availability to appear for witness conferences before trial, and how well he performs as a witness are all legitimate factors to consider in making the plea bargaining decision.[7] The defendant's prior record is another important factor. A first offender is more likely to receive a more generous plea offer than someone with a significant prior record.

There are also other factors that are not legitimate considerations but often may be the most influential. For example, if the prosecutor has a particularly good or bad relationship with the defense attorney, that fact will undoubtedly affect the plea bargain. Plea negotiations require give-and-take, which is unlikely if the parties don't get along. The media's interest in a particular case is another factor that always influences the prosecutor's decision to plea bargain. If a particular case has a high profile in the media, either because it involves a well-known defendant or because it involves a particularly horrific crime, the prosecutor may be less inclined to offer a plea. This decision may be based on the prosecutor's desire to appear "tough on crime" in cases the media has exposed to the public. And although they are rarely consciously or intentionally considered, the race and class of either the victim or the defendant may subconsciously influence a prosecutor's plea bargaining decisions.[8]

Overriding issues that influence the entire process are the philosophy and management style of the chief prosecutor. If the head of the prosecutor's office believes in long periods of imprisonment and is not inclined to support alternatives to incarceration, she may establish plea bargaining policies that limit the discretion of the prosecutors on her staff.[9] The chief prosecutor's management style will also influence the process, regardless of her philosophy of punishment. Even a chief prosecutor who believes in alternatives to incarceration will affect the process if she limits her staff's discretion by requiring prior approval of each plea offer.

With so many charging options and legitimate and illegitimate factors that may or may not be considered, it is no surprise that the plea bargaining process tends to be unsystematic and arbitrary. Some prosecution offices offer plea bargains more than others, and there are disparities in application within offices, depending on the proclivities of the chief prosecutor and the individual prosecutors on her staff. Some of the disparities break down along race and class lines, and some do not. The result is vagueness, inconsistency, and ultimately the inequitable treatment of defendants and victims, all of which create a sense of unfairness in the criminal justice system.

The absence of transparency in the process compounds the public's lack of confidence in plea bargaining. Although courtrooms are open to the public in adult criminal cases, it would be difficult to discover the types of plea bargains prosecutors offer without sitting in criminal courts every day. Even in the unlikely event the prosecutor's constituents had the interest and time to court-watch, they would not have an effective basis for determining whether similarly situated defendants and victims were treated equitably because so many of the important factors in making this determination would not be revealed in open court. Of course, the reality is that individuals do not have the interest or time to court-watch, and there is no mechanism to provide this information to the public. The public is informed about particular cases only when members of the media decide to report them.

UNFAIR DEALS

Andrew Klepper

The media discovered and reported the arrest and prosecution of Andrew Klepper, a white, middle-class young man who lived in a Maryland suburb outside Washington, D.C., with his parents. His father was a lawyer, and his mother was a high school guidance counselor. Andrew attended a prestigious high school with a reputation for high achievement among its students. When he was fifteen, Andrew and two friends who attended the same school hired a prostitute, invited her to Andrew's home, and proceeded to brutally assault and rob her. They struck her with a baseball bat, sodomized her with the bat handle and a large ink marker, and robbed her of over $2,000.[10]

Andrew was charged as an adult with first-degree sex offense, conspiracy to commit a first-degree sex offense, armed robbery, and conspiracy to commit armed robbery. All of these charges carry a maximum penalty of life in prison in the state of Maryland.[11] The evidence against Andrew was overwhelming and included his own confession to the crime.

Despite the horrific nature of the crimes, Andrew Klepper never served a day in prison. The prosecutor offered him a deal that involved his guilty plea to robbery, first-degree assault, and fourth-degree sexual offense. The prosecutor also agreed to support a suspension of his prison term and a five-year term of probation so that he could enroll in a facility for troubled youth in Tennessee called Peninsula Village. Peninsula Village treats severely troubled youth with six to eight weeks in a locked admissions unit followed by intensive group therapy in an outdoor setting. As part of the agreement, Klepper would spend an additional eighteen months at Peninsula before enrolling in an unspecified boarding school that specializes in treating troubled youth. Klepper's parents agreed to pay for the cost of the treatment. Ultimately, the Tennessee authorities declined to supervise Klepper's probation, so the Maryland judge resentenced Klepper and placed him on unsupervised probation so he could receive the rehabilitative treatment at the Tennessee facility.

First offenders are frequently offered deals that result in a probationary sentence, but rarely if they commit very serious offenses, and Klepper's crimes were among the most serious. Furthermore, Klepper's involvement in the offense was much more destructive than that of his codefendants. According to the victim, he seemed to be the leader of the group, and he performed the most heinous act—the sodomy with the baseball bat and marker. Yet, ironically, he was the only one of the three boys to avoid imprisonment. His nineteen-year-old less culpable accomplice, Young Jiun Song, was not present during the sexual assault and received a four-year sentence.[12] Even the fourteen-year-old accomplice, whose case was transferred to juvenile court, was detained in a juvenile facility.

Did Klepper's social status, wealth, and possibly his race influence the prosecutor's decision to offer him such a lenient plea bargain? It certainly may be reasonable to provide rehabilitative services rather than punishment for a juvenile first time offender.[13] But if Andrew Klepper was deserving of such help, then so are other young first offenders charged with the same offenses.

The prosecutor might respond that he gave Klepper a break because his parents found and paid for an alternative that provided rehabilitative services and that he would have given a similar break to other similarly situated defendants, regardless of their race or socioeconomic background, had they proposed to provide a similar appropriate alternative. The prosecutor might further argue that it is not his role to secure alternatives to incarceration for criminal defendants and that he is not responsible for the inequities in society that divide people along socioeconomic lines. Why should Andrew Klepper be denied rehabilitative treatment because others in his situation cannot afford it?

These arguments have some force, but they may not tell the whole story. Could the prosecutor have agreed to the plea bargain because he empathized with Andrew Klepper and his parents? Klepper's parents were well-educated professionals who hired a well-known criminal defense attorney to represent their son. Klepper was a popular student at one of the best high schools in the county. He was bound for college and had a bright future. Could the prosecutor have looked at Andrew and his parents and seen a life and family worth saving? Would the prosecutor have offered the same deal to a poor, African American male with no family support, no education, and no foreseeable future? The reality is that the poor African American male would never be able to afford such services, so prosecutors are rarely compelled to confront these issues.

The fact that few if any governmental entities provide free programs or services to treat defendants with problems and needs like those of Andrew Klepper is an indication that legislatures do not support such alternatives for individuals who commit crimes this serious.[14] The legislatures may be shortsighted or just plain wrong, but should an individual like Klepper be allowed to buy his way out of punishment with the assistance of the prosecutor while others who may be just as deserving of help are sent to prison?

Erma Faye Stewart

Erma Faye Stewart's case was much more typical. Ms. Stewart was a poor African American woman with very limited education and even less understanding of the criminal justice system. She was arrested on November 2, 2000, in Hearne, Texas, for drug distribution on the word of a confidential informant who later was proven to have lied. She was held in jail on a $70,000 bond pending the outcome of her case.

Stewart proclaimed her innocence steadfastly from the moment she was arrested. Nonetheless, her court-appointed attorney urged her to accept the prosecutor's plea offer. He told her that if she did not take the plea, she would be facing a ten-year prison term. When Stewart told her lawyer that she couldn't plead guilty to something she didn't do, he became impatient with her. According to Stewart,

> He was, like, pushing me to take the probation. He wasn't on my side at all. He wasn't trying to hear me. He wasn't trying to explain nothing to me. And I even had told him, you know, "My understanding, you know, is not that good, so, you know, you're just going to have to really break it down to me, for me to understand."[15]

Stewart's lawyer told her that if she pled guilty, she would be released and placed on probation. After almost a month in jail, she decided to plead guilty to something she insisted she didn't do.

> Even though I wasn't guilty, I was willing to plead guilty because I had to go home to my kids. My son was sick. And I asked him, "Listen, now, you know—you know, I can plead for five-year probation. You know, just—just let me go home to my kids."[16]

On the date of her guilty plea hearing, Stewart learned that the prosecutor insisted on a ten-year period of probation. Desperate to go home, she agreed and pled guilty. The judge imposed a fine and court costs. Three years after the plea, Ms. Stewart was working as a cook making $5.25 per hour. She was evicted from the housing project where she and her children had lived, and they were put in foster care. Because of her conviction, she was ineligible for food stamps or federal aid to pursue an education. She won't be able to vote until two years after her ten-year period of probation has ended. Needless to say, she was not able to pay the $1,000 fine or the court and probation costs.

Stewart was one of twenty-five people who were arrested on the word of the same confidential informant. The first trial of one who declined to plead guilty started on February 19, 2001. It was soon revealed that the informant had lied, and within a few weeks, all of the remaining cases were dismissed. Had Ms. Stewart not pled guilty, her case would have been dismissed as well. The prosecutor offered no assistance and expressed no regrets.[17]

Obviously, many people who plead guilty actually committed the offense to which they admit guilt. But Erma Faye Stewart's case illustrates the pressures that many defendants feel when facing long prison terms, especially when they are detained prior to their trials. Unfortunately, most defendants have lawyers more like Stewart's than Klepper's, without the time, resources, or desire to investigate the case and mount a viable defense, and prosecutors who are more than willing to offer a plea even when they are not confident that they can prove guilt beyond a reasonable doubt. No one should plead guilty under these circumstances, but it happens frequently.

PLEA BARGAINING WITH THE SNITCH

Another type of plea bargain involves the defendant promising to cooperate with the prosecutor by providing information that will assist in the prosecution of another defendant in exchange for a dismissal or reduction of his own charges. Cooperation may take many forms, including meeting with the prosecutor and providing information outside of court. It may also involve testifying under oath against another defendant and providing evidence of that person's guilt. The defendant is commonly called an informant or "snitch" and frequently has been involved in the crime along with the person he is testifying against. The snitch is motivated to testify against his accomplice to avoid conviction and imprisonment on all of the charges brought against him. Sometimes the snitch has not been involved in the same crime, but has access to information that is helpful to the prosecution's case and wishes to "trade" this information for assistance from the prosecution in getting a lighter sentence in his unrelated case. For example, the snitch may be someone who has been imprisoned or detained with the defendant and claims that he heard the defendant admit guilt to the crime or make other inculpatory statements that would be helpful to the prosecutor's case.

As with other plea bargains, either side may initiate these deals. If the potential snitch is a codefendant, the deal may depend on who is lucky enough to contact the prosecutor and offer assistance first. This factor has great importance in the federal system, where defendants frequently face lengthy terms of incarceration. Sometimes, the prosecutor may have more of an interest in one defendant than the other—either because that person has a more serious criminal history or because his involvement in the crime was more serious than that of his codefendants. Either of these factors may affect who initiates the negotiations and who ends up with the deal.

Does plea bargaining with snitches create more opportunities for similarly situated defendants to be treated differently? The potential for perjury is a troubling aspect of plea bargains that require testimony under oath. A defendant may know or believe that he will get a better deal from the prosecutor if he can provide information in the form of testimony that will corroborate and strengthen the prosecutor's case against another defendant. This belief may entice him to fabricate evidence such as a confession or other inculpatory statement. A defendant who is incarcerated will commonly contact the prosecutor, either directly or through his attorney, and claim that another defendant admitted his involvement in a crime. The snitch may offer to testify in exchange for some action on the part of the prosecutor that will decrease his prison time. Of course, individuals sometimes do, in fact, confess to others, but this type of evidence can easily be fabricated. The prospect of getting out of prison sooner provides a strong motivation to commit perjury.

There is a similar incentive and potential for perjury in cases involving an individual testifying against his accomplice. In such cases, the prosecutor presumably has independent evidence of each defendant's involvement in the crime, but sometimes detailed information about each individual's specific actions may be weak or nonexistent. For example, if the police catch two masked armed robbers fleeing the scene of the crime, the prosecutor may have enough evidence to convict both of them, but because the perpetrators were masked, the victim would not be able to identify which held the gun and which acted as the lookout. Although each individual would be guilty of armed robbery, the details about which individual played the dominant role might be important to the prosecutor, who may want to offer a deal to the one who was not in possession of the gun. She would be especially prone to do this if she believes that person's testimony would strengthen her case.

The potential for perjury raises critical questions about the prosecutor's role in presenting the testimony of a snitch. No lawyer may present the testimony of a witness she knows will commit perjury. Such an act is called suborning perjury, and it is a criminal offense.[18] Of course, a prosecutor may legitimately claim that she doesn't *know* the witness is lying, unless she has credible evidence that totally contradicts his testimony. Prosecutors are under no obligation to conduct thorough investigations to ensure the veracity of each witness. Thus, they may engage in willful blindness, presenting a witness who helps their case without testing the truthfulness of his testimony.

At least one federal court attempted to put an end to the use of accomplice testimony. In *United States v. Singleton*,[19] the defendant Sonya Singleton was convicted of conspiracy to distribute cocaine and seven counts of money laundering. One of the witnesses who testified against her, Napoleon Douglas, was originally charged as a coconspirator. Douglas made a deal with the prosecutor that involved him testifying against the defendant in exchange for the prosecutor's promise to forgo further charges against him and to advocate on his behalf at his sentencing hearing and with the parole board after his incarceration. Singleton appealed her conviction, alleging that the trial judge should not have permitted Douglas's testimony because it was in violation of section 201(c)(2) of title 18 of the United States code, which prohibits giving, offering, or promising anything of value to a witness for or because of his testimony. According to Singleton, the prosecutor violated this statute by promising lenient treatment to Douglas in exchange for his testimony.

A three-judge panel of the U.S. Court of Appeals, Tenth Circuit, created a firestorm among federal prosecutors across the country when it reversed Singleton's conviction, holding that the prosecutor had violated the federal statute when he made a deal with Douglas. Prosecutors saw the court's ruling as a threat to their successful prosecution of criminal cases by prohibiting one of their most common practices. Although the ruling technically applied only in the Tenth Circuit, it potentially created a precedent that other federal courts might follow.

The opinion of the three-judge panel was not in effect long enough to have any impact. Nine days after the opinion was issued, the court ordered that the case be reheard by the entire court.[20] It also ordered that the opinion be vacated pending the rehearing. The full court ultimately reversed the three-judge panel, maintaining the practice of federal prosecutors using the testimony of informants.[21]

The court held that Congress did not intend for the statute to apply to prosecutors and noted that the practice of offering leniency in exchange for testimony has deep roots in American legal history, dating back to the common law in England.

The same three judges who wrote the panel opinion dissented when the case was heard by the full court. According to the dissent:

> Contrary to the concerns expressed by some commentators and courts, *see United States v. Ware,* 161 F.3d 414 (6th Cir. 1998), a straight-forward interpretation of § 201(c), which encompasses a prohibition against the government buying witness testimony with leniency, actually aids the search for truth. In theory, the leniency is only in exchange for "truthful" testimony. *See United States v. Haese,* 162 F.3d 359, 366–67 (5th Cir.1998). But as the Supreme Court has recognized: "Common sense would suggest that [an accused accomplice] often has a greater interest in lying in favor of the prosecution rather than against it, especially if he is still awaiting his own trial or sentencing. To think that criminals will lie to save their fellows but not to obtain favors from the prosecution for themselves is indeed to clothe the criminal class with more nobility than one might expect to find in the public at large." *Washington v. Texas,* 388 U.S. 14, 22–23, 87 S.Ct. 1920, 18 L.Ed.2d 1019 (1967).[22]

The dissent further points out that there are other ways prosecutors can use accomplices to assist in the prosecution of cases that would not involve the risk of perjury:

> I accept the government's position that accomplices can provide important information and interpreting § 201(c) to include prosecutors might require some changes to elicit testimony of some witnesses. While it would be up to the Department of Justice to devise ways of compliance, the government is not precluded from offering leniency in exchange for information and assistance short of actual testimony at trial. Likewise, the government could prosecute accomplices first, then compel their testimony by subpoena against co-conspirators. Finally, the government could request that

the district court order an accomplice to testify under a grant
of immunity. Surely the Department has the ability and resources to come up with effective and lawful means for pro-
curing necessary accomplice testimony. However, I also accept the defense attorneys' position that government leniency
in exchange for testimony can create a powerful incentive to
lie and derail the truth-seeking purpose of the criminal justice
system.[23]

PLEAS AND MANDATORY MINIMUM SENTENCES

Although the plea bargaining process always has provided prosecutors
with a great deal of control over the outcome of criminal cases, their
discretion and power is even more significant in cases involving mandatory minimum sentencing laws. These laws require the sentencing
judge to impose a specific minimum term of incarceration for specified
offenses. Although there always have been some mandatory minimum
sentences, specifically for first-degree murder and other very serious
offenses,[24] mandatory minimum sentencing laws were passed in large
numbers on the federal level, and in most states, beginning in the early
1980s.[25]

Mandatory minimum sentencing laws, along with sentencing
guidelines, were passed with an eye toward limiting judicial discretion.
However, these laws did not eliminate the discretion that produces
disparities in sentencing. Instead, prosecutors assumed exclusive control over the discretion that was once shared with judges. Race, class,
and other disparities continued, but now prosecutors retained the
lion's share of the responsibility for these inequities. Prosecutors controlled the outcome of criminal cases through their charging and plea
bargaining decisions even before the passage of mandatory minimum
sentencing laws. However, after these laws were passed, the balance of
power in the criminal justice system was tilted even more in favor of
prosecutors.

Because almost all criminal defendants ultimately plead guilty, the
charging and plea bargaining decisions of prosecutors essentially predetermine the outcome in criminal cases with mandatory minimum
sentences. These decisions certainly narrow the range of penalties in
cases without mandatory sentences, but when there is a required

minimum sentence, the judge has absolutely no discretion. Of course, if the defendant decides to go to trial and is convicted, the result is the same—the judge must impose a minimum predetermined period of incarceration for each offense for which the defendant is convicted.

Mandatory minimum sentences not only have stripped judges of sentencing power but also have driven defense attorneys to advise clients to accept plea bargains that they may previously have advised against. Ideally, the plea bargaining process involves negotiation between prosecutors and defense attorneys, with each side reaping some benefits and suffering some losses. Although the prosecutor was always at an advantage because of her control over the process and ability to have the last word, defense attorneys would sometimes have a few bargaining chips. For example, upon investigation of the case, they might discover weaknesses in the government's evidence that would allow them to secure a better deal for their clients. Sometimes, the investigation revealed evidence causing the client to decide to go to trial rather than accept a plea offer. In the rare case, the prosecution might even agree to dismiss the case. Mandatory minimum sentences have produced a change in this more equitable plea bargaining process.

In cases involving mandatory minimum offenses, the stakes are often too high for a defendant to exercise his constitutional right to trial, regardless of the weakness of the prosecutor's plea offer. Even if he believes he has a good chance of being acquitted because of the weakness of the government's case or the strength of his own defense, the defendant can never be sure of what the verdict of a judge or jury will be. If the defendant is charged with several or many offenses and the jury convicts him of all of the charges, he faces a term of incarceration on each offense when he is sentenced. If the judge is permitted to exercise discretion when imposing sentence, the defendant at least has a chance of convincing the judge to show some leniency. However, if the defendant is convicted of one or more offenses, each of which requires a mandatory minimum term of incarceration, he faces a definite, long prison term.

Prosecutors frequently impose expiration dates on plea offers that make it impossible for defense attorneys to effectively counsel their clients. For example, a defendant might face charges that carry a minimum of fifteen mandatory years in prison. The prosecutor might offer a deal that would result in five mandatory years, but may require the defendant to accept the offer within forty-eight hours. If the offer is made soon after the charges were filed, the defense attorney may not have the opportunity to investigate the case. Although expiration dates may be imposed in any plea offer, they have a particularly devastating effect in cases involving mandatory minimum sentences.

Investigation is one of the most important responsibilities of the defense attorney. If she does not investigate the case, she may not discover weaknesses in the government's case or other information that might exonerate the defendant. But this investigation often takes time—witnesses may be difficult to locate, and scientific or medical evidence may need to be tested. A defendant may have a strong defense, but his attorney may not make a timely discovery of the supporting information. If the defendant is facing a minimum of fifteen mandatory years in prison, an otherwise lengthy five-year period of incarceration begins to look attractive. The always risky business of going to trial becomes even more treacherous when the judge has no discretion to show leniency at time of sentencing. Thus, defense attorneys are often in the uncomfortable position of advising clients to consider plea offers without providing them with all of the information they need to make an informed decision.

REFORMING THE PROCESS

Despite the inherent flaws in the process, plea bargaining is here to stay. The criminal justice system would never be able to accommodate trials in every case, nor is such an outcome necessarily desirable. Defendants who choose to accept responsibility for their criminal behavior should not be discouraged from doing so, as long as the decision is made voluntarily and with the benefit of the advice of counsel. Prosecutors should be willing to dismiss charges and support a reduced sentence to "reward" defendants for their acceptance of responsibility and for giving up their constitutional right to trial. However, the process is in great need of reform.

The plea bargaining process would be greatly improved if prosecutors were required to provide all of the relevant information that would enable the defendant to make an informed decision. The prosecutor should reveal the weaknesses in her case and inform the defendant of information that is helpful to the defense.[26] Defendants would undoubtedly continue to accept plea offers because of the risky nature of jury trials. However, the provision of this information would provide more fairness and balance to the process. Prosecutors also should be required to corroborate the testimony of cooperating witnesses to reduce the potential for perjury. These small but important reforms would improve the overall quality of plea bargaining—a practice that dominates and controls the criminal justice process.

FOUR

Prosecutors and the
Victims of Crime

The relationship between prosecutors and crime victims is complicated and frequently misunderstood. It doesn't fit neatly in the model
of our adversarial system—two parties, each represented by counsel,
battling before a neutral fact-finder to achieve their respective goals. In
fact, contrary to popular belief, the prosecutor does not represent the
victim—at least not in the way a lawyer represents a client. The prosecutor does not have a client. Instead, she represents the state, which
consists of everyone who lives in the jurisdiction she serves, including
the defendant. For that reason, her role is complicated and involves the
balancing of conflicting goals. As the Supreme Court has noted, the
prosecutor's role is to seek justice, not convictions.[1]

Crime victims have a tremendous impact on how prosecutors exercise discretion at the charging, plea bargaining, and sentencing stages
of the process. Likewise, the exercise of prosecutorial discretion has an
impact on victims and how they are treated throughout the process.
Do crime victims influence the exercise of prosecutorial discretion in
ways that produce unfair results for defendants? Does the exercise of
prosecutorial discretion lead to unjustifiable disparities in how victims
are treated in the criminal process? This chapter will explore these and
other questions about the relationship between prosecutors and crime
victims.

THE PROSECUTOR-VICTIM RELATIONSHIP

Prosecutors are not simply advocates for the state; they are also ministers of justice. In that sense, their role is very different from that of the
defense attorney, whose sole responsibility is to represent the interests
of her client. When a prosecutor brings criminal charges against an
individual and seeks to incarcerate that person, she is making a judgment that these actions serve the interests of justice. The person who
breaks a criminal law presumably is causing harm and violating the
community's moral standards. The prosecutor's decision to charge and
seek incarceration of that person is a subjective judgment that such
actions will serve the purposes of protecting society and punishing the
defendant.

Not all crimes involve direct harm to individual people. For example, possession of illegal drugs and driving under the influence of
alcohol are often referred to as "victimless crimes." They each create
the potential for harm to others, but the actions that constitute these
crimes do not cause a specific, identifiable harm to another person. By
criminalizing these behaviors, society has made a judgment either that
they cause harm to society in general or that they are morally wrong
and therefore worthy of punishment, regardless of the harm they may
cause.

Of course, many crimes do cause direct harm to individual
people—for example, the person who is robbed or assaulted or whose
property is damaged or stolen. These victims of crime clearly have a
greater interest in these cases than members of the community
who were not directly harmed. They also play a crucial role in the
prosecutor's case because they usually serve as witnesses if there is
a trial—either because they are able to identify the defendant and
testify about what they experienced or saw or because they are able
to provide information about property that was stolen or damaged.
The critical question is whether they should play a greater role in
the prosecution of a case than that of an ordinary witness whose
sole function is to provide evidence in support of the prosecutor's
case. Should the prosecutor consult with the robbery victim before
making a plea offer to the defendant? Should the victim have the
right to veto a plea bargain or decide whether a case should be dismissed?

As with most other prosecutorial issues, the role of the victim in the prosecution of criminal cases varies widely from office to office and even within individual offices. Some prosecutors consult with victims before making plea offers, and some don't. Some prosecutors consult with some victims and not others. Some prosecutors will not make a plea offer unless the victim "signs off" on the deal. Other prosecutors treat victims purely as witnesses and barely keep them informed of the status of the case. One former prosecutor described her relationship with crime victims as that of "a good parent" and sometimes "a benevolent dictator."[2]

A prosecutor's relationship with a victim in a particular case often depends on who the victim is. Although some prosecutors take great interest in the victims of crime and treat them with dignity and respect, others do not. Most prosecutors naturally feel more comfortable working with the victim who is cooperative, sympathetic, and interested in the prosecution of the case than with the victim who is uncooperative and difficult to reach. Class and cultural differences also play a role. The prosecutor may find it easier to communicate with a victim who is highly educated and articulate than with someone who has difficulty expressing himself and may feel intimidated by the court system and its procedures. The "squeaky wheel" theory operates in prosecution offices as elsewhere—the cases of the victims who call and show up for witness conferences and court appearances understandably will receive more attention than the cases of those who don't. Race and class issues sometimes affect charging and plea bargaining decisions, resulting in cases with poor victims and/or victims of color being prosecuted less zealously than other cases, as discussed in chapter 2.

On the other hand, if the prosecutor is sympathetic and attentive to a poor victim's needs, that victim sometimes will become the most enthusiastic and cooperative supporter of the prosecutor's case. One former prosecutor noted that poor victims were often unemployed and otherwise living dejected and difficult lives. They were often motivated to honor subpoenas to the grand jury and other court hearings because they knew they would be paid witness fees. In addition, in serious cases, the detectives would drive them to and from court and provide the attention and concern that was otherwise frequently missing from their lives. As this prosecutor put it, "Someone in the system finally treats them with humanity."[3]

PROSECUTORS AND THE VICTIMS'
RIGHTS MOVEMENT

The victims' rights movement evolved in the 1970s, primarily because many crime victims believed that the criminal justice system did not treat them with humanity, regardless of their race, class, or gender. Initially focused on the poor treatment of victims of sex crimes and domestic violence, the victims' rights movement began to address the concerns of all crime victims and ultimately was successful in its efforts to secure legislation requiring compensation and support for victims. The movement also has resulted in amendments to a number of state constitutions that guarantee certain rights for victims, including the right to be informed of, present at, and heard at critical stages of the criminal process.[4] The victims' rights movement has been one of the most successful political movements in recent history. According to one author, "there has been a literal explosion of federal and state action to increase crime victim access to and participation in the criminal justice process."[5]

Victims' rights advocates did not focus their criticisms of the criminal justice system solely, or even primarily, on prosecutors. Initially, the most vigorous criticism was aimed at police officers, because they are the criminal justice officials whom most victims first encounter. Rape and domestic violence victims voiced legitimate complaints about the way police officers treated them, with complaints ranging from a failure to arrest victims' abusers to a lack of sensitivity to the trauma they had endured. Many victims received no better treatment from prosecutors, who often chose to dismiss these cases for a variety of reasons, including their belief that the victim would change her mind about prosecution or that a jury would not convict.

The victims' rights movement was responsible for a culture change in the treatment of crime victims, especially among police officers and prosecutors. The state legislation and constitutional amendments that established and protected victims' rights undoubtedly helped to inspire this change. Although crime victims continue to have conflicts with various criminal justice officials, there is a consensus that the improvements have outweighed the problems.

Prosecutors generally have supported the victims' rights movement, and many have been active participants. Prosecutors have been instrumental in the passage of many state constitutional amendments and have supported the use of victim impact statements at sentencing hearings. Prosecutors' offices also have administered most compensational and support programs for victims.[6]

Not surprisingly, prosecutors do not hold uniform views on all issues that concern crime victim advocates. Plea bargaining and charging decisions are two of the issues that cause considerable disagreement between prosecutors and crime victims. Although some state laws require prosecutors to obtain victims' input and/or notify them of plea negotiations,[7] there is no legal remedy for victims if the law is not followed.[8] Consequently, practices vary from office to office, and, often, prosecutors who do confer with victims on plea bargains are inconsistent—notifying and conferring with victims in some cases but not others. Victims are even less involved in the charging decision. There are no laws or constitutional amendments that provide a right to be heard regarding the charging decision, and there is much less prosecutorial support for victim involvement at this stage of the process.[9]

WHEN INTERESTS CONFLICT

Although the prosecutor doesn't serve as the victim's lawyer, she usually represents the victim's interests. Most victims want the perpetrator of the crime to be convicted and punished, and the prosecutor almost always shares these goals. Sometimes, however, the victim has different or additional interests. For example, the victim may know the defendant and may be interested only in restitution. Or maybe she wants to see the defendant held accountable for his actions but doesn't want to go through the stress and inconvenience of a trial. In such cases, a victim may support some type of plea bargain or even dismissal on the condition that restitution is paid.

On the other hand, some victims appear almost fanatical in their desire to punish the defendant, showing up for every court appearance (even when their presence is not required) and demanding that the prosecutor seek the harshest punishment. One former prosecutor indicated that she was especially cautious when dealing with these cases, particularly if the victim and the defendant knew each other or had some type of prior relationship. "If the victim seemed too zealous, a

red flag would go up," she noted, explaining that these victims sometimes had an axe to grind, or some other less than honorable reason for
seeking prosecution.[10]

Because the prosecutor always represents interests broader than
those of the individual victim, she should not be governed by the
victim's desires in a particular case. Society's broad interest in enforcing the law is always an important factor to consider. Other practical interests that affect the fair and effective administration of justice
also play a part. For example, even if the victim is insistent that the
prosecutor seek a long prison term for a particular defendant, the prosecutor must make an independent judgment about whether such an
outcome serves the interests of justice, taking into account numerous
additional relevant factors. Such factors include the defendant's criminal record and the particular facts and circumstances of the case. If the
victim believes that the defendant should not serve time, the prosecutor
should likewise make an independent assessment of whether probation
is fair considering all of the circumstances, regardless of the victim's
desires. Thus, although the victim's wishes should be considered, they
should not govern the prosecutor's actions in a particular case. The
prosecutor must assess how much weight to give to the victim's concerns, and this assessment will vary, depending on the case.

Sometimes, the victim may seek an outcome that totally conflicts
with the prosecutor's view of how the case should be prosecuted. If a
victim opposes the prosecutor's approach to the case, she can be an
impediment to a successful prosecution. If a witness doesn't show up
for witness conferences or court appearances, some prosecutors feel
compelled to dismiss the case. However, the prosecutor may compel
the victim to appear if the victim has been served with a lawful subpoena. In such cases, the prosecutor may request that the judge issue a
bench warrant to authorize law enforcement officers to arrest her and
bring her to court. Obviously, most prosecutors would like to avoid
going to these lengths if for no other reason than to avoid having to put
an angry, hostile witness on the stand. What should prosecutors do
when the interests of crime victims conflict with their own?

Ray Jefferson's case illustrates the problems that can arise when a
victim actively opposes a prosecutor's approach to a case. Jefferson was
charged with simple assault[11] and possession of a prohibited weapon in
the District of Columbia.[12] The weapon was a carpet sweeper. Jefferson was charged under the section of the statute that made it a crime

to be in possession of any object when it is used as a weapon. The government alleged that Jefferson had beaten his wife with the carpet sweeper.[13] I was appointed to represent Jefferson, and despite the fact that the charges were simple misdemeanors, it was one of the most troubling cases I handled in my twelve years as a public defender.

After I was assigned to the case, I proceeded to conduct an investigation of the facts, as I did in all of my cases. The first and most important step in a defense investigation is to speak to the government's witnesses and attempt to secure a written statement from them. In this case, the victim was the only witness to the crime. My investigator and I went to the Jefferson home to speak with her.[14] When she opened the door to her apartment, I was stunned. Mrs. Jefferson's face was badly bruised and swollen. One eye was swollen shut, and several of her teeth were missing. She was holding an infant, and two young children were on either side of her, holding onto the tattered housecoat she was wearing. When I found my voice, I explained that I was her husband's lawyer and that I wanted to speak with her. To my surprise, she invited me and my investigator to come in and have a seat.

Before I could ask her permission to take a written statement, Mrs. Jefferson immediately told me that she didn't want to proceed with the prosecution. She said that she had been trying to reach the prosecutor to tell her that she didn't want charges brought against her husband. She had not been able to contact her by phone, and the prosecutor had not responded to her messages. I explained to her that I had no control or influence over this decision, and she would have to work it out with the prosecutor. She was not interested in talking about what her husband was charged with doing to her, but she did want to give a written statement indicating that she had no interest in prosecuting the case. I took a short written statement from her that expressed her desire that the case be dismissed. As I prepared to leave, she told me that she didn't see the point in sending her husband to jail. She needed him to keep his job, so he could provide financial support for the family. She said she didn't think he would hit her again, but somehow I didn't think she really meant it. I thanked her for her time and told her I would give the statement to the prosecutor.

When I showed the statement to the prosecutor, she was furious. She told me that she didn't care what Mrs. Jefferson wanted and that it wasn't up to Mrs. Jefferson to decide how the case was prosecuted. The prosecutor went on to say that she had a duty to fight domestic violence and that she was going to fulfill that duty, with or without Mrs. Jefferson's help.

I was as stunned by my meeting with the prosecutor as I was when I met with the victim. Most surprising was the virulent anger that she seemed to direct at the victim. The prosecutor seemed angrier with the victim than with my client. It was as if the victim was ruining *her* case and impeding *her* fight against domestic violence. Instead of viewing the victim as a person who was badly hurt and in need of assistance and compassion, the prosecutor seemed to view her as the enemy— someone standing in the path of her battle against domestic violence. There was a definite patronizing tone in her voice—a sense that this poor woman was too ignorant to know what was good for her.

When I left the prosecutor's office, I felt strangely conflicted. I felt no less committed to my client and was determined to fight for his interests and keep him out of jail. Nonetheless, I felt sorry for this victim as well because the prosecutor was treating her badly and re-fusing to consider her concerns. I also empathized with Mrs. Jefferson because she was a poor African American woman, and I felt that the prosecutor's attitude toward her was condescending.

Mrs. Jefferson began to call me, continuously seeking my assis-tance. At this point, I felt it necessary to clearly draw the line. I told her that I was very sorry about her situation but that I had been assigned to represent her husband, and if it appeared that I was in any way assisting her in avoiding her responsibilities to appear in court, I could be charged with obstruction of justice. I told her that there was a status hearing in the case in a few days,[15] and she was certainly free to come to the court and speak with the prosecutor in person. I gave her the date of the hearing, and she said that she would come.

Mrs. Jefferson showed up at the status hearing with her children in tow. When Mr. Jefferson's case was called, she came into the court-room and sat in the audience. When the judge asked if there would be a trial in the case, I decided to inform her of the victim's presence in the courtroom and of her lack of interest in prosecution. The prose-cutor responded with her now characteristic anger. She informed the judge that she had no plans to dismiss the case, that she planned to deliver a subpoena to Mrs. Jefferson, and that if Mrs. Jefferson didn't show up, she would ask the court to issue a warrant for her arrest. The judge sided with the prosecutor, using the occasion to inform

Mrs. Jefferson that she would grant the prosecutor's request for a warrant if she didn't appear on the trial date.

Although Mrs. Jefferson was not the prosecutor's client, the prosecutor certainly should have considered Mrs. Jefferson's concerns in her assessment of how to handle the case. Instead, she chose to totally ignore Mrs. Jefferson's attempts to explain her situation and ultimately threatened to seek her incarceration if she failed to appear on the trial date. Had the prosecutor taken the time to speak with Mrs. Jefferson, she might have been able to persuade her to pursue the prosecution. At a minimum, she might have come to some understanding of Mrs. Jefferson's concerns.

Ultimately, I persuaded the prosecutor to agree to a postponement of the case while Mr. Jefferson completed a program of rehabilitative therapy for batterers. After his successful completion of the program, she ultimately agreed to dismiss the case. Her decision undoubtedly was influenced by the prospect of trying to secure a conviction with a hostile and uncooperative victim.

Domestic violence cases epitomize the complexities of prosecutor-victim conflicts. There is a long and troubling history of law enforcement officers—police and prosecutors—failing to protect women who have been assaulted by their husbands or partners. As a result, some jurisdictions responded by passing laws or establishing policies that require arrest and prosecution in these cases, regardless of the preference of the victim. The laws and policies were designed to protect women from further abuse and to address situations in which women were requesting that cases be dismissed as a result of threats from their husbands and partners. These so-called no-drop laws and policies may serve an important function but sometimes result in the victims being treated like Mrs. Jefferson—ignored and disrespected throughout the process.[16]

The case of Ricky Joseph Langley illustrates the problem of prosecutor-victim conflict in a different context. Langley was charged with capital murder in the state of Louisiana for the murder of a six-year-old child. He was convicted in 1994, but his conviction was reversed, and he was granted a new trial. The second trial was not held until 2003. The district attorney, Rick Bryant, zealously pursued the death penalty again, despite the fact that the victim's mother, Lorilei Guillory, asked the prosecutor to agree to a guilty plea that would have required a mandatory prison sentence of life without the possibility of parole.

Guillory was clear that she had not forgiven Langley for the brutal murder of her son but noted that she didn't need him put to death to heal. She also stated that she wanted to avoid the stress and pain of going though another capital murder trial. She stated that she wanted the district attorney to accept the plea agreement to life in prison without parole but the district attorney declined Guillory's request.[17]

The district attorney certainly did not have to abide by the wishes of the victim's mother. Although it was his duty to consider her views, it was his responsibility to make this important decision independently, on the basis of all of the relevant factors. Bryant's behavior was noteworthy, however, in the same way as that of the prosecutor in the Jefferson case. He treated Guillory as the enemy and was vocally and publicly hostile to her. He even blamed her, in part, for the jury's verdict of second-degree murder—a verdict that does not permit the death penalty and requires the sentence that Mrs. Guillory had asked Bryant to accept. In a press conference, Bryant said, "[Lorilei Guillory] was against everything that we were trying to do to the point of trying to help Ricky Langley be found not guilty by reason of insanity, and we had a real problem with that."[18] Guillory expressed her belief that the prosecutor had made her life more difficult since the death of her son.

Prosecutors should neither ignore nor cater to the interests or desires of victims of crime. Victims are human beings who have suffered a direct harm as a result of criminal behavior. They deserve compassion and, if possible, restitution. They do have a greater interest in the case than the entire community that the prosecutor serves, and their interests and desires should be given greater consideration. However, victims' interests and concerns are but one set of factors among many that prosecutors must consider in making decisions about how to prosecute a case.[19] If the prosecutor has determined that the defendant poses a danger to society because of the seriousness of the offense and the defendant's prior record, it would be reasonable for him to go forward with the prosecution, even if the victim indicates that she wants the case dismissed. But if the defendant would not pose a danger, and the victim is not interested in prosecution, a dismissal might be a reasonable result. On the other hand, if a victim is insistent that the defendant should be punished to the full extent of the law, but the prosecutor believes that a plea offer to a misdemeanor is appropriate, either because the case is weak or because the defendant does not have a prior record, he should offer the plea, regardless of the victim's wishes. Common sense and a careful weighing of all of the relevant considerations should govern the prosecutor's decision-making process.

RACE, CLASS, AND THE "WORTHY" VICTIM

The subtle complexities of race and class frequently affect important prosecutorial decisions. Cases with articulate, cooperative, well-educated victims will more likely go to trial than cases with witnesses who don't show up for witness conferences, don't express themselves well, or have a criminal record that would be revealed to the jury during their testimony. Although these judgments appear to have a class or racial effect, one can point to legitimate race- and class-neutral reasons for them. It is reasonable for a prosecutor to take into account the victim's willingness to show up and jury appeal in her assessment of the likelihood of obtaining a conviction in a particular case.

However, do prosecutors treat some cases as more important solely because the victim is a more prominent or important person—someone more "worthy" of a vigorous prosecution than other crime victims? Do class and/or race sometimes coincide with "worthiness?" The case of James Robinson raises these issues. Robinson was charged with felony murder in the District of Columbia in 1991. He was accused of robbing an individual at gunpoint and killing him during the course of the robbery. Unfortunately for Robinson, his victim happened to be a young, white college student from Nebraska who was a summer intern in the District of Columbia. Felony murder is one of the most serious forms of homicide and is charged as first-degree murder, but there was nothing noteworthy or more heinous about this felony murder than any other. The only remarkable detail about the case was the fact that the victim was a young white man from the Midwest. At that time, the vast majority of murder victims in the District of Columbia were African American.

From the beginning, it was clear that this case would receive special attention from the prosecutor's office. There was attention from the press, and prosecutors always behaved differently in cases the press followed for at least one obvious reason—the public would be watching. The prosecutor's behavior also was affected by the fact that the victim had a prominent and assertive advocate—a congressman from his state, whom the victim's family had contacted after the murder. The congressman appeared at many court hearings in the case, no matter how routine. He was often joined by a Nebraska newsman who was assigned to his paper's Washington bureau. The congressman attended the initial bond hearing and appeared on the local news later that night. He later showed up for status hearings—the routine hearings where mundane issues like schedules for filing motions, evidentiary and other legal issues, and trial dates are discussed. He was not permitted to speak or otherwise participate in the hearings, but everyone knew who he was and noticed his presence. The prosecutor was often seen chatting with him before and after court hearings, so it was clear that the prosecutor was, at a minimum, listening to his views.

I was the director of PDS at that time, and our office was appointed to handle the case. As was typical with cases of this magnitude, this one was handled by an experienced trial lawyer and cocounseled by a junior lawyer whose role was to assist with the defense under supervision. It was clear that there would be no plea offer and that the case would be going to trial.

Almost one year after Robinson's arrest, the trial began. Robinson was represented by Tony Morris, one of the most experienced senior attorneys in our office. His junior co-counsel was Sara McCarthy. One of the government's witnesses was a former codefendant who had negotiated a deal to testify against Robinson. During this witness's direct testimony, he revealed that he had been involved in other criminal activity with the defendant. This testimony drew an immediate objection and a request by the defense for a mistrial. The court agreed that the witness's testimony was unduly prejudicial and granted the mistrial.

The trial court directed the parties to return to court on the following Monday to select a new jury and begin a new trial. The next morning the *Washington Post* prominently reported that a mistrial had been declared in the trial of James Robinson after a government witness revealed prejudicial information. The defense, already concerned about the amount of news coverage generated by the case, was alarmed about the most recent reports and the obvious impact such reporting would have on the ability to select a fair and impartial jury. Morris was prepared to raise this concern with the judge prior to jury selection on Monday morning. The defense request would be to postpone the trial. Recognizing that a continuance was unlikely, Morris was prepared to accept, if the prosecutor and the court would agree, a less suitable alternative—a more comprehensive questioning of potential jurors than is normally available to the parties. Before any such request was made by the defense, however, the prosecutor indicated that her cousin had died over the weekend and that she would be requesting a continuance. Morris did not object, and the judge granted the continuance.

Several months later, the trial began. In the early morning on the fifth day of the trial, I received a distressing phone call. Tony Morris had suffered a stroke and had been admitted to the intensive care unit of a local hospital. I was stunned and heartbroken. Tony Morris was one of the best and most well-liked attorneys in the office. I was very worried about his condition but knew that it was my responsibility to report the unfortunate news to the court and move for a mistrial. In his condition, there was no chance that Tony would recuperate in time to resume the trial.

I decided to go to court in my capacity as the agency's director to inform Robinson, the judge, and the prosecutor and to make what I thought would be a routine and unopposed motion for a mistrial.[20] I was in no way prepared for what occurred. After I went to the holding cell to inform Robinson of his attorney's illness, I decided to tell the prosecutor what had happened and inform her of my intention to seek a mistrial. The prosecutor, an African American woman I had known for some time, expressed concern for Tony's well-being. The judge entered the courtroom, and I approached counsel table as Robinson was brought out from the holding cell. I informed the court of the situation and moved for a mistrial. The judge turned to the prosecutor to ask if she opposed the motion. To my surprise, she did.

First, the prosecutor announced that a mistrial, which would entail aborting the trial, dismissing the jury, and rescheduling the trial to begin anew on a date some time in the future, would be far too inconvenient for the victim's family. They had traveled to Washington to attend the trial and were anxious to see the case resolved. The prosecutor suggested that we recess the trial for a few days to see if Morris would be able to resume his representation of Robinson. When I explained that Mr. Morris had suffered a serious stroke, was in intensive care, and was not expected to return to work for six to eight weeks at the earliest, the prosecutor began to question my representations. "Can he talk? Can he walk?" she asked. I was stunned and overcome with anger. Morris was barely holding on to life in a hospital bed, but the prosecutor showed no sensitivity or concern about his condition. I had asked for nothing more than what the same prosecutor had asked for and received when she had a death in her family. It was not as if I was asking for the case to be dismissed; a mistrial would involve dismissing the jury and rescheduling the trial for a later date. Nonetheless, the prosecutor opposed my request. She obviously was more concerned about inconveniencing her witnesses and the victim's family than about the life of someone who was critically ill or a fair trial for the defendant.

To my surprise and dismay, the judge did not grant my motion for a mistrial. Instead, he suggested that Sara McCarthy, the junior co-counsel in the case, continue and finish the trial on her own. I informed the judge that his suggestion was not a feasible option. McCarthy only had two years of experience as a lawyer and had never tried a case before a jury on her own. I reminded the judge of our office's policy of pairing inexperienced lawyers with senior attorneys, primarily as a learning tool for the junior lawyer. The judge, who was a former PDS attorney, was well aware of the policy but didn't seem to care. His second suggestion was equally untenable. He decided to appoint another senior attorney to the case, postpone the trial for a few days while the lawyer prepared and read the transcript of the first few days of the trial, and resume the trial with the new lawyer and McCarthy. Over my vehement objections, the trial proceeded with a new unprepared lawyer entering the trial midstream. Robinson was convicted of all counts. One of the grounds of his appeal was the judge's decision to proceed with the trial in the absence of his counsel of record. The appeal was denied.

I believed that the prosecutor's decision to oppose my motion for a mistrial was motivated by the status and influence of the victim's family. That year, there were a total of 443 homicides in the District of Columbia.[21] Almost all of the victims were young black men. All of these victims had families who loved and cared about them. Many of them had been killed under circumstances even more brutal and heinous than those of Robinson's case, yet it appeared that this case was prosecuted far more zealously than any other homicide that year.

Mistrials were granted in cases every day for reasons far less serious than the critical illness of the defense attorney. I had seen mistrials declared when one of the lawyers (either the prosecutor or the defense attorney) had the flu, a migraine, or just wasn't feeling well. It never occurred to me that the prosecutor would oppose a mistrial in this case, but it was quite clear to me why she did.

There are countless examples in the media of special treatment and empathy for certain victims of crime. We hear about these cases because members of the media choose them as worthy news stories, using their criteria for what will sell newspapers and attract an audience. They always report cases involving celebrities and other public figures as either defendants or victims. But what about the other cases that news outlets choose to report? If the case involves unusual or sensational facts, there is an obvious interest in reporting it—the Columbine school shooting or the woman who found and recognized her daughter ten years after she had been kidnapped as an infant, for example. But not all of these cases involve unusual facts.

Very few people have never heard of JonBenet Ramsey. She was murdered in her home in 1995, and her killer was never found. JonBenet was a cute, blond, six-year-old whose picture was on the cover of every major magazine for months. Every news outlet constantly reported the story of her death. She was not a celebrity, nor did the public know her parents before her death. Her death, although horrible and tragic, was not unusual,[22] yet the search for JonBenet's killer was the number one story in the media for quite some time. Despite the passage of time, occasional stories on the JonBenet Ramsey investigation continue to be featured in the news.

Elizabeth Smart is another previously unknown crime victim whose name and face are now recognized in most households across the nation. Elizabeth was kidnapped from her home in Salt Lake City, Utah, in June 2002. She was missing for nine months, and not a day passed when her face and the story of her kidnapping were not featured on the news, usually as one of the top stories. Like JonBenet Ramsey, Elizabeth Smart was blond, beautiful, and the child of wealthy parents. Pictures and videos of her riding a horse and playing her harp were frequently shown on the news. Her parents appeared on almost every major television news and talk show, tearfully pleading for the nation's help in finding their daughter's kidnapper. Fortunately, Elizabeth was rescued nine months later and returned to the safety of her parents' home.

There is no doubt that the media's decision to focus on certain cases moves them to the top of the prosecutor's priority list. What is unclear is what comes first—the media attention or the prosecutor's interest in the case. Does the media begin to focus on a case that law enforcement and prosecutors bring to their attention, or do prosecutors focus on a case when they know the media is informing the public? Either way, prosecutors give these cases more attention than others for reasons that cannot be justified. These cases are not more serious than other cases involving the same type of crime, nor are the victims or their families necessarily any more cooperative or interested in bringing the perpetrator of the crime to justice. These victims are simply more sympathetic because they are attractive, and they and their families present a more appealing image than the child of a poor, single mother who isn't shown in videos doing interesting things like singing in a pageant or playing an instrument.

There is no question that the cases involving JonBenet Ramsey and Elizabeth Smart deserved the attention they received, but so does every case involving a child or any other victim of crime, for that matter. Prosecutors certainly cannot control the actions of members of the media, but they don't have to follow them. Prosecutors should not ignore these cases, but they should take affirmative steps to assure that they are not prosecuting certain cases more vigorously simply because of the status of the victim.

In sum, prosecutors should certainly support crime victims, consult with them, and consider their views when making prosecutorial decisions. However, prosecutors should never assume the role of the victim's attorney. They represent the state, not the individual victim. Their goals are much broader than those of the victim and may sometimes even conflict with the victim's wishes. Prosecutors should work hard to make sure that they are not unduly influenced by media attention, politics, or other factors that may not be consistent with the fair administration of justice. They should consider a broad range of legitimate factors when making important decisions in criminal cases, including the safety of the community, fairness to the defendant, the allocation of resources in the criminal justice system, and the interests of the victim.

FIVE

Prosecutors and the Death Penalty

No issue makes the case for restraining prosecutorial power more forcefully than the death penalty. As with just about every other critical issue in the criminal process, prosecutors exercise a great deal of control over the death penalty, especially the decision to seek the death penalty in particular cases. However, unlike other important criminal justice issues, the death penalty is final and irreversible. If a mistake is made, the unthinkable could happen—an innocent person could be executed. Since 1973, over one hundred innocent people have been freed from death row,[1] suggesting that innocent people probably have been executed.[2] Although execution of the innocent is perhaps the greatest flaw of the death penalty, there are many others, leading former Supreme Court Justice Harry Blackmun to conclude:

> From this day forward, I no longer shall tinker with the machinery of death. For more than 20 years I have endeavored— indeed, I have struggled—along with a majority of this Court, to develop procedural and substantive rules that would lend more than the mere appearance of fairness to the death penalty endeavor. Rather than continue to coddle the Court's delusion that the desired level of fairness has been achieved and the need for regulation eviscerated, I feel morally and intellectually obligated simply to concede that the death penalty experiment has failed.[3]

Despite Justice Blackmun's grim conclusions, prosecutors—the most powerful and least accountable of all criminal justice officials—continue to make the decisions that set the machinery of death in motion.

The death penalty is probably the most controversial issue in the American criminal justice system. The Supreme Court has addressed the constitutionality of the death penalty in a variety of contexts and has reversed itself on controversial issues such as the execution of juveniles and the mentally retarded.[4] Frequently the votes have been close, demonstrating deep divisions on the Court. Recent discoveries of innocent people on death row and reports documenting racial disparities in the implementation of the death penalty have energized movements to abolish the death penalty or at least declare a moratorium on its implementation. Despite its problems and flaws, thirty-eight states authorize the use of the death penalty for murder in a variety of circumstances.[5] The federal government permits the death penalty for many types of murder and for treason, espionage, and even for certain narcotics offenses.[6] The United States maintains its status as the only country in the Western world to use death as a legal punishment.[7]

HOW PROSECUTORS CONTROL
THE DEATH PENALTY

There would be no death penalty without prosecutors, because only prosecutors may decide whether or not to seek the death penalty in a particular case. Neither judges nor jurors, nor any other individual or body, may initiate the process. Although a jury must make the ultimate execution decision, prosecutors, through their charging decisions, decide which cases will be tried as capital offenses. By making the initial death penalty charging decision, prosecutors present juries with an option they otherwise would not be able to consider. Thus, the importance of this initial decision cannot be overstated.

Although the federal government and several states permit the death penalty in cases that do not involve homicide,[8] it is sought most frequently in murder cases. Prosecutors may not seek the death penalty in *every* murder case. The death penalty statutes of each state restrict capital cases to murders involving certain specified circumstances but do not require that every case that fits within these circumstances be charged as a capital case. In fact, the Supreme Court has held that statutes that mandate the death penalty are unconstitutional.[9] Thus, prosecutors maintain broad discretion to decide which of the many cases that fall within the parameters of the statute will be charged as capital cases.

Most death penalty statutes list a number of circumstances, called "aggravating circumstances," that permit a prosecutor to charge a defendant with capital murder.[10] Presumably these are the most serious and heinous murders and are so much worse than others that they warrant the ultimate punishment. The Maryland statute lists the following aggravating circumstances, which are typical of most death penalty statutes:

> (i) one or more persons committed the murder of a law enforcement officer while the officer was performing the officer's duties;
>
> (ii) the defendant committed the murder while confined in a correctional facility;
>
> (iii) the defendant committed the murder in furtherance of an escape from, an attempt to escape from, or an attempt to evade lawful arrest, custody, or detention by:
> 1. a guard or officer of a correctional facility; or
> 2. a law enforcement officer;
>
> (iv) the victim was taken or attempted to be taken in the course of an abduction, kidnapping, or an attempt to abduct or kidnap;
>
> (v) the victim was a child abducted in violation of § 3-503(a)(1) of this article;
>
> (vi) the defendant committed the murder under an agreement or contract for remuneration or promise of remuneration to commit the murder;
>
> (vii) the defendant employed or engaged another to commit the murder and the murder was committed under an agreement or contract for remuneration or promise of remuneration;
>
> (viii) the defendant committed the murder while under a sentence of death or imprisonment for life;
>
> (ix) the defendant committed more than one murder in the first degree arising out of the same incident; or

(x) the defendant committed the murder while committing, or attempting to commit:
1. arson in the first degree;
2. carjacking or armed carjacking;
3. rape in the first degree;
4. robbery under § 3-402 or § 3-403 of this article; or
5. sexual offense in the first degree.[11]

As this list demonstrates, there are many different types of murders
for which a defendant may face the death penalty. Most prosecutors
rarely seek the death penalty because of the time and expense involved
in trying these cases and because most prosecutors maintain that the
death penalty should be reserved for the very worst, most egregious
murders.[12] However, since so many murders fall within the list of death
eligible cases, prosecutors maintain immense discretion to choose who
faces death at the hands of the state.

Federal and some state prosecutors make the death penalty decision
with much more care and precision than other charging decisions. Although the chief prosecutor always makes the final decision, in some
state prosecution offices, there is a formal process involving a number
of senior prosecutors. These prosecutors meet and discuss whether the
case under consideration should be brought as a capital offense. They
consider numerous factors, including the facts of the case, the defendant's prior criminal record, and the views of the victim's family.[13]

Federal prosecutors must follow the formal procedures set forth
in the criminal resource manual of the U.S. attorney's manual before
charging a capital offense.[14] The attorney general makes the final decision, after a formal review process involving consultation with the
Capital Case Unit of the Criminal Division of the Justice Department.
This formal review process involves the submission of a death penalty
evaluation form and formal memorandum outlining the facts and
circumstances of the case and any other relevant information. Defense
counsel may submit a written or oral presentation on why the attorney
general should not pursue the death penalty. The review process also
requires consideration of the views of the victim's family.

Although some prosecution offices have review and evaluation
procedures, these procedures do little to guide the discretion prosecutors exercise during the process and provide no external accountability for the choices they ultimately make. Not all prosecutors in

death penalty states use these procedures, but even among those that do, the procedures only provide for the consideration of various factors, leaving the prosecutors free to evaluate and interpret them as they see fit. Although the procedures may make the process seem less arbitrary, it is unclear whether they do much to control the subjective and sometimes subconscious judgments that influence these critical decisions.

PROSECUTORS, RACE, AND THE DEATH PENALTY

Much has been written about racial disparities in the implementation of the death penalty. African Americans, who are only 12 percent of the population, were 34 percent of the total number of persons executed as of December 14, 2005.[15] However, the race of the victim reveals the starkest disparity in how the death penalty is implemented. As of December 14, 2005, 80 percent of the victims in death penalty cases were white, while only 14 percent were black.[16] Of the numerous studies that have examined racial disparities in how the death penalty is implemented, the most consistent theme has been the disproportionately high number of death penalty cases with white victims, regardless of the race of the defendant.[17] According to a 1990 study by the General Accounting Office, in cases involving interracial murders, the death penalty was sought far more frequently in cases involving black defendants and white victims. The same study found very few death penalty cases involving white defendants and black victims.[18]

These startling racial disparities can be attributed, in large part, to death penalty charging decisions by prosecutors. Although the jury ultimately decides whether the death penalty should be imposed, some studies demonstrate that the prosecutor's pretrial charging decision often has already narrowed the number of death penalty cases to a pool consisting disproportionately of cases with white victims. For example, one study that examined murder cases in Kentucky between 1976 and 1986 concluded that prosecutors were heavily influenced by the race of the victim and defendant when making the death penalty decision.[19] Another study of New Jersey murder cases in the mid-1980s found similar results and concluded that prosecutors were much more likely to seek the death penalty in cases involving white victims.[20]

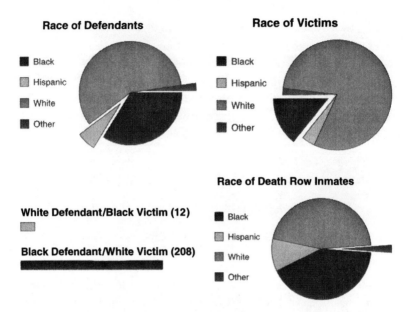

Figure 5.1. Racial Statistics of Executions and Death Row in the United States.
Source: Death Penalty Information Center (DPIC), www.deathpenaltyinfo.org.

The most well-known statistical analysis of racial disparity in the implementation of the death penalty was conducted by Professor David Baldus of the University of Iowa Law School. Known as the Baldus study, this analysis examined the implementation of the death penalty in the state of Georgia during the 1970s through an evaluation of over two thousand murder cases. Professor Baldus found that defendants charged with killing white persons received the death penalty in 11 percent of these cases, but defendants charged with killing blacks received the death penalty in only 1 percent of the cases. Baldus also divided the cases according to the race of the defendant and the race of the victim. He found that the defendants received the death penalty in 22 percent of the cases involving black defendants and white victims; 8 percent of the cases involving white defendants and white victims; 1 percent of the cases involving black defendants and black victims; and 3 percent of the cases involving white defendants and black victims.[21]

Professor Baldus's study demonstrated the significance of the prosecutor's role in these disparities. Baldus found that prosecutors sought the death penalty in 70 percent of the cases involving black defendants and white victims; 32 percent of the cases involving white defendants and white victims; 15 percent of the cases involving black defendants and black victims; and 19 percent of the cases involving white defendants and black victims.[22]

The Baldus study was presented as evidence in a case that was ultimately appealed to the Supreme Court and resulted in one of the Court's most well-known and controversial death penalty decisions—*McCleskey v. Kemp*.[23] Warren McCleskey was a black man who was convicted of the armed robbery and murder of a white police officer in the state of Georgia in 1978. The prosecutor sought the death penalty, and the jury sentenced McCleskey to death. During one of his post-conviction appeals in federal district court, McCleskey claimed that the death penalty was administered in a racially discriminatory manner and presented the Baldus study as evidence in support of his claim. McCleskey's claim was rejected, as were his appeals to the U.S. Court of Appeals and the Supreme Court. Interestingly, the Supreme Court accepted the validity of the Baldus study but held that there was no constitutional violation. According to the Court, McCleskey was not entitled to relief because he did not prove that the decision-makers in his case intended to discriminate against him because of his race.

In *McCleskey*, the Court discussed prosecutorial discretion in the death penalty context. The majority opinion sanctioned the unbridled discretion that permits prosecutors to make decisions that discriminate on the basis of race. According to Justice Powell, writing for the majority, "[p]rosecutorial decisions necessarily involve both judgmental and factual decisions that vary from case to case."[24] The dissenting opinions, on the other hand, soundly criticized the exercise of prosecutorial discretion in the implementation of the death penalty. Justice Brennan's dissent noted that the absence of guidelines governing the prosecutor's decision to seek the death penalty provided substantial opportunity for racial considerations, even if subtle or unconscious, to influence the charging decision.[25]

Justice Blackmun wrote a separate dissent, which focused on the prosecutor's role in the process to an even greater degree. He noted that the prosecutor is the primary decision-maker at each stage of the death penalty process and analyzed the evidence of abuse of discretion by the district attorney in McCleskey's case. Justice Blackmun cited the prosecutor's deposition, in which he acknowledged that there were no guidelines for when to seek the death penalty and that the only guidance was "on-the-job training." According to the district attorney, individual prosecutors made the death penalty decisions regarding their cases and were not even required to report these decisions to him.[26] Justice Blackmun noted the significance of the race of the victim at various stages of prosecutorial decision-making and urged the establishment of guidelines that might provide some procedural safeguards at these early stages of the criminal process.

The Baldus study is only one of many statistical analyses of racial disparities in the implementation of the death penalty. Another such study, published by the Death Penalty Information Center, suggests that these disparities occur, at least in part, because almost all of the chief state prosecutors are white.[27] At the time of the study, 98 percent of the chief District Attorneys in counties that use the death penalty were white, and only 1 percent were African American.[28] Although the study does not suggest that white prosecutors intentionally or even consciously pursue the death penalty primarily in cases involving white victims, it does suggest that they are more likely to have relationships with the families of white victims, and are therefore more receptive to these families' requests to seek the death penalty. Stephen Bright, the director of the Southern Center for Human Rights, suggests more unscrupulous dealings between at least one prosecutor and the family of a white victim:

> [F]rom 1973 to 1990 . . . in cases involving the murder of a
> white person, prosecutors often met with the victim's family
> and discussed whether to seek the death penalty. In a case
> involving the murder of the daughter of a prominent white
> contractor, the prosecutor contacted the contractor and asked
> him if he wanted to seek the death penalty. When the con-
> tractor replied in the affirmative, the prosecutor said that was all
> he needed to know. He obtained the death penalty at trial. He
> was rewarded with a contribution of $5,000 from the con-
> tractor when he successfully ran for judge in the next election.
> The contribution was the largest received by the District
> Attorney. . . . But prosecutors failed to meet with African-
> Americans whose family members had been murdered to de-
> termine what sentence they wanted. Most were not even no-
> tified that the case had been resolved. As a result of these
> practices, although African-Americans were the victims of 65

percent of the homicides in the Chattahoochee Judicial Circuit, 85 percent of the capital cases in that circuit were white
victim cases.[29]

WHEN PROSECUTORS OPPOSE
THE DEATH PENALTY

Robert Johnson

The Death Penalty Information Center's study exposing and criticizing the dearth of African American chief prosecutors suggests that if
there were more chief prosecutors of color, there might be less racial
disparity in the implementation of the death penalty. Ironically, one
chief African American district attorney was removed from a case when
he did not immediately seek the death penalty. The case was a high-
profile murder of a police officer. The district attorney was Robert
T. Johnson. Johnson was first elected as the Bronx district attorney
in 1988 and was repeatedly reelected by his constituents. Despite
Johnson's tough-on-crime approach, he was always open about his
opposition to the death penalty, a position with few political risks in
1988, when there was no death penalty in New York. However, in
1995, New Yorkers voted to include the death penalty as a sentencing
option.[30] Johnson maintained his opposition to the death penalty, and
in 1996, he faced a major challenge.

On March 14, 1996, Officer Kevin Gillespie, who was white, was
shot and killed after three men hijacked a car and led police officers on
a high-speed chase that ended on the Grand Concourse in the Bronx.
Angel Diaz, a Hispanic man, was identified as the gunman. Almost immediately after Diaz's arrest, Governor George Pataki made a number
of public statements suggesting that Johnson should seek the death
penalty against Diaz. Johnson made it clear that he would not be
rushed to make a decision, noting that the New York statute gave him
120 days to decide whether to seek the death penalty.[31]

Johnson and Pataki engaged in a very public dispute in the days
that followed, with Johnson maintaining that the governor would not
pressure him into hurriedly making a life-or-death decision and the
governor accusing Johnson of failing to enforce the law against someone who had viciously gunned down a police officer. The two men

even appeared on the *Today Show* and engaged in a very contentious debate. Pataki insisted that Johnson would not enforce the death penalty statute because of his personal opposition to capital punishment, and Johnson maintained that the governor was attempting to rush him into making a decision without carefully considering all of the appropriate issues.

Pataki ultimately ended the debate just seven days after the shooting when, on March 21, he issued an executive order removing Johnson from the case and assigning Attorney General Dennis C. Vacco to replace him. According to the executive order, Johnson's statements and swift rejection of the death penalty option in prior death eligible cases indicated that he had adopted a blanket policy against imposition of the death penalty.[32] The order stated that Johnson's policy violated his statutory duty to make death penalty determinations on a case-by-case basis and opened the possibility that future death sentences would be challenged as unconstitutional. The governor concluded that his immediate intervention through a superseding order was necessary in light of his obligation to assure that the death penalty law would be faithfully executed. Pataki argued that the district attorney would take action that would irrevocably foreclose the death penalty in the Gillespie matter.

Johnson sued the governor and challenged the legality of the executive order. The New York Civil Liberties Union filed a similar action on behalf of the Bronx voters and taxpayers, contending that the governor did not have the right to remove Johnson in the absence of corruption or similar illegal behavior. They argued that the governor's action disenfranchised the Bronx voters, who had reelected Johnson with full knowledge of his reluctance to impose the death penalty. Both lawsuits were dismissed, and the dismissals ultimately were affirmed on appeal. Angel Diaz was indicted for the murder of Officer Gillespie, and Vacco filed notice of his intention to seek the death penalty. The case ended in a strange twist when Diaz was found dead in his jail cell from an apparent suicide.

Ironically, Robert Johnson's public statements against the death penalty did not hurt him politically, before or after his conflict with the governor. His constituents reelected him repeatedly, knowing of his opposition to capital punishment. However, Johnson's battle with the governor raises the question of whether the electoral process can be effective as an expression of the will of the people in the selection of prosecutors, an issue discussed in more detail in chapter 9.

Kamala Harris

Several years later, a district attorney on the West Coast experienced a similar political battle involving the death penalty. Kamala Harris was elected district attorney for San Francisco in December 2003. Like Johnson, Harris is a person of color[33] who openly expressed her opposition to the death penalty before and after her election. Both prosecutors won elections in liberal pockets of death penalty states where strong support for the death penalty would not be expected.

Kamala Harris was compelled to confront the death penalty decision much sooner in her term of office than Johnson. Just a few months after her election, on April 10, 2004, San Francisco police officer Isaac Anthony Espinoza was gunned down with an AK-47. David Hill was arrested for the murder, and immediately demands for the death penalty poured in from a number of sources, including the Police Officers Association, the victim's parents, and even members of the state legislature. Officer Espinoza was Hispanic, and David Hill is African American.

Despite a great deal of political pressure, Harris declined to charge Hill with capital murder. She issued a statement explaining her decision:

> Some are demanding that death be the penalty. And I must admit that I, too, felt an immediate desire for revenge. I have been a member of law enforcement for my entire career, and so I take personally the outrageousness of violence against a police officer. Wanting an eye for an eye is also one of the oldest, and most natural, of emotions. But as one of America's greatest teachers, Dr. Martin Luther King Jr., said, "the old eye for an eye philosophy leaves everyone blind."
>
> The district attorney is charged with seeking justice, not vengeance. From my career in law enforcement and the law, it is clear to me that the death penalty is deeply flawed. Numerous studies have shown the death penalty is not

a deterrent to murder. It is prone to error, resulting in innocent people being sent to their death. It has been applied disproportionately. And it drains millions of dollars from efforts that more effectively protect public safety and promote justice.

The flaws of the death penalty are so deep, in fact, that when police chiefs were asked to rank the factors that reduce violent crime, they mention curbing drug use, putting more officers on the street, longer sentences and gun control. They ranked the death penalty as least effective. I am bound by oath and law to make decisions about what charges to bring—not based on emotion, anger or politics—within 48 hours of a suspect's arrest. Instead, I must use my long experience as a prosecutor combined with a review of the facts and the law in each case.

I have charged this case as a special circumstance homicide, which automatically carries a sentence of life in prison without possibility of parole. And, let's be clear about that sentence: It means exactly what is says. People who receive this sentence never see the light of day again. For those who want this defendant put to death, let me say simply that there can be no exception to principle. I gave my word to the people of San Francisco that I oppose the death penalty and I will honor that commitment despite the strong emotions evoked by this case. I have heard and considered those pleas very carefully and I understand and share the pain that drives them, but my decision is made and it is final.[34]

Harris was supported by a number of lawyers' associations,[35] but her explanation did not satisfy her opponents. The president of the Police Officers Association asked Harris to recuse herself from the case, and when she refused, sent a letter to California attorney general Bill Lockyer, asking that he review Harris's handling of the case. State Assemblyman Joe Canciamilla went even further, introducing a resolution in the state legislature urging state and federal officials to intervene. The resolution urged Attorney General Lockyer to determine whether he could legally intervene in the case and also asked the U.S. attorney for Northern California to review the case to determine whether the case could be prosecuted as a federal death penalty case.[36] Canciamilla's resolution did not pass, and the attorney general declined to intervene, concluding that although he would have sought the death penalty, Harris did not abuse her discretion by refusing to do so.[37]

The experiences of Johnson and Harris illustrate how prosecutors' discretionary decisions are affected by politics, especially in death penalty cases. Most state prosecutors are elected officials and thus very mindful of public perceptions of how they are performing their prosecutorial duties. Although most of their important decisions, such as charging and plea bargaining decisions, are made in private, the public pays attention to cases and issues that are exposed by the media. Death penalty cases almost always attract media attention, so prosecutors, aware of the political ramifications of their actions, are very careful about how they handle these cases publicly.

Most prosecutors in death penalty states garner political capital by seeking the death penalty in high-profile cases in an effort to show that they are tough on crime. Many of the same prosecutors will run for office on the promise of seeking the death penalty and boast about the number of death penalty sentences they secured when they run for reelection.[38] Very few will criticize the death penalty in any way, much less openly oppose it as Johnson and Harris did.

Whether a prosecutor seeks the death penalty or opposes it, these cases demonstrate the possibilities when the public is informed about the important decisions prosecutors make. When the media educates the public about an important prosecutorial decision, prosecutors often feel compelled to respond and explain their decisions, thereby providing their constituents with a basis for holding them accountable through the democratic process. Despite Governor Pataki's actions, Johnson's constituents reelected him, sending the message, at least in theory, that they approve of his decision concerning the death penalty. Time will tell if the same holds true for Harris.

ARBITRARY DECISION-MAKING

Like so many other prosecutorial decisions, the death penalty decision is far too arbitrary, often depending on the philosophy and proclivities of the chief prosecutor instead of on legal principles, standards, or guidelines. In most states, the chief prosecutor is a political animal who frequently considers the political consequences of his actions before, or instead of, standards or guidelines that are merely advisory. Given the political nature of the death penalty, it is not surprising that the decisions of Robert Johnson and Kamala Harris are the exception rather than the rule.

The arbitrariness of the death penalty charging decision is troubling for several reasons. First, the sheer gravity of the decision and its consequences cries out for some measure of process and consistent decision-making. Second, arbitrary decision-making can produce unjustified disparities, like the racial disparities documented in the Baldus study and others like it.[39] A "one-size-fits-all" approach rarely works in the criminal justice system, but notions of fairness require some consistency among similarly situated individuals.

Arbitrary decision-making causes disparities in the implementation of the death penalty on a number of levels—from case to case, from prosecutor to prosecutor, and from office to office. A study conducted by criminologist Raymond Paternoster of the University of Maryland illustrates the problem. Paternoster's study was strikingly similar to the Baldus study in methodology and results, but it focused more on the role of the prosecutor. The study found that Maryland state's attorneys are more likely to seek the death penalty in cases involving white victims and are significantly and substantially more likely to seek it in cases involving a white victim and a black defendant.[40] The study further found that the state's attorney for Baltimore County is significantly more likely to seek the death penalty than state's attorneys in any other county in Maryland.[41] Thus, according to the study, because of differences among prosecutors, whether one faces the death penalty in Maryland depends on totally fortuitous and inappropriate factors such as race and geography.

There is no evidence that any prosecutor in the state of Maryland consciously considers race when making the death penalty decision. According to Baltimore County state's attorney Sandra A. O'Connor, "[w]e knew going into the study that our policy was racially neutral, and the statistics back us up. We don't look at the race of the victim; we don't look at the race of the defendant. That has been in our policy for 20 years and will continue to be."[42] O'Connor seeks the death penalty in every death eligible case. In other words, instead of exercising discretion in making the death penalty decision, she seeks it in every murder case that falls within the parameters of the statute. This practice eliminates disparities in her county but causes tremendous disparities in the entire state, since state's attorneys in other counties rarely seek the death penalty.[43] Thus, the same law is applied and enforced in dramatically different ways, depending on where the crime is committed and the inclination of the prosecutor for that geographical area.

Some might suggest that the geographic disparities are not problematic because the prosecutors for each county must answer to the residents who elected them. In other words, if the residents of Baltimore County disagree with O'Connor's death penalty decisions, they have the power to remove her from office. Likewise, if the residents of the other counties want their prosecutors to seek the death penalty more frequently, they have the power to advocate for its greater use. These prosecutors would suggest that their constituents would complain or vote them out of office if they were displeased with the manner and frequency with which they sought the death penalty.

Does the democratic system of accountability for prosecutors function as it should? A true system of accountability requires transparency— the public must have information in order to make meaningful decisions. If the public does not know the facts and circumstances of death eligible cases, it cannot make a judgment about whether the prosecutor is exercising her discretion fairly. Currently, the public is entirely dependent on the media and the unpredictable nature of news reporting. The media picks and chooses the cases it investigates and does not have access to all of the relevant information. In the absence of a structure that regularly and systematically informs the public of prosecutorial decisions, can the public truly hold prosecutors accountable for their exercise of discretion in the implementation of the death penalty?

Accountability through transparency might improve the prosecutor's troubling role in the implementation of the death penalty, but it would not repair it entirely. Even with access to all of the relevant information, the public does not necessarily have the ability to make judgments about all of the complex legal decisions inherent in the death penalty and other important prosecutorial decisions. Although some combination of transparency and public accountability on the one hand and legal standards for prosecutors on the other might improve the prosecutorial decision-making process in death penalty cases, the many inequities that result from these decisions seem to confirm Justice Blackmun's conclusion that "the death penalty experiment has failed."

SIX

Federal Prosecutors and the Power

of the Attorney General

All of the problematic issues that affect the prosecutorial function—unbridled discretion, unrestrained power, and lack of accountability—apply to both state and federal prosecutors. The impact that these issues have on charging and plea bargaining decisions and the implementation of the death penalty affect the prosecutorial function on both the state and federal levels. These problems are played out much more intensely in the hands of federal prosecutors, however, and are thus more troubling in their sphere of power.

Beyond the expansive power of federal prosecutors, there are two primary reasons why they warrant particular attention. First, the federal government has an all-encompassing impact on everyone in the nation and a tremendous influence on state and local governments. The laws passed by the U.S. Congress govern all residents, and state and local governments often follow the lead of the federal government in the passage and implementation of their local laws and policies. Although the vast majority of criminal cases are prosecuted by state and local prosecutors,[1] in the past several decades Congress has passed an extraordinary number of federal criminal laws.[2] Many of these laws are very broad and authorize prosecution of individuals for what hardly seems a federal case.[3] Thus, federal prosecutors, as the enforcers of these laws, arguably wield even more power and control than state prosecutors.

The second basis for concern is the lack of accountability for federal prosecutors, an issue that will be explored in more detail in chapter 9. They are appointed rather than elected, and the appointments process provides for very little meaningful input from ordinary voters. The chief federal prosecutor for the nation, the attorney general, is the single most powerful federal prosecutor in the country. The attorney general's policies and decisions can have a monumental impact on the lives of ordinary people, even though the people have no meaningful system for holding the attorney general accountable.

THE ROLE OF THE FEDERAL PROSECUTOR

Federal prosecutors play a wide range of roles in various agencies and U.S. attorneys' offices across the country. The Department of Justice (often called Main Justice), located in Washington, D.C., is a massive federal structure, consisting of a broad range of offices and divisions. The organizational chart in figure 6.1 illustrates its enormity.[4]

In addition to the U.S. attorneys' offices, there are federal prosecutors in the Criminal Division of the Justice Department.[5] At one time, the Criminal Division ran "strike forces" to deal with organized crime. Today, however, the Criminal Division prosecutes a few specific crimes and assists U.S. attorneys, but its role in the mainstream of federal prosecutions is limited. There is a U.S. attorney for each of the ninety-three federal districts in the country. The president nominates the attorney general and the U.S. attorney for each district, and the Senate must confirm the appointments by a simple majority vote. Although federal law indicates that the attorney general appoints the assistant U.S. attorneys (AUSAs) who serve in each U.S. attorney's office,[6] the practical reality is that each U.S. attorney hires and fires the AUSAs in her office and has daily supervisory authority over them.

United States attorneys are responsible for enforcing the federal laws. Currently, there are over three thousand federal criminal offenses, many of which duplicate existing state criminal laws.[7] Since state and federal prosecutors have simultaneous jurisdiction over the same individuals, a decision must be made about which office will prosecute or whether there will be successive prosecutions, a practice that is legally permissible, despite the double jeopardy clause.[8] There are no rules or laws that govern how this decision should be made, and

U.S. DEPARTMENT OF JUSTICE

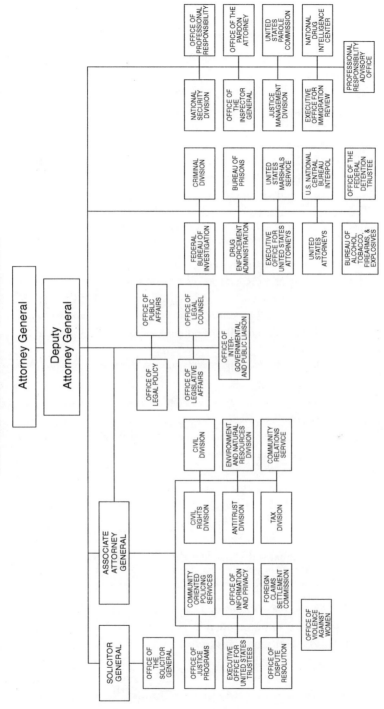

Figure 6.1. U.S. Department of Justice organizational chart.

despite the discretion and independence enjoyed by each U.S. attorney, the attorney general can set the tone and provide guidance on the types of cases each office should pursue.

The Justice Department publishes a U.S. attorneys' manual that sets forth policies and procedures for U.S. attorneys and other Justice Department lawyers in all of its divisions, including civil, tax, antitrust, environment and natural resources, civil rights, and criminal. Does the U.S. attorneys' manual effectively regulate and control the discretion of federal prosecutors? The criminal section of the manual establishes justice department policies on a wide range of criminal issues, including the circumstances under which federal prosecutors should commence or decline prosecution. Section 9-27.220 states:

> The attorney for the government should commence or recommend federal prosecution if he/she believes that the person's conduct constitutes a federal offense and that the admissible evidence will probably be sufficient to obtain and sustain a conviction, unless, in his/her judgment, prosecution should be declined because:
> 1. No substantial federal interest would be served by prosecution;
> 2. The person is subject to effective prosecution in another jurisdiction; or
> 3. There exists an adequate non-criminal alternative to prosecution.[9]

Of course, each of these exceptions is subject to the interpretation of the individual U.S. attorneys. As the comment to this section of the manual states, "[i]t is left to the judgment of the attorney for the government whether such a situation exists."[10] In fact, the introduction to the manual makes it clear that its policies and procedures are not required:

> The Manual provides only internal Department of Justice guidance. It is not intended to, does not, and may not be relied upon to create any rights, substantive or procedural, enforceable at law by any party in any matter civil or criminal. Nor are any limitations hereby placed on otherwise lawful litigative prerogatives of the Department of Justice.[11]

Ed Rosenthal's case demonstrates the extent to which the U.S. attorneys' manual controls when and under what circumstances U.S. attorneys seek federal prosecutions. Rosenthal was a medical marijuana advocate who was specifically authorized to grow marijuana for medical use by the city of Oakland in California. The California Compassionate Use Act, passed by the voters in 1996, legalized growing marijuana for this purpose. Federal prosecutors, fully aware of the legality of Rosenthal's actions under California state law, prosecuted him in federal court for violating the Controlled Substance Act, 21 U.S.C. §§ 841, 846, and 856. At his trial in federal court, U.S. District Court judge Charles Breyer prohibited Rosenthal from presenting a medical marijuana defense, so the jury never knew about the legal authority under which Rosenthal grew marijuana. He was convicted, but when the jurors discovered the facts after the trial ended, many of them were appalled. Several jurors held a press conference and expressed their dismay and outrage that they had not been permitted to consider Rosenthal's medical marijuana defense.[12] Although Rosenthal faced a maximum of sixty years under the federal sentencing guidelines, nine of the twelve jurors wrote a letter to the judge asking that he not sentence Rosenthal to prison. Even California's attorney general, Bill Lockyer, urged the judge to impose the minimum sentence permitted.[13] Nonetheless, the federal prosecutor asked for five years. Judge Breyer ultimately sentenced Rosenthal to one day in prison. The federal prosecutor appealed Judge Breyer's sentence.

Thus, the extent to which federal prosecutors in individual offices follow the policies and procedures in the U.S. attorneys' manual depends largely on the U.S. attorney in charge of each office. As with state prosecution offices, the chief prosecutor sets the tone and culture of the office and determines the extent to which individual prosecutors exercise their own discretion in individual cases. Some attorneys general have delegated substantial power and control to individual U.S. attorneys, while others have played a more significant role in the day-to-day prosecution of criminal cases. Regardless of whether the manual is followed, its language permits the broad exercise of discretion and neither requires nor prohibits particular practices or policies. Consequently, even though the criminal section of the manual encompasses numerous criminal issues, including the grand jury, indictments, capital cases, electronic surveillance, and plea bargaining, it merely provides internal guidance to the prosecutors who use it.

For example, the section on the grand jury indicates that "it is the policy of the Department of Justice to advise a grand jury witness of his or her rights if such witness is a 'target' or 'subject' of a grand jury investigation."[14] It further explains that although the U.S. Supreme Court has held that targets of grand jury investigations are not entitled to any special warnings,[15] the Justice Department will continue its longstanding policy of informing all grand jury witnesses of their right to remain silent, as follows:

Advice of Rights

* The grand jury is conducting an investigation of possible violations of Federal criminal laws involving: (State here the general subject matter of inquiry, e.g., conducting an illegal gambling business in violation of 18 U.S.C. § 1955).
* You may refuse to answer any question if a truthful answer to the question would tend to incriminate you.
* Anything that you do say may be used against you by the grand jury or in a subsequent legal proceeding.
* If you have retained counsel, the grand jury will permit you a reasonable opportunity to step outside the grand jury room to consult with counsel if you so desire.

Additional Advice to be Given to Targets: If the witness is a target, the above advice should also contain a supplemental warning that the witness's conduct is being investigated for possible violation of federal criminal law.[16]

Of course if a particular AUSA fails to give these warnings, neither the witness nor target is entitled to relief, nor does the AUSA suffer any consequences.

In sum, although the U.S. attorneys' manual appears to establish meaningful policies governing a broad range of criminal issues, its unenforceability renders it largely ineffective as a means of regulating prosecutorial power and discretion.[17] Like state prosecutors, AUSAs enjoy vast, unrestrained discretion and power in the prosecution of criminal cases. The difference lies in the fact that the exercise of federal prosecutorial discretion often has much greater consequences.

FEDERAL PROSECUTORS
AND THE WAR ON DRUGS

No phenomenon better illustrates the dire consequences of the exercise of federal prosecutorial discretion than the "War on Drugs." Launched during the 1980s,[18] the War on Drugs consisted of a series of tough anti-drug policies and laws that resulted in a massive increase in the prison population and unprecedented racial disparities at the arrest, prosecution, and sentencing stages of the criminal process. These laws and policies also resulted in a tremendous expansion of the power and discretion of federal prosecutors. First, the number of federal prosecutors increased tremendously during the War on Drugs—from twelve hundred to seven thousand.[19] And, although there has been an overall increase in the number of federal prosecutions in all offense categories, the greatest increase occurred in drug prosecutions, which tripled between 1981 and 1990.[20]

The Anti-Drug Abuse Act of 1986 provided prosecutors with the authority and incentive to pursue drug prosecutions in record numbers. Passed with alarming speed and no public hearings or consultation with experts, this law established long mandatory minimum prison terms for low-level drug dealing and possession of crack cocaine.[21] States passed laws with mandatory minimum terms before and after the federal law was passed. But the federal laws stand out because of the extreme harshness of the sentences—a mandatory five, ten, fifteen years or more as the minimum term of the sentence—laws far harsher than the state laws that penalize the same conduct.[22] Was there a need for a federal statute penalizing drug possession and distribution? State prosecutors had been effectively prosecuting drug offenses long before the 1986 law was passed, but Congress forged ahead in a highly politicized atmosphere on the heels of the death of Len Bias, a nationally known National Collegiate Athletic Association (NCAA) basketball star who died from a drug overdose.

The law was passed hurriedly without the preferred deliberation and consultation, but there was an effort on the part of the Subcommittee on Crime to provide some rational basis for the law. This Subcommittee attempted to assure that the law would be used to target "major" drug traffickers responsible for manufacturing and/or distributing very large quantities of drugs.[23] Unfortunately, their efforts did not prevail, and the final version of the law gave prosecutors broad authority to prosecute low-level users and dealers.

Although not a stated purpose, one of the most significant effects of the 1986 law was the intensification of the already considerable discretion and power of federal prosecutors. Together with the Sentencing Reform Act of 1984, which established the federal sentencing guidelines, this law effectively removed almost all of the sentencing discretion of federal judges in drug cases, while simultaneously transferring it to the officials least accountable to the people—federal prosecutors. Spurred on by the "tough on crime" politics of the Reagan and the first Bush administrations and armed with the Anti-Drug Abuse Act of 1986, the Justice Department pursued drug prosecutions with extraordinary vigor. The federal courts, previously reserved primarily for cases involving issues of national or federal interest, were flooded with cases involving small-time neighborhood drug dealers and their girlfriends and family members, who were often arrested and prosecuted for conspiracy on the scantiest of evidence.

The federal prosecution of drug offenses is probably the single most prominent example of federal intrusion into an area previously left to the states. There is no "substantial Federal interest" in prosecuting low-level drug dealers selling small quantities of cocaine or other drugs, and state prosecutors have prosecuted these drug offenses consistently and effectively on all levels—before and after the passage of the 1986 law.[24] The U.S. attorneys' manual clearly states that federal prosecution should be declined if "no substantial Federal interest would be served by prosecution; the person is subject to effective prosecution in another jurisdiction; or there exists an adequate non-criminal alternative to prosecution."[25] Reasonable minds may differ on whether criminal prosecution is a necessary response to drug use and distribution, but the first two factors suggest that federal prosecution of these offenses should be declined.

Although there are no rules or laws that determine when federal prosecutions should take precedence in cases involving concurrent jurisdiction, state prosecutors generally defer to the Justice Department when it has expressed interest in the prosecution of particular drug cases. The facts and circumstances of the cases prosecuted in federal court are not significantly different from those brought in state court, yet the results and consequences are strikingly different.

Does the exercise of discretion by federal prosecutors in drug cases produce unfair disparities? *United States v. Armstrong*[26] provides a compelling example. In this case, nine African American defendants in Los Angeles were charged in federal court with conspiring to distribute and conspiring to possess with intent to distribute more than fifty grams of crack cocaine. They also were charged with various firearms offenses. The defendants filed a motion to dismiss the indictment for selective prosecution based on race. Their claim was based on evidence that the U.S. attorney prosecuted virtually all African Americans charged with crack offenses in federal court, leaving all white crack defendants to be prosecuted in state court.[27] Since the federal law penalizes crack trafficking much more harshly than the California state law,[28] this decision by the federal prosecutor resulted in African Americans receiving harsher punishment than their white counterparts charged with the same criminal conduct.

The defendants filed a discovery motion to obtain information in support of their claim. The information requested included the U.S. attorney's criteria for deciding whether to bring charges in federal court and the number and racial identity of all defendants charged with crack offenses in both federal court and state court. The prosecution opposed the discovery motion, explaining that the facts of the case met the criteria for prosecution and denying that the defendants were prosecuted because they were black. Interestingly, the prosecution neither admitted nor denied the claim that there were no federal prosecutions of white defendants charged with these offenses. Despite the prosecution's opposition, the district court granted the motion.

The U.S. attorney went to remarkable lengths to avoid turning over the requested information. If he had not singled out African Americans for prosecution in federal court, then why not provide the requested information? The defendants did not request names or other identifying information about specific defendants, so privacy concerns were not at issue. Specifically, the district court ordered the government: (1) to provide a list of all cases from the last three years in which the government charged both cocaine and firearms offenses, (2) to identify the race of the defendants in those cases, (3) to identify what levels of law enforcement were involved in the investigations of those cases, and (4) to explain its criteria for deciding to prosecute those defendants for federal cocaine offenses.[29] Even though the prosecutors never explained how the discovery of this information would harm the prosecution of the case, their determination to prevent the discovery of the information was unrelenting. They appealed to the Court of Appeals for the Ninth Circuit, and when they lost this appeal,[30] they appealed the decision all the way to the Supreme Court.

Armstrong's federal prosecutors finally found support in the U.S. Supreme Court. The Court reversed the Ninth Circuit decision, holding that, in order to establish entitlement to discovery in selective prosecution cases based on race, a defendant must produce credible evidence that similarly situated defendants of other races could have been prosecuted, but were not.[31] The Court held that the defendants in *Armstrong* did not meet this threshold and reiterated the equal protection standard applicable in selective prosecution claims. The Court noted that in selective prosecution cases, the claimant must show discriminatory effect and purpose, and explained that, to establish discriminatory effect, the claimant must show that "similarly situated individuals of a different race were not prosecuted."[32] In other words, the Court placed the burden of demonstrating selective prosecution on the defendants, and it made that burden extremely heavy.

The *Armstrong* case illustrates how federal prosecutions can produce unjustified racial disparities. The prosecutors in that case never explained their criteria for choosing certain drug cases over others, and they spent considerable time and resources defending their right not to explain these disparities. The Supreme Court's decision in *Armstrong* empowers federal prosecutors to proceed with these prosecutions. According to the Court:

> The Attorney General and United States Attorneys retain
> " 'broad discretion' " to enforce the Nation's criminal laws.
> *Wayte v. United States*, 470 U.S. 598, 607, 105 S.Ct. 1524,
> 1530–1531, 84 L.Ed.2d 547 (1985) (quoting *United States v.
> Goodwin*, 457 U.S. 368, 380, n. 11, 102 S.Ct. 2485, 2492, n. 11,
> 73 L.Ed.2d 74 [1982]). They have this latitude because they are
> designated by statute as the President's delegates to help
> him discharge his constitutional responsibility to "take Care
> that the Laws be faithfully executed." U.S. Const., Art. II, § 3;
> see 28 U.S.C. §§ 516, 547. As a result, "[t]he presumption of
> regularity supports" their prosecutorial decisions and, "in the
> absence of clear evidence to the contrary, courts presume that

they have properly discharged their official duties." *United States v. Chemical Foundation, Inc.*, 272 U.S. 1, 14–15, 47 S.Ct. 1, 6, 71 L.Ed. 131 (1926). In the ordinary case, "so long as the prosecutor has probable cause to believe that the accused committed an offense defined by statute, the decision whether or not to prosecute, and what charge to file or bring before a grand jury, generally rests entirely in his discretion." *Bordenkircher v. Hayes*, 434 U.S. 357, 364, 98 S.Ct. 663, 668, 54 L.Ed.2d 604 (1978).[33]

Although the Court states that prosecutors must exercise discretion in accordance with the equal protection clause of the U.S. Constitution, its holdings in *Armstrong* and *McCleskey*[34] make it practically impossible to challenge prosecutorial decisions that produce unwarranted racial disparities.

THE FEDERAL SENTENCING GUIDELINES

The U.S. Congress passed the Sentencing Reform Act of 1984 in response to widespread discontent with the sentencing practices of federal judges.[35] Liberals and conservatives alike bemoaned the great variances in sentences imposed for similarly situated individuals convicted of the same offenses. Liberals complained that wealthy, well-educated defendants frequently received little or no prison time while poor defendants and defendants of color were sentenced to lengthy prison terms. Conservatives complained that liberal judges should not be permitted to show leniency to poor, uneducated defendants merely because they had suffered disadvantages in their lives. Hence legislation was passed to eliminate the variances in sentences for the same or similar offenses.

The Sentencing Reform Act of 1984 established the United States Sentencing Commission to create sentencing guidelines for federal judges with the goal of establishing uniformity in sentencing practices. In 1987, the Commission completed its initial work, and Congress passed the first version of the Federal Sentencing Guidelines on November 1, 1987. What the guidelines lacked in compassion they made up for in complexity. Judges, prosecutors, and defense attorneys were required to learn a complex graph system from an 845-page manual.

The sentences are calculated on a grid consisting of two intersecting axes—one measuring the severity of the offense and the other determining the criminal history of the defendant. The offense axis consists of forty-three levels, and the criminal history axis determines the number of prior convictions. In January 2005, in a case called *United States v. Booker*,[36] the Supreme Court ruled that the guidelines would be advisory rather than mandatory. But before *Booker* was decided, the point at which the two axes intersect indicated a narrow range of months within which the judge was required to sentence the defendant. The following description of a federal sentencing hearing in Galveston, Texas, where U.S. district judge Samuel Kent sentenced twenty-four-year-old Martin Jarvis Jackson for illegal firearms possession, illustrates how complicated guidelines sentencing can be:

> "The court finds that the base offense level is 20," the judge
> began. "Pursuant to Guideline 2K2.1(B)(4), the offense level is
> increased by two levels [to 22]. . . . The court notes that the
> criminal convictions . . . result in a total criminal history cate-
> gory score of 18. At the time of the instant offense . . . the
> defendant was serving a parole sentence in two causes of action.
> And pursuant to Sentencing Guidelines 4A1.1(D), 2 points
> are therefore added. The total criminal history points is 20. And
> according to the sentencing guidelines Chapter 5, Part A,
> 20 criminal history points establish a criminal history cate-
> gory of 6. . . . [As a result] the guideline range for imprison-
> ment is 84 to 105 months."[37]

Before *Booker*, the only relevant factors that judges could consider to reduce or increase the sentence within the prescribed range related to either the charge itself or the defendant's criminal history. The guidelines permit a limited number of "departures," including whether the defendant has provided "substantial assistance" to governmental authorities in the prosecution of others (downward departure), whether his conduct caused death or serious injury (upward departure), and whether his conduct was unusually extreme or cruel (upward departure).[38] Judges were not permitted to reduce the sentence based on factors such as drug addiction, lack of education or opportunity, emotional abuse or illness, or socioeconomic disadvantage.[39] Among the many Supreme Court decisions interpreting the Federal

Sentencing Guidelines since their inception in 1987 is a case that permitted judges to increase the prescribed sentence not only for criminal convictions but for arrests not resulting in a conviction and behavior with which the defendant has been charged but not convicted.[40]

Few criminal justice initiatives have been criticized more than the Federal Sentencing Guidelines.[41] Not only are they mechanical and extremely complicated, but the sentencing ranges for specific categories of offenses are exceptionally high, and there are very few offenses for which a probationary sentence is permitted.[42] Moreover, in some cases the lengthy sentences prescribed by the guidelines can be further increased by the mandatory minimum sentencing laws. And the Sentencing Reform Act required not only the establishment of rigid guidelines but also the abolition of parole, requiring defendants to serve at least 85 percent of these long sentences.

One of the most frequent criticisms of the Federal Sentencing Guidelines has been their elimination of judicial discretion and the corresponding enhancement of prosecutorial discretion and power. Although some have described the outcome of the guidelines as a "transfer" of discretion from judges to prosecutors, a more accurate description is the "concentration" of discretion in the hands of prosecutors. Prosecutors exercised vast discretion before the guidelines. Since the guidelines stripped judges of discretion, and the defense attorney's role never involved the exercise of discretion, before the *Booker* decision, prosecutors were left with exclusive control over this important function.

In the pre-*Booker* world, federal prosecutors' charging and plea bargaining decisions effectively predetermined the outcome of most criminal cases. Although state prosecutors wield similar power, these decisions have more serious ramifications in federal court, where the risk of exercising one's right to a jury trial is much greater due to the harshness of federal sentences. Since the sentencing guidelines and mandatory minimum sentencing laws required judges to impose a specific sentence based on limited, charge-based information, unless the defendant exercised his right to trial and was acquitted of all of the offenses, the prosecutor's charging and plea bargaining decisions determined whether he would be incarcerated and how long the term of incarceration would be. Judges had no power to show leniency at the sentencing hearing.

The vast majority of criminal defendants plea bargain in federal court because going to trial is risky business. Before *Booker*, if a defendant was charged with several offenses, the guidelines ensured that each offense would carry a lengthy term of imprisonment. For most defendants, the possibility that a jury or judge might acquit them of the charges was too risky and uncertain. If a defendant accepted a plea offer, he knew how much time he faced. Even if that term of imprisonment was lengthy, it would be significantly less than the guaranteed term of imprisonment he would serve if he was convicted of all charges after a trial. In some of these cases, the prosecutors were less than confident that they would secure a conviction at trial, but it was the rare prosecutor who would reveal those doubts to the defense. U.S. attorney Jay McCloskey of Maine described how he persuaded defendants to plead guilty simply by confronting them with the maximum sentence they could get under the federal guidelines:

> Only the U.S. attorney knows the strengths and weaknesses of his case but you don't have to show that hand. I don't know how many cases I've had where a defendant pleaded guilty when he saw how we'd charged him and where I thought I'm lucky they didn't know how weak my case was if I'd had to take it to trial.[43]

"SUBSTANTIAL" ASSISTANCE

Prior to the *Booker* decision, section 5K1.1 of the guidelines afforded extraordinary power and discretion to federal prosecutors. This section discusses one of the few means by which a judge could sentence a defendant to less prison time than the guidelines required, and it was left entirely within the discretion of the prosecutor. According to section 5K1.1, "[u]pon motion of the government stating that the defendant has provided substantial assistance in the investigation or prosecution of another person who has committed an offense, the court may depart from the guidelines."[44] In other words, unless the prosecutor filed a 5K1.1 motion, the judge could not grant a lower sentence.

Prosecutors file 5K1.1 or "substantial assistance" motions in the same arbitrary fashion with which they perform most of their important functions. There are no rules or criteria in the guidelines or the U.S. attorneys' manual governing the circumstances under which these motions should be filed. There is no definition of "substantial assistance," leaving this important interpretation totally within the discretion of the prosecutor. It is defined different ways by different prosecutors and offices. Individual prosecutors even interpret the term differently from case to case. For example, some offices will only file 5K motions if the defendant provides information that leads to an arrest and/or conviction, while others will file the motion as long as valuable information is provided, whether or not the prosecutor secures additional convictions. Individual prosecutors may file the motion for one defendant who provides minimal information while denying it to another who provides substantial information. Challenges to these decisions have rarely been successful.

Prosecutors have nothing to lose and everything to gain by offering to file a 5K motion in exchange for a defendant's cooperation. Before *Booker*, however, defendants agreed to these deals at almost as great a risk as exercising their right to trial. The defendant pled guilty up front and agreed to cooperate and provide information to assist the prosecutor. However, the prosecutor filed the 5K motion requesting a departure from the guidelines only after he or she was satisfied that the defendant had provided "substantial assistance."

There are countless examples of prosecutors declining to file 5K motions after defendants have provided information, often at great peril to the defendant's own safety. Ernest Ganz was one such defendant. In 1991, Ganz, a commuter pilot, was indicted for attempting to import several hundred pounds of marijuana into south Florida. If he chose to go to trial, he risked conviction on all charges and a 97- to 121-month prison term under the guidelines. The federal prosecutor offered him a deal. If he agreed to tell the prosecutor everything he knew about drug deliveries and work undercover, the prosecutor would dismiss one count and consider filing a 5K motion. Ganz cooperated to the fullest, secretly tape-recording conversations with drug dealers who threatened to kill him if he "snitched" and meeting over thirty times with federal customs agents. One of the customs agents even offered testimony about how helpful Ganz had been. But it wasn't enough for AUSA William Michael. Without explanation, Michael declined to file the 5K motion. Fortunately for Ganz, his case was one of the rare instances where the judge found that the prosecutor acted

in bad faith—the standard by which judges may override the prosecutor's decision. Judge Shelby Highsmith ordered Michael to file the
5K motion and sentenced Ganz to twenty-four months.[45]

Mark Forney's case was much more typical. Forney pled guilty to
conspiracy with intent to distribute cocaine and agreed to cooperate
with the government in exchange for the prosecutor's agreement to
file a 5K motion. Forney provided the government with significant
information about other individuals and identified photographs of the
perpetrators. Nonetheless, the prosecutor declined to file a 5K motion,
claiming that Forney's information had not led to any arrests. However, the information provided was sufficient as a basis for arrest
warrants; the prosecutor simply chose not to pursue the arrests because
he believed the crimes were too minor to prosecute. At his sentencing
hearing, Forney asked the judge to depart from the guidelines, noting
that had he known that the prosecutor might take this position, he
never would have pled guilty. The judge refused to depart, stating that
the decision was up to the prosecutor and that there was nothing he
could do.[46]

CONTINUED DISPARITY

The enhanced power of federal prosecutors created by the guidelines
not only granted them almost exclusive control over the outcome of
most cases; it failed to achieve the primary goal of the guidelines—
uniformity in sentencing. The sentencing disparities the guidelines
were designed to eliminate are now worse than ever. A year-long
investigation conducted by the *Washington Post* included the analysis of
seventy-nine thousand criminal sentencing hearings and three hundred court opinions in fiscal years 1994 and 1995 and concluded that
sentencing disparities persisted since the implementation of the
guidelines.[47] Black defendants are more likely than whites to receive
the severest sentences, and female defendants receive slightly more
lenient sentences than men for the same crimes committed under
similar circumstances. There are also geographical disparities, with
defendants in one part of the country receiving longer sentences than
their similarly situated counterparts in other states.[48] The racial and
geographical disparities result from the discretionary nature of charging
and plea bargaining decisions among federal prosecutors—from case to

case, courtroom to courtroom, and from city to city. In 1994, the Sentencing Commission studied how prosecutors made decisions about which cases to pursue and when to award leniency. Ilene H. Nagel, an original commission member and the study's coauthor, noted: "There appeared to be disturbing hints of social class, race and gender distinctions."[49]

THE FEENEY AMENDMENT

Despite extensive criticisms of the guidelines, Congress has taken little action to amend its provisions or rectify the harsh, unfair consequences it produces. In fact, Congress required the Sentencing Commission to amend the guidelines to provide even more power for prosecutors at the expense of judicial independence. In April 2003, Congress amended the Sentencing Reform Act of 1984 by passing the "Feeney Amendment"[50] to the "Prosecutorial Remedies and Tools Against the Exploitation of Children Today Act," or "PROTECT Act."[51] Pursuant to the amendment, in any case in which a judge gives a downward departure, or sentence lower than the guidelines recommendation, the judge was required to file a written report of their reasons for the lesser sentence. The chief judge of that district was required to file a report with the Sentencing Commission, which included the judge's statement of reasons, the presentence report, and the plea agreement, and provide that report to the Department of Justice and/or Congress, on request. The Feeney Amendment also required the Justice Department to send a report to Congress on every case in which there is a downward departure for reasons other than substantial assistance to the prosecutor. This report from the Justice Department included the facts of the case, the identity of the sentencing judge, the judge's stated reasons for departure, and the parties' position on the downward departure.[52]

The Feeney Amendment was a very clear threat to judges—if you dare to exercise judicial independence and stray from the mandates of the Federal Sentencing Guidelines, you will have to justify your actions, not only to Congress but to the prosecutors who appear before you. Although federal judges have lifetime tenure, many critics of the Feeney Amendment viewed it as a sort of "blacklist" that threatened judicial independence.[53] Some of Congress's actions corroborate this view. For example, after Chief Judge James Rosenbaum of Minnesota testified against the amendment before the House Judiciary Committee, some of the Committee's members threatened to subpoena his records in all cases in which he departed from the guidelines.[54] Since Congress must approve all judicial nominations, the amendment served as a threat to any judge with aspirations of ascension to a higher federal court. Another fear was that the Feeney Amendment's new requirements would chill judicial discretion by intimidation.[55] For fear of being reported, judges would be compelled to issue a harsher guideline sentence, even if they strongly believed a departure was warranted.[56]

Many federal judges resisted the amendment's requirement that they cede even more of their independence to prosecutors and the Congress. In June 2003, Judge John Martin, Jr., of the U.S. District Court in Manhattan announced that he would take early retirement, relinquishing his lifetime appointment, in part to protest the unfairness of the sentencing process.[57] In December 2003, twenty-seven federal judges from around the country signed a statement calling for repeal of the Feeney Amendment.[58] Even conservative judges, such as Supreme Court Chief Justice Rehnquist and Justice Kennedy, expressed vehement opposition to the amendment. The Judicial Conference of the United States voted unanimously to support overturning the law. One of the boldest responses came from U.S. District Court judge Sterling Johnson, Jr., who issued an order forbidding Congress from examining any of the court documents required in the amendment without his approval.[59]

Some judges expressed their outrage in open court. Judge Guido Calabresi of the U.S. Court of Appeals for the Second Circuit addressed the prosecutor during an oral argument: "You're telling me that the system we have set up, that has been set up by Congress, which removes discretion from the judges, has given discretion to your office. . . . This case is a perfect example of you telling me that your office made some decisions with respect to what is right and just and true, and the district court is thereby prohibited from having any say in the matter."[60] Before the assistant U.S. attorney could respond, Judge Robert Miner, another judge on the panel hearing the case stated that if the panel didn't follow the prosecutor's recommendations, the prosecutor would "probably take our names and report them to the attorney general." Another judge on the panel facetiously added, "Be sure you spell them correctly."[61]

The Feeney Amendment not only reinforced prosecutorial power and control over the sentencing process, but it arguably threatened one of the most basic constitutional tenets of democratic government—the separation of powers. The Feeney Amendment was in direct conflict with and in violation of the doctrine of separation of powers. It required judges to report and explain their decisions to both the executive and legislative branches of government.

One court found a portion of the Feeney Amendment to be unconstitutional, in part because it violated the separation of powers doctrine. On January 12, 2004, U.S. District Court judge Dickran Tevrizian of the Central District of California concluded that section 401(l)(1)(2) and (3) (Report by Attorney General) and the attorney general's memorandum of July 28, 2003, offends "judicial independence by allowing individual judges to be singled-out, threatened, intimidated and targeted."[62] Section 401, the judge wrote, "chills and stifles judicial independence to the extent that it is constitutionally prohibited. The chilling effect resulting from such reporting requirements is sufficient to violate the separation of powers limitations of the U.S. Constitution."[63]

There have been many legal challenges to various provisions of the Federal Sentencing Guidelines,[64] and although the Supreme Court on occasion upheld some defense challenges to the guidelines,[65] it repeatedly upheld their constitutionality.[66] However, on July 12, 2005, the Supreme Court issued its decision in *United States v. Booker.*[67] Not only does the *Booker* decision make the Feeney Amendment irrelevant but also it has the potential to fundamentally change federal sentencing by returning discretion to federal judges.

THE EFFECT OF *BOOKER* ON PROSECUTORIAL POWER

In *Booker,* the Court held that the Federal Sentencing Act was unconstitutional, in that it required the judge to sentence a defendant to a period of incarceration higher than the statutory maximum upon the judge's determination of certain facts by a preponderance of the evidence. Before *Booker*, the guidelines required judges to enhance the defendant's sentence above the maximum sentence for charges to which the defendant pled guilty or that he was convicted of beyond a reasonable doubt, as long as the judge made a determination of certain facts by a preponderance of the evidence. The Supreme Court found that this requirement violated the defendant's Sixth Amendment right to a jury trial. The Court remedied the constitutional violation by severing the section of the Federal Sentencing Act that made the guidelines mandatory. *Booker* requires judges to consider the guidelines but allows them to depart as long as they give reasons. Sentences may be appealed and overturned for unreasonableness.

Because *Booker* no longer requires judges to slavishly follow the guidelines when sentencing defendants, the prosecutor's charging and plea bargaining decisions, at least in theory, do not necessarily predetermine the outcome of most criminal cases in federal court. Nonetheless, *Booker* may not significantly alter federal prosecutorial power. Much depends on the extent to which federal judges continue to follow the guidelines. *Booker* permits judges to continue to mete out the sentences suggested by the guidelines and in fact requires them to consider them. In the months immediately following the Court's ruling, federal judges continued to sentence defendants within the guideline range, with a few exceptions.[68]

After *Booker* was decided, federal prosecutors expressed concern that the decision would hamper their ability to plea bargain. Some suggested that because defendants knew that judges could depart from the guidelines, they might decide to take their chances at trial and attempt to persuade the judge to depart from the guidelines if they were convicted of more charges than the prosecutor offered in the plea bargain.[69] This concern seems unfounded. It is highly unlikely that if a defendant went to trial and was convicted of numerous counts of distribution of cocaine, for example, the judge would sentence him to significantly less time than the guidelines suggest—especially if the prosecutor had offered the defendant a plea to lesser charges.

Booker will probably have its greatest effect on section 5K1.1 "substantial assistance" motions. Before *Booker*, this section provided that judges could reward a defendant for cooperating with the government only if prosecutors filed a motion stating that the defendant had provided substantial assistance in the investigation or prosecution of another person. Judges in a post-*Booker* world may now depart based on a defendant's cooperation, even if the prosecutor declines to file such a motion, providing potential relief for defendants like Mark Forney.

In sum, it is unlikely that *Booker* will have a noticeable effect on how prosecutors conduct business in the federal system or on the impact of their decisions. They will continue to have unfettered charging and plea bargaining discretion and those decisions will continue to greatly influence the outcome in all criminal cases, even those in which judges decide to depart. Judges will continue to consult the guidelines before sentencing, and will probably follow them in most cases. However, *Booker* now permits judges to exercise discretion in cases where justice cries out for a departure.

THE ATTORNEY GENERAL

The attorney general is the chief prosecutor for the entire nation. In principle, he or she has supervisory authority over all of the U.S. attorneys and the AUSAs who work in each office. In practice, much like that of the chief district attorneys on the state level, the authority the attorney general exercises depends on his or her management style and how much discretion he or she chooses to impart to each of the ninety-three U.S. attorneys. Several attorneys general in recent history have wielded their power freely, making decisions that have affected not only the U.S. attorneys under their authority but also the nation as a whole. These decisions range from issuing memoranda dictating policies and practices in the U.S. attorneys' offices across the country to implementing courses of action that affect individual citizens and residents in their daily lives. Should a single individual who is not directly accountable to the people wield such expansive power? Might the exercise of this broad power and discretion by attorneys general produce unwarranted disparities or other abuses? This section explores these issues by examining some of the decisions made by two former attorneys general—Richard Thornburgh and John Ashcroft.

The Thornburgh Memo

Richard Thornburgh, who served as attorney general from 1988 to 1991, was responsible for one of the most controversial decisions by an

attorney general for the United States. In 1989, Thornburgh issued a
memorandum to all of the U.S. attorneys that declared that internal
Justice Department rules and policies preempted the ethical rules of the
states in which federal prosecutors practiced. Known as the Thornburgh Memo, it specifically exempted federal prosecutors from rule
4.2 of the ABA Model Rules of Professional Conduct, which states:
"In representing a client, a lawyer shall not communicate about the
subject of the representation with a person the lawyer knows to be
represented by another lawyer in the matter, unless the lawyer has the
consent of the other lawyer or is authorized to do so by law or a court
order."[70] The organized bar strongly opposed the Thornburgh Memo,
and in 1990, the ABA House of Delegates passed a formal resolution
denouncing it. Courts also rejected Thornburgh's rule.[71] Attorney
General Janet Reno reissued the Thornburgh Memo as a proposed
rule for public comment in July 1993, and it was codified in a series of
regulations in 1994. This version softened the Justice Department's
original stance, but, under certain circumstances, continued to allow
contact with represented persons.[72]

Thornburgh issued the memorandum in response to complaints by
defense attorneys across the country that federal prosecutors were violating a sacrosanct ethical rule, namely, the rule prohibiting a lawyer
from communicating with a party in a civil or criminal case who is
represented by counsel. Defense attorneys claimed that prosecutors
were communicating with criminal defendants who had pending
charges without the consent or knowledge of their attorneys. Almost
all states have ethical rules prohibiting this behavior, but federal
prosecutors routinely ignored these rules. Thornburgh responded to
the widespread, vehement opposition to the practice by issuing a
memorandum unilaterally declaring that federal prosecutors were
exempt from following state ethical rules.

It literally took an act of Congress to overcome the Thornburgh
Memo. In 1998, Congress passed the Citizens Protection Act (CPA),
which states, in part, that "[a]n attorney for the Government shall be
subject to State laws and rules, and local Federal court rules, governing
attorneys in each State where such attorney engages in that attorney's
duties, to the same extent and in the same manner as other attorneys in
that State."[73] Despite its sweeping language, the CPA has provided
very little control over prosecutors, because defense attorneys and
judges rarely refer prosecutors to bar counsel for unethical behavior.[74]

John Ashcroft

Post–September 11 Powers

The bombing of the World Trade Center and the Pentagon on September 11, 2001, presented John Ashcroft with one of the greatest challenges to any attorney general in American history. Characterized as an act of war against Americans on American soil, the terrorist acts of September 11 not only gave rise to two wars[75] but resulted in a drastic curtailment of the civil liberties of many innocent American citizens and residents. Ashcroft was largely responsible for initiating and implementing policies and legislation that not only diminished civil liberties but also vastly expanded prosecutorial power.

Just two weeks after September 11, 2001, Ashcroft submitted written testimony to Congress requesting sweeping new powers to fight the "War on Terrorism." About a month later, on October 26, 2001, Congress passed the Uniting and Strengthening America by Providing Appropriate Tools Required to Intercept and Obstruct Terrorism (USA Patriot Act),[76] and President Bush signed it into law the following day. The speed with which the law was passed was rivaled only by its length and breadth. It is over three hundred pages long. The expanded powers it authorizes include searches and seizures without a warrant or even prior notice; interception of email, internet communications, and voicemail; expansion of roving wiretaps without prior judicial authority; and monitoring of confidential attorney-client communications. Opposition to the Patriot Act was vehement and widespread, even among the politically conservative.[77] Among the criticisms voiced was a concern that the Act would be used as an end run around constitutional requirements in ordinary domestic criminal cases. Newt Gingrich, former Republican Speaker of the House, expressed the following view:

> I strongly believe Congress must act now to rein in the Patriot
> Act, limit its use to national security concerns and prevent
> it from developing "mission creep" into areas outside of na-
> tional security. Similarly, if prosecutors lack the necessary
> legislation to combat other serious domestic crimes, crimes not
> connected to terrorism, then lawmakers should seek to give
> prosecutors separate legislation to provide them the tools they

need, but again not at the expense of civil rights. But in no case
should prosecutors of domestic crimes seek to use tools intended for national security purposes.[78]
Rep. Dick Armey, Republican former House Majority Leader
and Chair of the House Select Committee on Homeland Security, stated, "I told the President I thought his Justice Department was out of control. . . . Are we going to save ourselves
from international terrorism in order to deny the fundamental liberties we protect to ourselves? . . . It doesn't make sense
to me."[79]

The concerns expressed by these conservative critics were proven
to be well founded. A study by the General Accounting Office reported
that 75 percent of the convictions the Justice Department classified as
"international terrorism" were wrongly labeled and that many dealt
with common domestic crimes like document forgery.[80] Many suspected that Ashcroft used the tragic events of September 11 as an opportunity to expand prosecutorial and law enforcement power beyond
constitutional limits. According to Elliot Mincberg, legal director for
People for the American Way, "[w]hat the Justice Department has really done is to get things put into the law that have been on prosecutors' wish lists for years. They've used terrorism as a guise to expand law
enforcement powers in areas that are totally unrelated to terrorism."[81]
   The Patriot Act was by no means Ashcroft's only tool for expanding prosecutorial power. When the perpetrators of the September
11 bombings were identified as members of the terrorist group Al
Qaeda, Ashcroft began a sweeping, large-scale detention of innocent
Arab and Middle Eastern men living in the United States. His first act
was to round up and arrest over a thousand men on unspecified
charges. Almost all were of Middle Eastern descent. Ashcroft declined
to release any information about them, only indicating that some were
believed to be members of the Al Qaeda terrorist network. Many of
these men were not allowed to see their families or consult with
attorneys. On November 27, 2001, Ashcroft announced that 603 of
these men were still in custody—548 charged with immigration violations and 55 charged with unspecified federal crimes.[82] He claimed
that some were material witnesses but would provide no further information, claiming national security concerns and even contending
that he was protecting the privacy of the detainees.

Ashcroft simultaneously engaged in an even broader racial profiling policy that targeted a larger group of Middle Eastern men. On November 9, 2001, he asked local law enforcement agents to help round up and interrogate approximately five thousand Middle Eastern men. These men, listed by name, had all entered the United States from Middle Eastern countries on student, tourist, or work visas. None were suspected of terrorist or other criminal activity. Ashcroft was immediately criticized for engaging in racial profiling but denied the accusation, claiming that he chose these men not because of their race or ethnicity but because they were from countries with a known Al Qaeda presence.

Although some local police departments cooperated with Ashcroft, several declined. The Portland, Oregon, police chief was among the latter. He noted that complying with Ashcroft's request would violate his department's policy against racial profiling. It also would violate local laws that prohibit police officers from acting as immigration officers and from collecting information on any individual or group not suspected of criminal activity. Police departments in Arizona and California took similar positions. Most local departments complied with Ashcroft's request. Some chose to send letters of invitation to the men in their jurisdiction with a policy of ending the interrogation if and when the men declined to answer a question.

Ashcroft claimed that the purpose of the interrogations was to compile intelligence against Al Qaeda operatives by asking the individuals whether they had knowledge of persons involved with the organization or the events of September 11. But some individuals report that they were asked questions about whether they supported the attacks of September 11 or the Al Qaeda network. Others were asked personal questions about their religion, finances, and personal habits. Arab American and Muslim organizations criticized the policy as a blatant form of racial profiling. Other critics noted the policy's resemblance to the McCarthyism of the 1950s and its ineffectiveness in fighting terrorism.

Despite broad criticism, Ashcroft persisted in practices designed to detain even larger numbers of Middle Eastern men. On January 25, 2002, Deputy Attorney General Larry Thompson sent a memorandum to antiterrorism officials announcing that the Justice Department would seek to detain and interrogate approximately 6,000 men of Middle Eastern descent who were on a much larger list of 314,000

so-called absconders—individuals who had ignored preexisting deportation orders.[83] The vast majority of these "absconders" were from
Latin American countries, but Thompson was clear that agents should
seek out the six thousand Middle Eastern ones. He also indicated that
prosecutors should seek to charge them with any applicable criminal
offense so they could be detained and interrogated rather than sent to
their home countries in compliance with the outstanding deportation
orders.[84] Thompson urged law enforcement agents to offer money
and/or so-called S-visas ("snitch visas") in exchange for valuable information about the Al Qaeda network or other terrorist organizations.[85] Khalil E. Jahshan, vice president of the American-Arab Anti-
Discrimination Committee, criticized the policy as a clear form of
racial profiling,[86] as did legal scholars, who noted the unconstitution-
ality of selectively prosecuting individuals of a certain race.[87]

Controlling Plea Bargaining

Ashcroft frequently exerted his power in matters unrelated to terrorism and national security. In a memorandum issued to all U.S. attorneys
in September 2003, he directed them to charge defendants with "the
most serious, readily provable offense" in every case and strictly limited the discretion of AUSAs to offer plea bargains.[88] The memorandum defined the most serious offenses as "those that generate the
most substantial sentence under the Sentencing Guidelines, unless a
mandatory minimum sentence or count requiring a consecutive sentence would generate a longer sentence."[89] Ashcroft claimed that the
purpose of this memorandum was to assure that the Federal Sentencing
Guidelines would be implemented exactly as written and to counter
lenient sentencing practices by federal judges.[90]

Ashcroft's directive provoked harsh criticism from a variety of
sources, including federal prosecutors themselves. The requirement
that prosecutors seek the most serious charges in every case and the
prohibition against dismissing charges pursuant to plea bargains except
under very narrow circumstances could have provoked a vast increase
in jury trials. Since well over 90 percent of federal cases were resolved
through pleas before Ashcroft's memorandum, his directive could not
have been carried out without a drastic increase in federal prosecutors,
judges, defense attorneys, and courts.[91] The memorandum ultimately

was amended to permit federal prosecutors to make exceptions with
the approval of a supervisor.

The Sniper Trials

Ashcroft's handling of the "sniper" cases in the Washington, D.C.,
area presents another example of his authoritarian style. John Allen
Muhammad, a forty-one-year old man, and John Lee Malvo, his
seventeen-year-old companion, were arrested for a series of frighten-
ing "sniper"-style shootings in the Washington area and beyond.
Thirteen people were killed, and six were wounded, with most of
the shootings in Maryland and others spread between the District of
Columbia, Virginia, Alabama, Georgia, Louisiana, and Washington.
Although the prosecutors in each of these localities were capable of
handling these cases, Ashcroft filed charges against Muhammad and
Malvo under the Hobbs Act, a 1946 antiracketeering law that makes
robbery or extortion a federal offense when it obstructs interstate
commerce.[92] Since the suspects allegedly delivered a note demanding
$10 million and police searches tied up federal highways, Ashcroft used
the Hobbs Act to obtain custody of them. Clearly Ashcroft would
never consider prosecuting Muhammad and Malvo for mere extortion
when there was evidence that they had committed at least twelve
murders. Instead, he used the Hobbs Act arrest as a pretense to gain
custody of the suspects, attempt to interrogate them, and, most important, assure that they were prosecuted for murder in a state where they
would most likely be executed. Just nine days after they were taken into
federal custody, Ashcroft dismissed the federal charges and dispatched
them to Virginia—among the choices, the state with the highest execution record. In essence, Ashcroft filed federal charges solely to gain
control over the defendants and to shop for the jurisdiction of his choice.

Ashcroft boldly proclaimed his motives. Maryland prohibits the
death penalty for juveniles, and at the time of the arrests, there was a
moratorium on the death penalty in Maryland.[93] Virginia, on the other
hand, ranks second in the nation for the number of people put to death
since the death penalty was reinstated by the Supreme Court in 1976,
and three of them were juveniles at the time they committed their
crimes.[94] "We believe the first prosecutions should occur in those
jurisdictions that provide the best law, the best facts and the best range

of available penalties," Ashcroft said.[95] On the subject of the death penalty, he stated, "It is appropriate. It is imperative that the ultimate sanction be available."[96]

Forum shopping, or choosing a jurisdiction, court, or judge to achieve a particular outcome, is frowned on in the legal profession, and even considered unethical by some legal scholars.[97] Yet the attorney general, the top law enforcement officer in the nation, blatantly engaged in this behavior. With the exception of some criticism in legal circles and the media,[98] his behavior was never challenged. There is absolutely no authority for an attorney general choosing the state where a suspect will be prosecuted and tried. The fact that Ashcroft filed pretextual Hobbs Act charges to accomplish his goals indicates the impropriety of his actions. Yet he suffered no consequences.

CONCLUSION

The U.S. Constitution guarantees all citizens certain basic freedoms and civil rights. Although states have the power to pass their own state constitutions and may even afford citizens of their states more rights than those guaranteed by the federal constitution, they may not curtail the rights guaranteed by the U.S. Constitution. Basic concepts of federalism assure that state and federal governments operate within their own spheres without interfering with each other or exerting power or control over each other.[99]

The relationship between state and federal prosecutors has not traditionally conformed to the basic federalist concept of noninterference. As a result of the huge increase in the number of federal crimes, federal prosecutors now exercise simultaneous jurisdiction with state prosecutors over large numbers of crimes, and, in practice, the feds have the upper hand. They choose the cases they want to prosecute, and the vague, nonbinding language of the U.S. attorneys' manual permits them to make these choices arbitrarily and without accountability. Although state and federal prosecutors may sometimes work cooperatively, state prosecutors often bow to the wishes of their federal counterparts, without recourse. The U.S. attorneys are accountable to the attorney general, who is accountable, at least in theory, to the president. In practice, he or she is accountable to no one, since the president of the United States rarely interferes with matters that do not involve national security, and at any rate, certainly not with ordinary criminal prosecutions in the Justice Department. In the absence of major reform, federal prosecutors and the attorney general will continue to exercise broad, far-reaching power without effective accountability to the people they are obligated to serve.

SEVEN

Prosecutorial Misconduct: The Abuse
of Power and Discretion

Brian was a fifteen-year-old African American boy charged in the District of Columbia juvenile court with assault with intent to kill, burglary, and related charges. The government claimed that Brian and two adult men had severely beaten an older man during a burglary of his home. Brian's adult codefendants were charged with the same offenses and faced up to life in prison in adult court, where the office of the U.S. attorney for the District of Columbia prosecuted them.[1] As a juvenile, the Office of the Corporation Counsel prosecuted Brian,[2] and he faced a maximum punishment of two years in the juvenile correctional facility upon conviction. The juvenile court rules protected his anonymity and offered the possibility of rehabilitative treatment if needed.

The AUSA handling the case against the adult codefendants sought Brian's assistance in their prosecution. He contacted the assistant corporation counsel in charge of Brian's case and Brian's court-appointed attorney to arrange an "off-the-record" conversation. The prosecutor hoped to secure Brian's cooperation in the prosecution of the adults in exchange for lenient treatment, including possible dismissal of Brian's case. During the meeting, the prosecutor questioned Brian about the events surrounding the assault and burglary. Brian's attorney and mother were present during the meeting. Brian denied that either he or the adult codefendants had participated in the crimes.

The prosecutor expressed his displeasure with Brian's denials and pressured him to testify that the adults were involved. When Brian refused to submit to pressure, the prosecutor threatened to charge Brian as an adult if he declined to testify against the codefendants, warning him that he could receive a life sentence in an adult prison if convicted in adult court. Brian maintained that he knew nothing about the offenses, and the meeting ended without a deal. Soon thereafter, the prosecutor made good on his threats. The juvenile case was dismissed, and Brian was charged as an adult.

I was appointed to represent Brian in adult court. He immediately told me about the meeting with the prosecutor. I interviewed his mother, who verified the prosecutor's threats and expressed her shock and dismay at what the prosecutor had done. "Can he get away with that?" she asked. I agreed that his behavior was unscrupulous, and after consulting with other lawyers at PDS, I decided to file a motion to dismiss the indictment for prosecutorial vindictiveness.

The judge assigned to Brian's case scheduled a hearing, and Brian's mother testified. She described the prosecutor's threats in great detail, explaining how he had yelled at Brian and had threatened to charge Brian as an adult if he did not corroborate the government's story that he had helped the two adults beat and rob the complainant. The prosecutor representing the government at the hearing was not the same prosecutor who had threatened Brian. To my surprise, he declined to cross-examine Brian's mother. Instead, he began to argue, in a very dismissive manner, that Brian's mother was lying and that the threats were never made. The judge interrupted the prosecutor's argument and asked whether he planned to present any evidence. The prosecutor appeared surprised and informed the judge that he would just "make representations" as an officer of the court. This prosecutor apparently believed that he was not required to present testimony under oath and that the judge should simply accept his word to rebut the testimony of Brian's mother. When it became clear that the judge planned to follow the rules of evidence and only consider the undisputed testimony of Brian's mother, the prosecutor asked if he might have additional time to locate the prosecutor and present his testimony. The judge declined his request.

The hearing ended late on a Friday afternoon, and Brian's trial was scheduled to begin the following Monday morning. The judge declined to rule on the motion, indicating that she would take the matter under advisement. I warned my client and his mother that they should not get their hopes up, that these motions were rarely granted, and that we should prepare to start the trial on Monday.

On the following Monday morning, the case was called, and my client and I joined the adult codefendants and their lawyers at counsel table. The case had been assigned to another judge. He looked in my client's court file and announced, "Ms. Davis, your client's case has been dismissed. There is an order issued by Judge Williams granting your motion to dismiss the indictment for prosecutorial vindictiveness." I was shocked. Although I had challenged prosecutorial misconduct on many occasions during my years as a public defender, this was the only time a judge granted the relief I had requested.

The vindictiveness in Brian's case is just one of the many forms of prosecutorial misconduct and is by no means the most common. Numerous articles and books have been written about prosecutorial misconduct.[3] Such misconduct may take many forms, including:

- Courtroom misconduct (making inappropriate or inflammatory comments in the presence of the jury; introducing or attempting to introduce inadmissible, inappropriate or inflammatory evidence; mischaracterizing the evidence or the facts of the case to the court or jury; committing violations pertaining to the selection of the jury; or making improper closing arguments);
- Mishandling of physical evidence (hiding, destroying or tampering with evidence, case files or court records);
- Failing to disclose exculpatory evidence;
- Threatening, badgering or tampering with witnesses;
- Using false or misleading evidence;
- Harassing, displaying bias toward, or having a vendetta against the defendant or defendant's counsel (including *selective* or *vindictive prosecution*, which includes instances of denial of a speedy trial); and
- Improper behavior during grand jury proceedings.[4]

I do not attempt to present a comprehensive discussion of prosecutorial misconduct in this one chapter, as such a task would be impossible in light of the breadth of the problem. Instead, I attempt to demonstrate that the line between legal prosecutorial behavior and illegal prosecutorial misconduct is a thin one. I explore whether a number of factors, including the Supreme Court's jurisprudence and the prosecutorial culture of power and lack of accountability, create a climate that fosters misconduct. I focus on *Brady* violations—the most common form of misconduct—and examine how and why prosecutors continue to engage in illegal behavior with impunity.

THE BREADTH OF THE PROBLEM

Much of what passes for legal behavior might in fact be illegal, but because prosecutorial practices are so rarely challenged, it is difficult to define the universe of prosecutorial misconduct. Because it is so difficult to discover, much prosecutorial misconduct goes unchallenged, suggesting that the problem is much more widespread than the many reported cases of prosecutorial misconduct would indicate. As one editorial described the problem, "[i]t would be like trying to count drivers who speed; the problem is larger than the number of tickets would indicate."[5]

One of the most comprehensive studies of prosecutorial misconduct was completed in 2003 by the Center for Public Integrity, a nonpartisan organization that conducts investigative research on public policy issues. A team of twenty-one researchers and writers studied the problem for three years and examined 11,452 cases in which charges of prosecutorial misconduct were reviewed by appellate court judges. In the majority of cases, the alleged misconduct was ruled harmless error or was not addressed by the appellate judges. The Center discovered that judges found prosecutorial misconduct in over two thousand cases, in which they dismissed charges, reversed convictions, or reduced sentences.[6] In hundreds of additional cases, judges believed that the prosecutorial behavior was inappropriate but affirmed the convictions under the "harmless error" doctrine.[7]

The cases investigated by the Center for Public Integrity only scratch the surface of the issue, as they only represent the cases in which prosecutorial misconduct was discovered and litigated. Most of the prosecutorial practices that occur behind closed doors, such as charging and plea bargaining decisions and grand jury practices, are never revealed to the public. Even after cases are indicted, defense attorneys are not entitled to discover what occurred behind the scenes.

In the rare cases in which practices that appear to be illegal are discovered, it is often impractical to challenge them, in light of the Supreme Court's pro-prosecution decisions on prosecutorial misconduct. Of course, there is no opportunity to challenge any misconduct that may have occurred in the over 95 percent of all criminal cases which result in a guilty plea, since defendants give up most of their appellate rights when they plead guilty.

Why is prosecutorial misconduct so widespread and how did it reach this stage? An examination of the Supreme Court's jurisprudence in this area may shed some light. The Court has shielded prosecutors from scrutiny in a series of cases that have narrowly defined the universe of behaviors that constitute prosecutorial misconduct and the circumstances under which victims of such behaviors are entitled to relief. Might these cases have emboldened prosecutors to engage in misconduct, since they know that even if their behavior is discovered and challenged, courts will most likely find the behavior to be "harmless error?" This chapter will consider these questions.

THE SUPREME COURT—PROTECTING PROSECUTORIAL POWER

The Supreme Court has established nearly impossible standards for obtaining the necessary discovery to seek judicial review of some forms of prosecutorial misconduct.[8] Inappropriate or unethical charging decisions, intimidating conversations with witnesses, selective and vindictive prosecutions, and grand jury abuse all occur in the privacy of prosecution offices—away from the public and the parties whose cases are affected by the harmful behavior. As a result of the Supreme Court's rulings,[9] prosecutors know that it is highly unlikely that any of these behaviors will be discovered by defense attorneys or anyone who might challenge them.

On the rare occasion when such misconduct is discovered, judicial review is extremely limited. Under the harmless error rule, appellate courts affirm convictions if the evidence supports the defendant's guilt, even if she did not receive a fair trial.[10] This rule permits, perhaps even unintentionally encourages, prosecutors to engage in misconduct during trial with the assurance that so long as the evidence of the defendant's guilt is clear, the conviction will be affirmed.

In addition to its constitutional power to reverse lower court convictions, the Supreme Court's supervisory authority to oversee the implementation of criminal justice grants the Court powers to regulate lower court procedures. For example, in *McNabb v. United States*, the Court concluded that when determining the admissibility of evidence, it obeys the Constitution, and, under its power of judicial supervision, formulates "civilized standards of procedure and evidence."[11] These standards are to be applied in federal criminal prosecutions, in an effort to deter governmental misconduct and preserve judicial integrity. The Court's standards are satisfied by more than simple adherence to due process laws and are derived from considerations of "evidentiary relevance" and justice.[12]

In *United States v. Russell*,[13] however, the Supreme Court drastically curtailed the supervisory power doctrine by reversing a lower court's use of the power in a case involving questionable law enforcement tactics. The Court invoked the separation of powers doctrine as it warned lower courts not to meddle in the business of law enforcement.[14] In a further effort to limit the reach of a federal court's supervisory power, in *United States v. Hasting*, the Court held that judges may not use the supervisory power doctrine to reverse convictions because of prosecutorial misconduct in cases involving harmless error.[15]

Civil lawsuits have proven equally ineffective as remedies for prosecutorial misconduct. The Supreme Court established a broad rule of absolute immunity from civil liability for prosecutors in *Imbler v. Pachtman*.[16] This rule immunizes prosecutors from liability for acts "intimately associated with the judicial phase of the criminal process."[17] The Court expressed concern that prosecutors might be deterred from zealously pursuing their law enforcement responsibilities if they faced the possibility of civil liability and suggested that prosecutorial misconduct should be referred to state attorney disciplinary authorities.

The Supreme Court's decision to avoid the problem and pass it on to state bar authorities has proven totally ineffective.[18] All attorneys, including prosecutors, must abide by their state's Code of Professional Responsibility. Attorneys who violate the Code are subject to various forms of discipline, including disbarment. However, the Center for Public Integrity found only forty-four cases since 1970 in which prosecutors faced disciplinary proceedings for misconduct that infringed on the constitutional rights of criminal defendants. The misconduct in these cases included:

- Discovery violations;
- Improper contact with witnesses, defendants, judges or jurors;
- Improper behavior during hearings or trials;
- Prosecuting cases not supported by probable cause;
- Harassing or threatening defendants, defendants' lawyers or witnesses;
- Using improper, false or misleading evidence;
- Displaying a lack of diligence or thoroughness in prosecution; and
- Making improper public statements about a pending criminal matter.[19]

Out of the 44 attorney disciplinary cases,

> In 7, the court dismissed the complaint or did not impose a punishment.
> In 20, the court imposed a public or private reprimand or censure.
> In 12, the prosecutor's license to practice law was suspended.
> In 2, the prosecutor was disbarred.
> In 1, a period of probation was imposed in lieu of a harsher punishment.
> In 24, the prosecutor was assessed the costs of the disciplinary proceedings.
> In 3, the court remanded the case for further proceedings.[20]

For many years, federal prosecutors refused to abide by state disciplinary rules. As mentioned earlier, in 1989, the Thornburgh Memo declared that federal prosecutors would abide by internal Justice Department rules rather than the ethical rules of the state in which they practiced.[21] Although this memorandum was overturned by the Citizens Protection Act of 1998, the Act simply returned prosecutors to the status quo, which has proven highly ineffective in deterring or punishing misconduct.[22]

It is not surprising that very few prosecutors are referred to state disciplinary authorities. In many ways, the phenomenon brings to mind the old saying "If you shoot at the king, you'd better kill him." Since over 95 percent of criminal cases result in guilty pleas,[23] every defense attorney knows that her future clients are at the mercy of the prosecutor, whose unfettered discretion determines what plea offers will be made and to whom. Challenging the bar license of an official who holds all the cards is risky business, especially given the odds of prevailing. Prosecutors are powerful and often popular political figures. Even when referrals are made, bar authorities frequently decline to recommend serious punishment, as the statistics from the Center for Public Integrity indicate.[24] Thus, referring prosecutors to state bar authorities has proven to be a dismal failure.[25]

The Court's rulings have sent a very clear message to prosecutors— we will protect your practices from discovery; when they are discovered, we will make it extremely difficult for challengers to prevail; and as long as you mount overwhelming evidence against defendants, we will not reverse their convictions if you engage in misconduct at trial. Prosecutors are well aware of these facts, and although they may not always intentionally set out to engage in misconduct, it leads one to question whether the Supreme Court has provided prosecutors with a comfort zone that fosters and perhaps even encourages a culture of wrongdoing.

BRADY VIOLATIONS: WITHHOLDING EXCULPATORY EVIDENCE

The obligation of a prosecutor to reveal favorable, exculpatory information about a criminal defendant is not only fair; it is a constitutional requirement. In *Brady v. Maryland*,[26] the Supreme Court held that a prosecutor's failure to disclose evidence favorable to the defendant violated due process rights when the defendant had requested such information. The Court expanded this rule in *United States v. Agurs*,[27] requiring prosecutors to turn over exculpatory information to the defense even in the absence of a request if such information is clearly supportive of a claim of innocence.[28] Professional ethical and disciplinary rules in each state and the District of Columbia reiterate and reinforce the duty to turn over information. The obligation to reveal

Brady information is ongoing and is not excused even if the prosecutor acts in good faith.

Brady violations are among the most common forms of prosecutorial misconduct. Because the obligation is expansive, continuing, and not limited by the good faith efforts of the prosecutor, great potential for wrongdoing exists. The failure to provide *Brady* information can have dire consequences for the defendant. In capital cases, *Brady* violations have resulted in the execution of arguably innocent persons. At the very least, withholding *Brady* information can determine the outcome of a trial.

Ken Armstrong and Maurice Possley, staff writers for the *Chicago Tribune,* conducted a national study of eleven thousand cases involving prosecutorial misconduct between 1963 and 1999.[29] The study revealed widespread, almost routine, violations of the *Brady* doctrine by prosecutors across the country.[30] They discovered that since 1963, courts had dismissed homicide convictions against at least 381 defendants because prosecutors either concealed exculpatory information or presented false evidence.[31] Of the 381 defendants, 67 had been sentenced to death.[32] Courts eventually freed approximately 30 of the 67 death row inmates, including two defendants who were exonerated by DNA tests.[33] One innocent defendant served twenty-six years before a court reversed his conviction.[34] Armstrong and Possley suggest that this number represents only a fraction of cases involving this type of prosecutorial misconduct, since the study only considered cases where courts convicted the defendant of killing another individual.[35] They also reported that the prosecutors who engaged in the reported misconduct were neither convicted of a crime nor barred from practicing law.[36]

Another study by Bill Moushey of the *Pittsburgh Post-Gazette* found similar results.[37] In his examination of over fifteen hundred cases throughout the nation, Moushey discovered that prosecutors routinely withhold evidence that might help prove a defendant innocent.[38] He found that prosecutors intentionally withheld evidence in hundreds of cases during the past decade, but courts overturned verdicts in only the most extreme cases.[39]

Few defense attorneys have the time, resources, or expertise to conduct massive investigations of prosecution officials. Nor should the discovery of prosecutorial misconduct depend on investigative reporting. However, the current law and practices result in the random and infrequent discovery of *Brady* violations. Even when discovered, remedies for the accused are inadequate, and punishment of the offending prosecutor is rare.

MISCONDUCT THAT LEADS
TO A DEATH SENTENCE

Prosecutorial misconduct in any case is reprehensible and can lead to the wrongful conviction of the innocent. When misconduct occurs in a capital case, however, the stakes are the highest because an innocent person might be sentenced to death. In fact, prosecutorial misconduct has been discovered in an extraordinary number of capital cases.[40] Although various types of misconduct have been reported in capital cases, a high percentage of these cases, 16–19 percent,[41] involve *Brady* violations. Delma Banks's case is one example.[42] The misconduct in Banks's case was so egregious that even the U.S. Supreme Court, which had been unreceptive to claims of prosecutorial misconduct in the past, provided relief.[43]

In 1980, Texas authorities charged Delma Banks with the death of sixteen-year-old Richard Whitehead. Prior to Banks's trial, the prosecutor informed Banks's defense attorney that he had turned over all discoverable information.[44] In fact, the prosecutor failed to reveal key exculpatory information about two of its primary witnesses—Charles Cook and Robert Farr. During the trial, Cook testified that Banks had confessed to killing Whitehead and that he had seen Banks with blood on his leg and in possession of a gun soon after Whitehead's death.[45] On cross-examination, Cook denied that he had rehearsed his testimony with law enforcement officials.[46] Farr testified during the trial as well and corroborated key aspects of Cook's testimony.[47] During Farr's cross-examination, he denied that law enforcement officials had promised him anything in exchange for his testimony.[48] Farr also testified during the penalty phase of Banks's trial in support of his death sentence.[49] Banks was sentenced to death.[50]

Banks filed several postconviction motions in Texas state courts.[51] The court denied the first two motions on grounds unrelated to alleged *Brady* violations, but the third motion alleged that the prosecutor had failed to reveal exculpatory information about Cook and Farr.[52] The third motion was denied, but Banks raised the allegations of *Brady* violations again in 1996 in a petition for a writ of habeas corpus in the U.S. District Court for the Eastern District of Texas.[53] Prior to an evidentiary hearing on Banks's motion, the magistrate judge ordered the prosecutor to turn over the prosecutor's trial files.[54] Information in the prosecutor's files, affidavits signed by Cook and the deputy sheriff, and evidence uncovered at the hearing proved extraordinary and egregious prosecutorial misconduct.[55]

Hidden in the prosecutor's file was a seventy-four-page transcript of Cook's interrogation by law enforcement officers and prosecutors.[56] During this interrogation, Cook was coached repeatedly on what to say at trial and how to reconcile his many inconsistent statements.[57] In his affidavit, Cook stated that he was warned that if he did not conform his testimony to the state's evidence, he would "spend the rest of his life in prison."[58] The deputy sheriff testified at the hearing, and revealed, for the first time, that Farr, the other witness, was a paid police informant who received $200 for his assistance in Banks's case.[59]

The prosecutor obviously knew that Cook's testimony had been coached, even scripted, and that Farr was a paid informant. These facts were clearly exculpatory and should have been revealed to the defense prior to trial. Furthermore, the prosecutor knew that Cook and Farr had committed perjury when they denied these facts under oath during the trial, yet he allowed these lies to become part of the record and stressed them heavily in the punishment phase.[60]

The magistrate judge granted partial relief after the evidentiary hearing, recommending a writ of habeas corpus as to the death sentence, but not the guilty verdict.[61] The district court adopted the magistrate's recommendation, but the Court of Appeals for the Fifth Circuit reversed the district court's grant of partial relief to Banks.[62] In March 2003, just ten minutes before Banks's scheduled execution by lethal injection and after he had been strapped to the gurney, the Supreme Court issued a stay of execution while it decided whether to review Banks's case.

The Court ultimately decided to hear Banks' claims and overturned his death sentence on February 24, 2004, by a vote of seven to two.[63] In reversing the Fifth Circuit's decision, the Supreme Court held that Banks had demonstrated all three elements of a *Brady* prosecutorial misconduct claim: "The evidence at issue must be favorable to the accused, either because it is exculpatory, or because it is

impeaching; that evidence must have been suppressed by the State,
either willfully or inadvertently; and prejudice must have ensued."[64]
The Court used particularly harsh language in criticizing the prosecutor's conduct:

> The State here nevertheless urges, in effect, that "the prose-
> cution can lie and conceal and the prisoner still has the burden
> to . . . discover the evidence." [. . .] A rule thus declaring
> "prosecutor may hide, defendant must seek," is not tenable in a
> system constitutionally bound to accord defendants due pro-
> cess.[65]

Brady violations are very common in prosecutors' offices, even
violations as egregious as those in Banks's case.[66] The Supreme Court
and lower courts have affirmed convictions in cases involving similar
violations.[67] So why did the Court provide relief for Delma Banks?
There are a number of possible explanations.

First, Banks faced death at the hands of the state in a case where
prosecutors deliberately withheld evidence. The Court has always
noted that "death is different,"[68] and has provided more protections
for defendants facing death than for others.[69] The Supreme Court
undoubtedly has been affected by the growing evidence of innocent
people being freed from death row as a result of DNA evidence and
investigative reporting.[70] Its death penalty jurisprudence in recent years
reflects more sensitivity to the rights of death row inmates.[71]

Second, the Banks case garnered widespread national attention and
support for Banks from an unusual combination of groups and individuals. One of the amicus briefs for Delma Banks was submitted by a
group of former federal judges, prosecutors, and public officials, including federal judges John Gibbons, Timothy Lewis, and William
Sessions. Sessions is a former director of the Federal Bureau of Investigation. Thomas Sullivan, a former U.S. attorney for the Northern
District of Illinois, also joined this brief; and the ABA also filed an
amicus brief.

Third, some have speculated that the Supreme Court has taken
umbrage in what it perceives as defiance of its jurisprudence by the
Court of Appeals for the Fifth Circuit.[72] There is certainly language in
Banks that lends some credence to this theory. In *Banks*, the Court
cites and relies on its holding in *Strickler v. Greene* and chides the Fifth

Circuit for ignoring it: "Surprisingly, the Court of Appeals' *per curiam* opinion did not refer to *Strickler v. Greene*, 527 U.S. 263, 119 S.Ct. 1936, 144 L.Ed.2d 286 (1999), the controlling precedent on the issue of 'cause.' "[73]

Regardless of its reasons, the Court's holding in *Banks* is a departure from its usual deference to prosecutors. It remains to be seen whether *Banks* is the beginning of a trend toward holding the fire to prosecutors' feet or an anomaly attributable to Banks's death row status at a time when the death penalty is under particular scrutiny. The latter characterization is more likely, in light of the large body of Supreme Court jurisprudence that defers to prosecutorial power and discretion.

WHY PROSECUTORS ESCAPE PUNISHMENT

Prosecutors are rarely punished for misconduct, even when the misconduct causes tremendous harm to its victims. Of the eleven thousand cases of alleged prosecutorial misconduct examined by the Center for Public Integrity, the appellate courts reversed convictions, dismissed charges, or reduced sentences in just over two thousand.[74] However, in these cases, most of the prosecutors suffered no consequences and were not held accountable or even reprimanded for their behavior.[75]

Ken Armstrong and Maurice Possley found the same lack of punishment and accountability in their 1999 study:

> With impunity, prosecutors across the country have violated
> their oaths and the law, committing the worst kinds of de-
> ception in the most serious of cases. . . . They have prosecuted
> black men, hiding evidence the real killers were white. They
> have prosecuted a wife, hiding evidence her husband com-
> mitted suicide. They have prosecuted parents, hiding evidence
> their daughter was killed by wild dogs.
>   They do it to win.
>   They do it because they won't get punished.[76]

Armstrong and Possley found that a number of the prosecutors not only totally escaped punishment or even a reprimand but also advanced in their careers.[77] In the 381 cases they examined in which

appellate courts reversed convictions based on either *Brady* violations
or prosecutors knowingly allowing lying witnesses to testify, the courts
described the behavior in terms such as "unforgivable," "intolerable,"
"beyond reprehension," and "illegal, improper and dishonest."[78] Yet,
of those cases,

> [o]ne was fired, but appealed and was reinstated with back
> pay. Another received an in-house suspension of 30 days. A
> third prosecutor's law license was suspended for 59 days, but
> because of other misconduct in the case. . . . Not one re-
> ceived any kind of public sanction from a state lawyer disci-
> plinary agency or was convicted of any crime for hiding evi-
> dence or presenting false evidence, the *Tribune* found. Two
> were indicted, but the charges were dismissed before trial.[79]

None of the prosecutors were publicly sanctioned or charged with a
crime. It is unclear whether any were sanctioned by state bar authorities, because these proceedings are not a matter of public record if the
sanction was minor. Several of the offending prosecutors advanced
significantly in their careers:

> In Georgia, George "Buddy" Darden became a congressman
> after a court concluded that he withheld evidence in a case
> where seven men, later exonerated, were convicted of mur-
> der and one was sentenced to death. In New Mexico, Virginia
> Ferrara failed to disclose evidence of another suspect in a
> murder case. By the time the conviction was reversed she
> had become chief disciplinary counsel for the New Mexico
> agency that polices lawyers for misconduct.[80]

If state bar authorities are hesitant to bring disciplinary actions against
prosecutors, it is not surprising that criminal charges are even more
infrequent. Yet much of prosecutorial misconduct is criminal behavior.
When prosecutors knowingly put witnesses on the stand to testify falsely,
they suborn perjury. Subornation of perjury is a felony in all fifty states.[81]
Prosecutors are not above the law or immune from prosecution. In fact,
as the chief law enforcement officers, they should be held to the highest
standard of conduct. Yet despite overwhelming evidence that prosecutors routinely break the law, they are not punished.

One of the rare prosecutions for prosecutorial misconduct occurred in 1999 in DuPage County, Illinois.[82] Three former prosecutors and four sheriff's deputies were indicted and tried for various criminal offenses, including obstruction of justice and subornation of perjury. The charges grew out of allegations that the prosecutors had hidden exculpatory evidence and knowingly put witnesses on the stand to lie under oath in the trial of Rolando Cruz. Cruz, Alejandro Hernandez, and Stephen Buckley faced the death penalty for the abduction, sexual assault, and murder of a ten-year-old girl.[83] The facts of the case were particularly gruesome, and there was much pressure to find and convict the perpetrators.

The prosecutors' behavior in the Cruz case was particularly egregious. They hid exculpatory evidence from defense counsel, including a confession to the crime by a convicted murderer and forensic reports from several experts demonstrating that the shoe print in the victim's home did not belong to any of the defendants. In addition, the deputies involved in the case allegedly fabricated an incriminating statement that they claimed Cruz had made while in jail. In fact, two DuPage sheriff's investigators and an assistant Illinois attorney general were so convinced of wrongdoing by the prosecutors and deputies that they resigned rather than support the prosecution of Cruz. Charges against Buckley were ultimately dismissed, but Cruz and Hernandez were tried and convicted. Their convictions were overturned, and they were tried and convicted a second time, only to have their convictions reversed again. Neither reversal was based on allegations of prosecutorial misconduct. At Cruz's third trial, there was overwhelming evidence of perjury by the sheriff's deputies, and he was acquitted.[84]

After Cruz's acquittal, the chief judge of the DuPage County Circuit Court appointed a special prosecutor to investigate the sheriff's deputies. The special prosecutor expanded his investigation to include the prosecutors and ultimately returned the indictment that led to their trial. The trial received relatively little national coverage, despite its historic significance. According to Armstrong and Possley, only six prosecutors have been prosecuted in this century for the type of misconduct alleged against the Cruz prosecutors.[85] Two were convicted of minor misdemeanors and fined $500, two were acquitted, and charges against the other two were dismissed before trial.[86]

All seven of the defendants—the prosecutors and the sheriff's deputies—were acquitted of all charges.[87] A number of the jurors spent the better part of the evening of the acquittal celebrating with the defendants in a local steakhouse.[88] The former prosecutors—Patrick King, Thomas Knight, and Robert Kilander—went on to pursue successful legal careers. Patrick King became an assistant U.S. attorney in the Northern District of Illinois.[89] Thomas Knight practiced law in the private sector, and Robert Kilander became a judge in the very court where he had faced criminal charges.[90] Thomas Knight eventually filed a lawsuit against Armstrong, Possley, and the *Chicago Tribune*.[91] There was a jury trial, and on May 20, 2005, the jury returned a verdict in favor of Possley and the newspaper.[92]

Most prosecutors who engage in misconduct not only escape punishment but also advance in their careers. Paul Howes, a former U.S. attorney in the District of Columbia, was accused of prosecutorial misconduct on several occasions.[93] After a two-year investigation of Howes's behavior, the Justice Department's Office of Professional Responsibility (OPR) concluded that Howes had abused the witness stipend system by doling out excessive payments to cooperating witnesses and their family and friends, who were not witnesses. Acknowledging that Howes's behavior constituted criminal conduct, investigators declined to prosecute him, instead agreeing to drastically reduce the sentences of the defendants convicted in the cases in which misconduct was found.[94] Howes later became a partner at the San Diego firm of Lerach, Coughlin, Stoia, Geller, Rudman & Robbins.

Howes's experience is typical. Cook County, Illinois, prosecutors Carol Pearce McCarthy, Kenneth Wadas, and Patrick Quinn were all scathingly criticized in appellate opinions for misconduct during trial. All three were promoted to supervisor positions, and all three became judges.[95]

Why do prosecutors escape punishment for prosecutorial misconduct? The responses of the Supreme Court, state and federal disciplinary authorities, and the general public provide some insight. The Supreme Court's deference to prosecutors and the harmless error doctrine might be attributable to the fact that the remedy generally sought is reversal of a criminal case. The Court's hesitancy to reverse criminal convictions when there is substantial evidence of a defendant's guilt indicates that it places a higher premium on affirming convictions than in punishing prosecutors who do wrong. In addition, some might argue that reversing a criminal conviction does not directly or sufficiently punish prosecutors for wrongdoing.

State and federal bar authorities rarely punish prosecutors for the reasons previously mentioned. First, they seldom receive formal complaints about prosecutors, because the people most likely to discover the misconduct—defense attorneys—fear retaliation from prosecution offices that will continue to wield power and exercise considerable discretion in their clients' cases. Second, even when complaints are made, the punishment is light—perhaps because of the deference and respect prosecutors generally receive from the legal profession.

But what about the general public? On the rare occasions that the public has been informed about prosecutorial misconduct, there has not been public outcry, nor have prosecutors been voted out of office for their behavior. The *Chicago Tribune* and *Pittsburgh Post-Gazette* articles reported egregious behavior by local prosecutors, yet these articles did not result in the public taking action against the offending prosecutors. There are a number of possible reasons for the lack of response. Perhaps members of the general public did not read the articles. Or they may have read about the misconduct but dismissed or excused it, indicating a disturbing support of ignoring the rule of law in the interest of catching criminals. On the other hand, the public may not endorse prosecutorial misconduct, but may not know how to take action to stop it.[96] Even if the prosecutor is an elected official who may be voted out of office, the next election may be years away, and the misconduct may be long forgotten.

The public may certainly punish prosecutorial misconduct if the offending prosecutor is charged and exercises his or her right to trial. But these prosecutions are extremely rare, and the few in this century have not resulted in serious punishment. It would be unwise to draw any broad conclusions about the general public's reaction to prosecutorial misconduct from these few prosecutions, primarily because there are too few to draw a conclusion from, and also because the public did not play a part in the outcome of most of the cases, since most of them never went to trial. The acquittal of the Cruz prosecutors may not indicate an acceptance of prosecutorial wrongdoing. Because there are so many factors that affect a jury verdict, in the absence of firsthand information from the jurors themselves, one cannot know with certainty what factors or issues led them to acquit.

An informal poll conducted by the *Chicago Tribune* after the publication of its series on prosecutorial misconduct may offer some guidance on the public's view of prosecutorial misconduct. The *Tribune* posted the following question: "An investigation by the *Chicago Tribune* found that prosecutor misconduct is commonplace in felony cases brought in Cook County. But Chicago is not alone. Scores of murder convictions have been thrown out around the country because of dishonest prosecutions. What do you think should be done to remedy this situation?" Readers responded as follows:

> "[Prosecutors] should be prosecuted for their crimes."

> "We need more effective checks and balances on the unfettered discretion about what and whom to charge. We also need a more certain sanction for those prosecutors found guilty of fudging or hiding the evidence."

> "The first thing to do is eliminate the immunity that they and our prosecutors, judges, and other bureaucrats do not deserve. . . . At a minimum we need to raise the standard of proof in order to execute someone accused of murder. . . . Last, but not least, prosecutors need to be prevented from buying testimony from criminals to help prosecute others."

> "We need institutional reform."

> "Our judicial system as a whole, needs to be overhauled."[97]

These responses may suggest that, even in cases involving serious criminal behavior, the American public ultimately wants the laws to be enforced fairly. The poll also suggests that the lack of public outrage over prosecutorial misconduct may be a result of lack of information about what prosecutors do and how they behave.

THE THIN LINE

Prosecutors wield incredible power and exercise broad discretion in the important decisions they make every day—especially charging and plea bargaining decisions. Their decision-making is often arbitrary, hasty, and impulsive, sometimes resulting in disparities among similarly situated defendants and crime victims. Because prosecutors make these decisions in private without meaningful supervision or accountability, they are rarely punished when they engage in misconduct. In fact, they are often rewarded with promotions and career advancement as long as their conviction rates remain high. This system suggests a cycle of misconduct that is continually reinforced. It is easier for prosecutors to secure a conviction when they withhold exculpatory evidence, and since they suffer no consequences for withholding it and are rewarded for securing convictions, they continue the misconduct.

When misconduct is neither acknowledged nor punished, the line between acceptable behavior and misconduct begins to blur. Some prosecutors may not actually realize the illegality of their behavior, especially inexperienced prosecutors in offices that foster a culture of winning at any cost. If a prosecution office does not train its prosecutors to reveal *Brady* information and otherwise play by the rules, these prosecutors may unknowingly cross the line from acceptable to illegal behavior. Even when prosecutors know their behavior is illegal, the harmless error doctrine and the absence of meaningful oversight by bar disciplinary authorities serve to encourage the offending behavior.

CONCLUSION

When the law is broken by the very people the public trusts to enforce the law, meaningful action must be taken. Prosecutorial misconduct is widespread and unchecked, and it is unlikely that either the courts or the general public will take action to eliminate it. Prosecutors certainly have not policed themselves. Thus, the legal profession must take the lead in instituting meaningful reform that will assure oversight and strict accountability when prosecutors break the law. Although criminal lawyers in individual cases may not have the ability to affect meaningful reform, other lawyers, through local and national bar associations, should advocate for legislation and binding professional rules that will be enforced against wrongdoers.[98] Lawyers have a vested interest in improving the reputation of the profession and in the fair administration of justice for everyone. They also have the expertise and responsibility to institute reforms to eliminate misconduct among prosecutors.

EIGHT

Prosecutorial Ethics

The Supreme Court has suggested that the most appropriate remedy for prosecutorial misconduct is disciplinary action by state bar authorities.[1] However, the Court's suggestion has proven to be woefully inadequate and ineffective.[2] The lack of transparency in prosecution offices has made discovery of prosecutorial misconduct extremely difficult, and even when misconduct is discovered, referrals to state disciplinary authorities have been few and far between. As discussed in chapter 7, in the relatively few cases that have been referred to state authorities, prosecutors rarely receive serious discipline.

Chapter 10 discusses ways the disciplinary process might be reformed to more effectively root out prosecutorial misconduct. However, before addressing the issue of reforming the process, it is useful to explore whether the disciplinary rules themselves adequately address the prosecution function. Given the very different role that prosecutors play, as compared to lawyers who represent clients in both civil and criminal cases, do the disciplinary rules that govern attorney conduct provide sufficient guidance to prosecutors or adequate bases for holding prosecutors accountable for misconduct? This chapter will explore these issues.

THE RULES OF PROFESSIONAL CONDUCT

The rules that govern the professional conduct of lawyers are promulgated by the ABA, a private organization and the largest voluntary

bar association in the country. The ABA has drafted several comprehensive codes of ethical conduct over the past one hundred years that
have provided the model for the rules adopted by state courts. When a
state court adopts a code of ethical conduct, it may then be enforced
against the lawyers in that jurisdiction.

The first code of ethical conduct was the Canons of Professional
Ethics, promulgated by the ABA in 1908. The Canons of Professional
Ethics were vague and contradictory and were enforced selectively.
Nonetheless, they remained in effect for over sixty years. It was not
until 1969 that the ABA adopted a new code of professional conduct,
called the Model Code of Professional Responsibility. Almost all jurisdictions adopted the Model Code, and it remains in effect in a few
states, including New York. In 1977, the ABA began yet another
reconsideration of the rules of professional conduct. A commission was
appointed and ultimately proposed the Model Rules of Professional
Conduct in 1983.[3] Most jurisdictions adopted these.

Just fourteen years after the adoption of the Model Rules, the ABA
undertook yet another project to revise the rules governing attorney
conduct. In 1997, then–ABA president Jerome Shestack, his immediate predecessor, N. Lee Cooper, and his successor, Philip S. Anderson,
persuaded the ABA House of Governors that the Model Rules were in
need of review and revision. They established what became known as
the Ethics 2000 Commission to undertake this project.[4] According to its
proponents, a commission was needed to review and revise the rules
because there was substantial lack of uniformity among the various state
versions of the Model Rules and new legal issues were being raised by
the influence of advancements in technology on the delivery of legal
services.[5] In 2002, the ABA House of Delegates adopted a series of
amendments as a result of the Commission's work. Forty-seven states
and the District of Columbia have adopted some version of the
amended Model Rules.[6]

The Model Rules cover a wide range of attorney conduct, and
many of the rules apply only to lawyers who represent clients. As
representatives of the state, prosecutors represent "the people" (including the defendants they prosecute) and are charged with "doing
justice" rather than zealously pursuing the interests of individual clients. Thus, the Model Rules address an entire range of issues, including
attorney fees, conflicts among clients, selling a law practice, advertising,

and solicitation,[7] that have no applicability to the performance of prosecutorial duties and responsibilities.

On the other hand, the Model Rules include provisions that apply to all lawyers, including prosecutors. These rules govern issues such as making false statements, offering false evidence, concealing evidence, asking a witness not to cooperate with the adversary, and publicity during litigation.[8] These provisions all use the term "lawyer," even though the prohibitions regarding attorney behavior apply to prosecutors as well.

The only rule that specifically addresses the conduct and behavior of prosecutors is Model Rule 3.8: Special Responsibilities of a Prosecutor. The Ethics 2000 Commission recommended no substantive changes to Model Rule 3.8 and only one substantive change to the rule's comment. This change resulted in fewer restrictions on prosecutorial behavior than the original rule.

MODEL RULE 3.8

The role of the prosecutor is clearly distinct and fundamentally different from that of lawyers who represent clients. The ABA and the Association of American Law Schools (AALS) recognized this distinction in their Joint Conference Report on Professional Responsibility, concluding that a "prosecutor cannot take as a guide for the conduct of his office the standards of an attorney appearing on the behalf of an individual client. The freedom elsewhere wisely granted to partisan advocacy must be severely curtailed if the prosecutor's duties are to be properly discharged."[9] Presumably, Model Rule 3.8, the only rule specifically directed solely to prosecutors, should adequately address their distinct duties and responsibilities. According to Model Rule 3.8:

The prosecutor in a criminal case shall:

   (a) refrain from prosecuting a charge that the prosecutor knows is not supported by probable cause;
   (b) make reasonable efforts to assure that the accused has been advised of the right to, and the procedure for

obtaining, counsel and has been given reasonable opportunity to obtain counsel;

(c) not seek to obtain from an unrepresented accused a
waiver of important pretrial rights, such as the right to a
preliminary hearing;

(d) make timely disclosure to the defense of all evidence or
information known to the prosecutor that tends to negate the guilt of the accused or mitigates the offense,
and, in connection with sentencing, disclose to the defense and to the tribunal all unprivileged mitigating
information known to the prosecutor, except when the
prosecutor is relieved of this responsibility by a pro-
tective order of the tribunal;

(e) not subpoena a lawyer in a grand jury or other criminal
proceeding to present evidence about a past or present
client unless the prosecutor reasonably believes:

(1) the information sought is not protected from disclosure by any applicable privilege;

(2) the evidence sought is essential to the successful completion of an ongoing investigation or prosecution;
and

(3) there is no other feasible alternative to obtain the
information;

(f) except for statements that are necessary to inform the
public of the nature and extent of the prosecutor's action
and that serve a legitimate law enforcement purpose,
refrain from making extrajudicial comments that have a
substantial likelihood of heightening public condemn-
ation of the accused and exercise reasonable care to
prevent investigators, law enforcement personnel, em-
ployees or other persons assisting or associated with the
prosecutor in a criminal case from making an extrajudicial statement that the prosecutor would be prohibited
from making under Rule 3.6 or this Rule.[10]

Rule 3.8 addresses some of the prosecutor's most important responsibilities, such as the charging decision (3.8(a)) and the duty to
disclose exculpatory information to defense counsel (3.8(d)). However, rule 3.8 fails to address a number of equally important prose-

cutorial issues, including conduct before the grand jury, relations with the police and other law enforcement officers, relations with victims and government witnesses, and selective prosecution. In fact, these critical issues are not addressed anywhere in the Model Rules. In addition, some of the language of rule 3.8 is vague and subject to interpretation, providing very little clear guidance to prosecutors and making it difficult to sustain complaints against prosecutors before disciplinary authorities.

As discussed in previous chapters, there have been many claims of prosecutorial misconduct regarding charging decisions, grand jury issues, witness relations, and other issues. The Supreme Court has created a very high standard for the reversal of criminal cases based on misconduct and has suggested that claims of misconduct that do not meet this standard be referred to bar disciplinary authorities.[11] Chapter 7 discussed some of the reasons why there have been so few referrals of prosecutors to disciplinary authorities and even fewer sustained complaints. However, the rules themselves may present an additional impediment.

Rule 3.8(a) permits prosecutors to bring charges that are based on the very low standard of probable cause. Although probable cause is the standard that the grand jury must use in deciding whether to issue an indictment, shouldn't ethical rules require that prosecutors meet a higher standard in the exercise of the charging decision? After all, prosecutors must meet a much higher standard—proof beyond a reasonable doubt—to obtain a conviction. If they are permitted to bring charges on the minimal standard of probable cause, there is a greater potential that the charging power will be used improperly— perhaps to intimidate, harass, or coerce a guilty plea in a case in which the government cannot meet its burden of proof at trial. However, prosecutors have argued that if the reasonable doubt standard were imposed as an ethical requirement, prosecutors would be subject to claims of unethical behavior in every case involving an acquittal.[12]

Despite the minimal requirements of Rule 3.8(a), some prosecutors use a higher standard in deciding whether to bring charges.[13] Prosecutors usually do not know whether the defendant would be inclined to accept a plea offer, so if the defendant decides to exercise his right to a trial, the prosecutor must be prepared to meet the higher reasonable doubt standard. In addition to the ethical issues, it would be a waste of time and resources for a prosecutor to present a case to the grand jury if she did not believe that she could prove the case beyond a reasonable doubt.

The standards promulgated by the National District Attorneys Association seem to establish a slightly higher charging standard than the Model Rules. According to standard 43.3, "[t]he prosecutor should file only those charges which he reasonably believes can be substantiated by admissible evidence at trial."[14] Since prosecutors are permitted to present hearsay and other otherwise inadmissible evidence to a grand jury to establish probable cause, the NDAA standard seems to require a greater level of certainty than the Model Rules. Nonetheless, the NDAA standards, like the ABA prosecution standards, are aspirational and not enforceable. Furthermore, the commentary to NDAA standard 43 may neutralize its slightly more rigorous requirements. According to the commentary, "[t]he charging decision is not an exact science, since the prosecutor, in deciding what he feels to be the maximum charge supported by the available evidence, necessarily operates with less than total knowledge of the facts and possible trial situation. As a result, the initial charging decision may have to be modified and reduced to a lesser charge as the prosecutor gains additional information about the offense and offender."[15] This language seems to endorse prosecutors bringing charges before they are fully informed about the facts and may be interpreted as permitting prosecutors to "overcharge"—a practice that may have devastating and unfair consequences for criminal defendants, as discussed in chapter 2.

Even if it were demonstrated that most prosecutors abide by a higher charging standard than either the Model Rules or the NDAA standards, the Model Rules are the only ethical rules that are enforceable by law, and they leave the door open for unethical practices. An indictment alone may significantly damage an individually personally, professionally, and financially. As one former prosecutor stated, "[a] prosecutor's power to damage or destroy anyone he chooses to indict is virtually limitless."[16] An unethical prosecutor may decide to bring an indictment against an individual that she may easily accomplish under a probable cause standard, even if she knows that she would not be able to prove that person's guilt beyond a reasonable doubt. There is nothing in rule 3.8 or anywhere in the Model Rules that specifically prohibits such behavior.

Model rule 3.8(d) requires prosecutors to disclose all evidence or information that tends to negate or mitigate the defendant's guilt. This rule essentially imposes the same requirements on prosecutors as did the U.S. Supreme Court in *Brady v. Maryland*.[17] In *Brady*, the Court held that "the suppression by the prosecution of evidence favorable to an accused upon request violates due process where the evidence is material either to guilt or to punishment, irrespective of the good faith or bad faith of the prosecution."[18] Arguably, the model rule may go further than *Brady* in that it requires disclosure even when there has not been a request. Thus, in jurisdictions that have adopted the Model Rules, prosecutors may be referred to disciplinary authorities for *Brady* violations. Yet such referrals are rare. There are many reasons why lawyers, judges, and ordinary citizens may not be inclined to bring claims of unethical behavior against prosecutors,[19] but even if a claim were brought, it would be difficult to sustain in light of the imprecise language of the rule.

Rule 3.8(d) requires "timely disclosure" of exculpatory information. This phrase alone demonstrates the imprecision of the rule. Neither the rule nor the comment to the rule defines what is meant by "timely." Defense attorneys would suggest that such information is of no help to the defense unless it is disclosed long before the trial date. For example, if there is a witness who identified someone other than the defendant as the perpetrator, the defense would need time to locate, interview, and possibly subpoena that witness for trial. Yet many prosecutors might withhold such information until the trial date, arguing that as long as the defense attorney knows about it before trial, she will be able to use it in defense of the accused.

A prosecutor who believes that exculpatory information need not be disclosed until the time of trial has no incentive to disclose the information if she offers the defendant a plea to a lesser offense before trial and the defendant accepts the offer. The plea bargaining process, although controlled by the prosecutor, is one of negotiation.[20] If the defense attorney knows that there is information that tends to exculpate her client, she will be in a much better bargaining position during the plea bargaining process. Or, depending on the information, the defense attorney may advise the client that he has a good chance of an acquittal at trial. The prosecutor who makes a plea offer while withholding such information arguably is engaging in unethical conduct. Yet the vagueness of the term "timely disclosure" makes it unlikely that such behavior would be sufficient to sustain a claim that the prosecutor violated rule 3.8(d).

Rule 3.8(d) refers to "evidence or information known to the prosecutor." This phrase is also subject to interpretation. Are prosecutors required to disclose information known to police officers or other law enforcement agents? Do they have an affirmative obligation to ask police officers, law enforcement agents, or other individuals involved in the investigation and prosecution of the case whether there is any exculpatory information? These questions have been the subject of much litigation.[21] The fact that there is so much disagreement about this issue makes it unlikely that disciplinary authorities would punish a prosecutor in the absence of proof that she had actual knowledge of exculpatory information. The rule does not require prosecutors to make efforts to discover such information from anyone, so the failure to do so would not likely constitute an ethical violation.

The part of the rule that is probably the most important is also the vaguest. Neither the rule nor the comment to the rule clarifies what is meant by information "that tends to negate the guilt of the accused or mitigates the offense." Prosecutors and defense attorneys are likely to have very different views of what information this phrase covers. For example, defense attorneys likely would argue that any contradictory or inconsistent statements made by any government witness should be disclosed. They would suggest that such information impeaches the credibility of these witnesses and thus "negate[s] the guilt of the accused."[22] Prosecutors would argue that contradictory statements by a witness may not negate the guilt of the accused. In an armed robbery case involving codefendants, a defense attorney may argue that information showing that government witnesses disagree about who carried the gun should be disclosed. For example, if one witness claims a codefendant was the gunman and all other witnesses identify the defendant as the gunman, the defense attorney would argue that this information negates his client's guilt or at least mitigates the offense. A prosecutor would argue that such information would not tend to "negate the guilt of the accused" and should not be disclosed, since an accomplice who stands beside the gunman during an armed robbery is just as guilty of the offense.

In sum, model rule 3.8 does not adequately address the conduct and behavior of prosecutors. The rule does address, albeit inadequately, the charging decision and the duty to disclose exculpatory evidence. In addition, sections e and f address controversial issues that prosecutors regularly confront—subpoenas to defense attorneys and extrajudicial statements by prosecutors. The other sections, b and c, concern issues that, though important, do not rank among the most pressing concerns regarding prosecutorial behavior. In most jurisdictions, judges assume responsibility for the appointment of counsel. As for pretrial waivers, the comment makes it clear that this section does not apply to the questioning of uncharged suspects—an issue of greater concern to defense attorneys than preliminary hearings. It is unclear why the rule would address these issues while ignoring those about which prosecutors clearly need guidance, such as the grand jury, relations with witnesses and victims, and selective prosecution.

The rule's inadequacy lies not only in its failure to address critical issues but also in the vagueness of its language. Much of it is subject to interpretation, providing very little guidance to prosecutors or disciplinary authorities. The comment to the rule also contains vague language that provides no more guidance than the rule itself. According to the comment:

> A prosecutor has the responsibility of a minister of justice and not simply that of an advocate. This responsibility carries with it specific obligations to see that the defendant is accorded procedural justice and that guilt is decided upon the basis of sufficient evidence. Precisely how far the prosecutor is required to go in this direction is a matter of debate and varies in different jurisdictions. Many jurisdictions have adopted the ABA Standards of Criminal Justice Relating to the Prosecution Function, which in turn are the product of prolonged and careful deliberation by lawyers experienced in both criminal prosecution and defense. Applicable law may require other measures by the prosecutor and knowing disregard of those obligations or a systematic abuse of prosecutorial discretion could constitute a violation of Rule 8.4.[23]

THE ETHICS 2000 COMMISSION—
A LOST OPPORTUNITY?

The Ethics 2000 Commission made very few recommendations that specifically addressed prosecutorial responsibilities. The only change to rule 3.8 involved a consolidation of two of the existing sections into one.[24] However, there were several amendments to the comment to rule 3.8. Two dealt with sections c (prohibiting prosecutors from soliciting waivers from unrepresented persons) and f (prohibiting prosecutors from making certain extrajudicial statements). The other amendment to the comment weakened prosecutors' responsibilities under 3.8(d). The original comment made it clear that prosecutors should disclose information exculpatory to the defense to grand juries.[25] The Ethics 2000 Commission deleted this clarification from the comment, choosing to follow the Supreme Court's holding that such information need not be disclosed to grand juries[26] rather than the ABA Standards, which recommend disclosure.[27]

Although many of the recommended changes adopted by the ABA apply to both lawyers who represent clients and prosecutors, most do not specifically address the duties and responsibilities unique to the prosecution function. The only other amendment (other than the amendments to the comment to rule 3.8) that specifically addressed a prosecution issue was the amendment to rule 4.2. This rule states:

> In representing a client, a lawyer shall not communicate
> about the subject of the representation with a person the law-
> yer knows to be represented by another lawyer in the matter,
> unless the lawyer has the consent of the other lawyer or is
> authorized to do so by law or a court order.

Rule 4.2 was the subject of great controversy when Richard Thornburgh issued the memo in 1989 that exempted federal prosecutors from the rule. The Commission held numerous meetings about the rule with the ABA Standing Committee on Ethics and Professional Responsibility and attempted to draft an amendment that would provide clarity as to how prosecutors should interpret the rule.[28] However, the Justice Department never supported the Commission's efforts, so it abandoned the amendment.[29] Instead, the Commission added the words "or a court order" to the end of the previous rule to give prosecutors the opportunity to convince a court to permit communication with represented persons.

Many organizations and individuals submitted suggestions and comments to the Commission on various aspects of the Model Rules, but very few commented on the duties and responsibilities of prosecutors. A few bar associations and individuals commented on rule 3.8.

For example, Rex Heinke, then-president of the Los Angeles County Bar Association, sent a letter objecting to proposed language in the comment that suggested that prosecutors' discovery obligations in rule 3.8 went beyond what was required by the Constitution.[30] In addition, Robert O'Malley, then-chair of the District of Columbia Bar Rules of Professional Conduct Review Committee, sent a letter to the ABA Commission on Evaluation of the Rules of Professional Conduct recommending changes to strengthen the independence of the grand jury and require prosecutors to submit exculpatory information to the grand jury.[31] However, none of the national prosecutor or defense organizations submitted comments.[32]

The Commission did solicit comments from the ABA Criminal Justice Standards Committee. Niki Kuckes, then-chair of the Committee, submitted a report that was critical of model rule 3.8.[33] The report suggested the need for a number of amendments, including raising the standard for bringing charges. It also suggested the need to add provisions that address important issues that rule 3.8 is silent about but various state ethics codes address. These include provisions prohibiting selective prosecution and the use of peremptory strikes against jurors based on race, religion, sex, ethnicity, or nationality.[34] Nonetheless, the report discouraged the Commission from recommending a comprehensive overhaul of the rule, instead suggesting that there should be a separate, long-term review of the rule with participation of prosecutors, defense attorneys, and the courts, in light of the controversial nature of the suggested changes.[35] The Commission obviously acted in accordance with the Standards Committee's recommendation.

One of the stated reasons for the latest revision of the Model Rules was the lack of uniformity among state ethics codes. There are few areas of legal practice more lacking in uniformity than the performance of prosecutorial duties and responsibilities. Because of the discretionary nature of prosecutorial practice, complete uniformity is neither possible nor necessarily desirable. However, vast disparities in how prosecutors perform fundamental duties and responsibilities suggest a need for guidance. The fact that there has been so much litigation and controversy around issues of grand jury practice, selective prosecution, disclosure of exculpatory information, and contact with represented persons suggests the need for more guidance in the ethical rules. Yet the ABA chose to pass on the opportunity to provide that guidance during its last revision of the Model Rules. This decision is especially troubling in light of the Supreme Court's suggestion that state disciplinary authorities should bear the responsibility for addressing prosecutorial misconduct. If both the Supreme Court and the ABA choose to sidestep the responsibility for holding prosecutors accountable, all that is left is a reliance on the electoral and appointments processes, which have proven ineffective due to the lack of transparency in prosecution offices and the lack of interest by the general public.[36]

THE REGULATION OF FEDERAL PROSECUTORS

As with many other issues involving prosecutorial power, the regulation of the professional conduct of federal prosecutors is even more difficult than that of their state and local counterparts. As already mentioned, despite the dearth of disciplinary referrals of either state or federal prosecutors, in 1989, former attorney general Richard Thornburgh issued his extraordinary memo, which Attorney General Janet Reno reissued for public comment with some modifications (the "Reno Rule"), and it was codified in a series of regulations in 1994.[37]

Thornburgh issued his memo in response to a controversy surrounding the extent to which federal prosecutors should be required to comply with disciplinary rule 7-104(A)(1) of the ABA Model Code of Professional Responsibility and its successor, rule 4.2 of the ABA Model Rules of Professional Conduct. According to rule 7-104(A)(1):

> During the course of his representation of a client a lawyer shall not: Communicate or cause another to communicate on the subject of the representation by a lawyer in that matter unless he has the prior consent of the lawyer representing such other party or is authorized by law to do so.

Rule 4.2 of the Model Rules is quite similar:

> In representing a client, a lawyer shall not communicate about the subject of the representation with a person the lawyer knows to be represented by another lawyer in the matter, unless the lawyer has the consent of the other lawyer or is authorized by law to do so.

Defense attorneys complained that federal prosecutors were routinely violating the rule, which had been adopted in almost all states. Some of these attorneys filed motions to suppress evidence in cases in which prosecutors violated the rule, and others referred the prosecutors to the state disciplinary authorities.[38]

Most of these alleged violations involved either undercover or overt communications with individuals who were targets of a criminal investigation. Thornburgh took the position that, even though these individuals were represented by counsel in their pending cases, the challenged communications were about criminal behavior that had not yet been charged. Thus, according to Thornburgh, these defendants were not represented by counsel in the matters about which they were being questioned.

In the memo, Thornburgh contended that prosecutors were carrying out their lawful responsibilities as federal law enforcement officers when they engaged in these communications and that these actions were protected by the Supremacy Clause of the U.S. Constitution:

> Indeed, the Department has consistently taken the position that the Supremacy Clause of the Constitution does not permit local and state rules to frustrate the lawful operation of the federal government. *See Ethical Restraints of the ABA Code of Professional Responsibility on Federal Criminal Investigations*, 4B Op. Off. of Legal Counsel 576, 601-02 (1980). The Department has taken the position that, although the states have the authority to regulate the ethical conduct of attorneys admitted to practice before their courts, *Nix v. Whiteside*, 106 S.Ct. 988, 994 (1986), that authority permits regulation of federal attorneys only if the regulation does not conflict with the federal law or with the attorneys' federal responsibilities, *see Sperry v. Florida*, 373 U.S. 379, 402(1963).[39]

The Thornburgh Memo and the Reno Rule sparked litigation that challenged the supremacy clause argument and other grounds of the Justice Department's exemption of federal prosecutors from rule 4.2. Some courts rejected the Justice Department's arguments,[40] and others did not.[41]

The Thornburgh Memo and the Reno Rule became moot in 1998, when Congress passed the CPA, requiring federal prosecutors to

abide by the ethics rules of the states in which they practiced, providing, in part, that

> (a) [a]n attorney for the Government shall be subject to State
>   laws and rules, and local Federal court rules, governing
>   attorneys in each State where such attorney engages in
>   that attorney's duties, to the same extent as other attorneys
>   in that State.
> (b) The Attorney General shall make and amend rules of
>   the Department of Justice to assure compliance with this
>   section.[42]

The CPA was introduced by former congressman Joseph McDade, who
had been indicted on bribery-related charges in federal court in 1992.
During the pendency of his case, McDade filed numerous motions
alleging prosecutorial misconduct and violations of state ethical rules. All
of the motions were denied, and in 1996, McDade was acquitted of all
charges after a jury trial. Motivated by what he believed to be unethical
behavior by the federal prosecutors in his case, McDade began his
campaign to secure passage of various versions of the CPA, and finally
succeeded with the current version in 1998.

Not surprisingly, federal prosecutors have been highly critical of
the CPA. Its express purpose was to overrule the Justice Department
policy that purported to exempt federal prosecutors from state ethical
rules that, in the Justice Department's view, conflict with their responsibilities as federal law enforcement officers. However, the expansive language of the bill potentially reaches much further. Section
530B is entitled "Ethical Standards for Attorneys for the Government," but the language of the section does not limit federal prosecutors to compliance with state ethical rules, instead declaring that
they are subject to all "State laws and rules."[43] What should federal
prosecutors do when federal and state laws conflict, as they frequently
do? Federal prosecutors would have a good argument that the federal
law should prevail if there is a clear conflict.[44] However, what if
particular state laws impose additional obligations on federal prosecutors? For example, if a state's discovery rules require prosecutors to
disclose more information than the federal rules, would a federal
prosecutor violate the CPA by merely complying with the federal
rules?[45]

The purpose of the CPA was a good one—to ensure that federal prosecutors comply with ethical rules. However, the statute does not provide adequate guidance to federal prosecutors and leaves too many questions unanswered. The language is broad, unclear, and subject to interpretation. One of the main concerns involves federal investigations that have crossed state lines. If a prosecutor were involved with such a multi-jurisdictional investigation, which state's ethical rules should she follow? Although most states ultimately passed some version of the Model Rules of Professional Responsibility, not all states did so, and how should a prosecutor proceed if she is involved in a multistate investigation involving conflicting ethical rules?

The Justice Department does not suggest that its prosecutors should not be required to comply with ethical standards. Instead, it points to its own OPR as evidence that it should and does require its lawyers to act ethically and responsibly in the implementation of their duties and responsibilities. The Justice Department describes the OPR as follows:

> The Office of Professional Responsibility, which reports directly to the Attorney General, is responsible for investigating allegations of misconduct involving Department attorneys, investigators, or law enforcement personnel, where the allegations relate to the exercise of the authority of an attorney to investigate, litigate, or provide legal advice.
>
> The objective of OPR is to ensure that Department of Justice attorneys continue to perform their duties in accordance with the high professional standards expected of the Nation's principal law enforcement agency.
>
> The Office is headed by the Counsel for Professional Responsibility. Under the Counsel's direction, OPR reviews allegations of attorney misconduct involving violation of any standard imposed by law, applicable rules of professional conduct, or Departmental policy. When warranted, OPR conducts full investigations of such allegations, and reports its findings and conclusions to the Attorney General and other appropriate Departmental officials.[46]

The duties and responsibilities of all prosecutors clearly are distinguishable from lawyers who represent clients, and there are obviously differences in how federal and state prosecutors practice—both in form and in substance.[47] Federal prosecutors typically handle more ongoing, complex investigations that may span several jurisdictions. They also may handle a different genre of criminal offense, such as environmental, corporate, or organized crime. State and local prosecutors govern their own jurisdictions without centralized direction,[48] whereas federal prosecutors are expected to abide by the U.S. attorneys' manual and any directives from the attorney general. Although it might be argued that the more centralized governance of federal prosecutors makes it more likely they will act ethically, the argument ultimately boils down to "Trust us because we are federal prosecutors"—an argument that ultimately rings hollow.[49]

There are undoubtedly many defense attorneys who would never refer a federal prosecutor to OPR because they would not have faith that the office would provide an unbiased assessment of the prosecutor's behavior. In my twelve years at PDS, I never referred a federal prosecutor to OPR, nor did I hear of other public defenders making such referrals, despite the fact that I was aware of many cases of prosecutorial misconduct. Instead, my colleagues and I chose to litigate the issues before judges and seek remedies for the clients whose cases were affected by the misconduct.[50]

The OPR issues an annual report each year, in which it describes its process and provides information about the complaints it receives— the number and type of complaints, how they are resolved, and so on. The OPR receives complaints from a number of sources, including judges, lawyers, private individuals, and other federal agencies. Some referrals come from the Justice Department itself. In fact, Department attorneys are required to refer all cases in which judges make a finding of prosecutorial misconduct.[51] In each investigation, the prosecutor accused of misconduct is interviewed on the record under oath. If there is a finding of misconduct, the lawyers issue a report with a recommendation, which may consist of a reprimand, suspension, or even termination. This report is sent to the attorney general and the hiring authority of the accused prosecutor's office. The prosecutor's office then conducts its own disciplinary proceedings. If that office sustains the finding of misconduct and the misconduct implicates that state's disciplinary rules, the OPR will refer the matter to the state's disciplinary authority.[52]

The most obvious criticism of OPR is a recurring theme in how the prosecution function operates—lack of accountability. Can prosecutors be trusted to discipline themselves? Even though OPR may ultimately refer its prosecutors to state disciplinary authorities, it only does so if its own investigation and the disciplinary process of the prosecutor's office sustain a finding of misconduct. Does OPR truly hold federal prosecutors accountable if it only refers them to an independent authority after it has made its own determination of misconduct? Might OPR be less inclined to find misconduct than an independent authority?

According to OPR's 2003 annual report, "[t]he majority of complaints reviewed by OPR each year are determined not to warrant further investigation because, for example, the complaint is frivolous on its face, is outside OPR's jurisdiction, or is vague and unsupported by any evidence."[53] The fact that the majority of complaints are dismissed is not, in and of itself, evidence of bias. Frivolous complaints should be dismissed, and in any disciplinary entity, someone has to make these judgments. However, the risk of actual and perceived bias in the decision-making process is high when the ultimate decision-makers have a vested interest in demonstrating that most of its prosecutors do not engage in misconduct.

The sheer number of complaints that OPR dismissed in 2003 creates at least the perception that there is a culture of the Justice Department protecting its own. In the 2003 annual report, OPR summarizes its intake and evaluation of complaints as follows:

> In fiscal year 2003, OPR received 913 complaints and other letters and memoranda requesting assistance, an increase of approximately 33% from fiscal year 2002. OPR determined that 342 of the matters, or approximately 37%, warranted further review by OPR attorneys. OPR opened full investigations in ninety-two of those matters; the remaining 250, which are termed "inquiries," were resolved with no findings of professional misconduct, based on further review, responses from the subjects, and other information. When information developed in an inquiry indicated that further investigation was warranted, the matter was converted to a full investigation.
>
> The remaining 571 matters were determined not to warrant an inquiry by OPR because, for example, they related to matters outside the jurisdiction of OPR; sought review of issues that were being litigated or that had already been

considered and rejected by a court; were frivolous, vague, or unsupported by any evidence; or simply requested information. Those matters were addressed by experienced management analysts through correspondence or referral to another government agency or Department of Justice component. A supervisory OPR attorney and the Deputy Counsel reviewed all such dispositions.[54]

Only ninety-two of the 913 complaints resulted in an investigation. Of the ninety-two complaints, only thirteen attorneys were found to have engaged in professional misconduct. Disciplinary action, including suspension without pay and written reprimands, was taken against twelve of the thirteen attorneys. The annual reports do not provide information about the number of federal prosecutors who resign either during an investigation or after learning that they will be investigated.[55]

The OPR also has been criticized for its failure to provide adequate information when it refers cases to state disciplinary authorities. The OPR staff often decline to provide complete reports on the prosecutors they refer, redacting classified or grand jury information and other information that may fall under certain privacy acts.[56] However, it is difficult and sometimes impossible for the independent authority to conduct an adequate investigation when OPR staff redact relevant information from their reports or delay referrals for many years after the initial complaint.[57]

Can independent oversight of federal prosecutors ever be achieved if OPR fails to provide full disclosure to the appropriate state disciplinary authority in all cases involving allegations of misconduct? Despite the failure of the Model Rules of Professional Responsibility to provide adequate guidance and discipline to prosecutors (state or federal), there is at least a recognition that the conduct of prosecutors should be independently regulated. State disciplinary authorities can and do investigate federal prosecutors in the absence of OPR referrals,[58] but OPR is certainly in the best possible position to facilitate these investigations. The OPR serves a useful purpose—there is certainly a value in the Justice Department devoting an entire office to assuring that its lawyers perform their duties legally and ethically. However, unless this office cooperates more fully with state and local authorities, true accountability cannot be achieved.

SEPARATE RULES AND PROCEDURES
FOR PROSECUTORS

The current disciplinary system for lawyers does not adequately address the conduct and behavior of prosecutors. For all the political and practical reasons previously discussed, lawyers rarely refer prosecutors to state disciplinary authorities when they have legitimate complaints of misconduct. Even if there were more referrals, the rules themselves fail to address many of the most important prosecutorial functions.

Professor Bruce Green has suggested that the judiciary should consider drafting separate ethical rules for prosecutors that recognize their unique role as ministers of justice.[59] Green's suggestion should be seriously considered. Many of the model rules, which have been adopted in most states, either don't apply to prosecutors or are not easily applied because they don't take into account the special role of prosecutors in the justice system. The one rule that does apply to prosecutors is inadequate because it fails to address many of the most important prosecutorial functions. A separate code of prosecutorial conduct would address specific prosecutorial functions, offering guidance to prosecutors and providing a basis for holding them accountable when they engage in misconduct.

Green suggests that the judiciary oversee the development of the rules rather than the ABA, to reduce opposition from prosecutors' offices.[60] Judicial oversight may or may not reduce prosecutorial opposition, but it should reduce the appearance of bias for or against prosecutors. Prosecutors should play a major role in the rule-making process, but criminal defense attorneys and the general bar should participate as well. There should be a parallel separate process for federal prosecutors involving the federal judiciary. A separate code of conduct for federal prosecutors would specifically address the unique responsibilities of federal prosecutors.

There must be a multifaceted approach to reform of the prosecutorial function. Reform of the disciplinary rules and process for prosecutors is just one method of promoting greater accountability for prosecutors. Codification of a separate set of rules and a separate disciplinary process for prosecutors would be a long and tedious process but would produce a more effective system that would benefit prosecutors and the public at large.

NINE

Prosecutorial Accountability

The previous chapters demonstrate the immense power and discretion of the American prosecutor and how that power and the arbitrary exercise of discretion often contribute to injustices in the criminal justice system. Even when prosecutors set out to do justice in good faith, the arbitrary nature of their decisions and the absence of a meaningful system of accountability frequently result in widely varying consequences for similarly situated victims and defendants. As chapter 7 demonstrates, some prosecutors intentionally break the rules, and the absence of meaningful punishment of these prosecutors may foster and encourage a continuing climate of misconduct.

How and why does the current system of prosecution persist and thrive in a democratic society of which the accountability of governmental officials is an essential component? How effective is the current system in holding prosecutors accountable to the people they purport to serve? To the extent the system falls short, why is there such a lack of interest in reform? This chapter explores these difficult issues by discussing the current mechanisms of accountability and the role the media plays in perpetuating the current paradigm.

HOLDING PROSECUTORS ACCOUNTABLE

Separation of powers and a system of checks and balances were core values of the framers of the Constitution.[1] The distribution of power among the three branches of government was meant to ensure efficient government and to prevent any single branch from exercising arbitrary power.[2] The prosecutorial function falls within the executive branch of government.[3] Our system of checks and balances suggests that the judicial and legislative branches have the power to hold prosecutors accountable for abuse of power. For the most part, however, they have not done so on either the federal or state levels. Thus, the constitutional design has not prevented prosecutors, as members of the executive branch, from exercising "arbitrary power."

There is no historical or constitutional support for the de facto unaccountable twenty-first-century prosecutor. The Constitution is silent on the point.[4] The evidence suggesting that the prosecutorial function was at times unstructured and unaccountable to the people before and immediately after the ratification of the Constitution does not mandate the conclusion that the framers would endorse the current model of prosecution. In fact, an examination of constitutional values in light of the vast changes in our criminal justice system over time suggests that the current model offends these core principles.

Accountability is a core constitutional value[5]—one that should be preserved despite changes in the constitutional context. The framers viewed a strong, unitary executive as advancing accountability, because a fragmented executive branch could more easily escape review.[6] The modern prosecution model is fragmented within the executive branch. Crime and criminal law enforcement have expanded immensely since the eighteenth century.[7] Indeed, it is undoubtedly safe to suggest that the framers could not have imagined the numerous state and federal law enforcement agencies and the complex set of criminal laws enacted during the twentieth century.[8] This vast expansion in crime and law enforcement necessarily occasioned a corresponding increase in the size, number, and fragmentation of prosecutorial entities on both the state and federal levels. While more prosecutors were obviously necessary, more prosecutorial discretion and power were not.[9] In fact, the increase in crime, criminal laws, and prosecutors suggest a need for tightening, rather than expanding, prosecutorial power.

In sum, neither the history of the development of the American prosecutor nor an examination of the intent of the framers of the Constitution justifies the current model of the prosecution function.[10] Our system of checks and balances has proven ineffective in restraining prosecutorial power. The judicial branch has failed to check prosecutorial overreaching, and the legislative branch traditionally has passed laws that increase prosecutorial power.[11]

The breadth of prosecutorial discretion and the prevalence of prosecutorial misconduct demonstrate the importance of effective mechanisms of accountability. However, prosecutors require a certain level of independence to make their decisions without inappropriate and extraneous political pressures. These conflicting goals—accountability and independence—create a difficult tension. So far, independence has prevailed overwhelmingly.

It is difficult to strike the appropriate balance between independence and accountability in the prosecution function. Independence is extremely important to the appropriate exercise of prosecutorial discretion and power. Thus, prosecutors should perform their duties and responsibilities independently, on the basis of all of the appropriate considerations that promote the effective and efficient enforcement of the criminal laws, including the input of victims and the circumstances of defendants in particular cases. On the other hand, prosecutors should be accountable to the constituents they serve without allowing the prospect of reelection to improperly influence their decisions in individual cases. Prosecutors should be accountable to their constituents as they formulate policies on general issues such as charging, plea bargaining, and sentencing. However, ultimately they must make decisions in individual cases independently, taking into account all of the relevant considerations and ignoring inappropriate factors such as class, race, ethnicity, or politics, with the goal of achieving a fair and just result in all cases. All prosecutors face the difficult challenge of effectively implementing these conflicting goals.

Prosecutorial discretion is an important and essential ingredient of a fair and impartial criminal justice system. Mandatory minimum sentencing laws demonstrate the dangers of eliminating discretion from a decision-making process. Laws mandating that certain charging or plea bargaining decisions be made in every case or even every case in certain categories would surely result in injustices in some cases. A "one-size-fits-all" approach rarely, if ever, works in the criminal justice system. The facts and circumstances of each individual case must be considered to achieve a fair and just result.

The arbitrary exercise of discretion without careful consideration of only the relevant factors ultimately will produce unwarranted disparities, as demonstrated in the previous chapters. Even prosecutors who do not engage in intentional prosecutorial misconduct and try very hard to make decisions free of bias and political pressure often unintentionally exercise discretion in ways that produce inequitable results for similarly situated victims and defendants, for all of the reasons discussed in chapter 2. When there is no system in place to monitor whether there are race and/or class disparities in charging and plea bargaining, the prosecutor herself may not be aware of these disparities, and the public certainly won't know about them.

Although prosecutor offices do not routinely monitor race and class disparities in the implementation of the prosecution function,[12] all offices are subject to several mechanisms that purport to hold prosecutors accountable to their constituents. Do these systems work effectively? Are prosecutors held accountable for practices and policies that produce injustices in the system? Do the existing mechanisms of accountability—the electoral process, budgetary restrictions, and time and jurisdictional limitations—fall short of accomplishing this important goal?

The Electoral Process

Forty-three states hold popular elections for attorney general—the statewide prosecutor who, in most states, focuses on consumer protection, antitrust, and related matters, and has little or no involvement in the prosecution of ordinary street crimes.[13] At the county and municipal level, more than 95 percent of the chief prosecutors are elected.[14] These positions are highly political, and candidates usually campaign on general "tough on crime" themes, not on specific proposals about how they plan to exercise their prosecutorial power.[15] Prosecutors are usually elected in the same general elections as other public officials. The state and county prosecutors hire assistant district attorneys to handle the caseloads of their offices.

Ironically, the current system of choosing state and local prosecutors through the electoral process was established for the purpose of holding prosecutors accountable to the people they serve. This model of the elected prosecutor, which emerged during the rise of Jacksonian democracy in the 1820s, has not proven effective.[16] The public's access to information about prosecutorial decisions has not expanded since the 1820s. The electorate has very little information about a prosecutor's specific charging and plea bargaining practices or how he plans to exercise his discretion before electing him to office or, in the case of appointed prosecutors, before commenting on his appointment.[17] Because of the paucity of such relevant information, the Jacksonian democratic ideals that inspired the first elections of prosecutors in the 1820s have never been achieved.[18] Although the electorate can and does vote prosecutors out of office, it is not making these decisions in a fully informed manner.

Very few people understand the day-to-day responsibilities of prosecutors, nor do they seem to be interested in what prosecutors do. Unless a person has the unfortunate experience of becoming involved in the criminal justice system as a victim or witness, she would not have the opportunity to observe prosecutorial practices. And victims and witnesses are able to observe only so much. They ordinarily are not privy to the inner workings of the prosecutor's office, where charging and plea decisions are hidden from view. Certainly the many instances of prosecutorial misconduct discussed in chapter 7 rarely come to the public's attention. Even defense attorneys involved in the cases where those abuses occur have trouble discovering them. The public cannot hold the prosecutors accountable for behavior of which they are unaware.

The appointment process for federal prosecutors ensures that they are even less accountable to the people than their state and local counterparts. The president appoints the attorney general, who oversees the Justice Department,[19] and a U.S. attorney for each of the federal judicial districts.[20] Each U.S. attorney hires AUSAs for her office, and the attorney general may appoint additional AUSAs.[21] All U.S. attorneys serve at the pleasure of the sitting president and may face removal if a new president is elected, regardless of their conduct and record as federal prosecutors.[22] The president also retains the power to remove a particular federal prosecutor during his term as president, but would probably do so only in the unlikely possibility that the people become aware of prosecutorial abuses and demand her dismissal.

After the president nominates the attorney general and the U.S. attorney for each district, the Senate must confirm the appointments. Members of the public certainly have the right to provide input and comment during the confirmation process by communicating with their senators, but they rarely do. If the nominee has prior experience as a prosecutor, her record theoretically would provide a basis for evaluation. Of course, the nominee's record would not reflect his or

her most important prosecutorial decisions, such as charging and plea
bargaining, because they are made in private and rarely revealed to the
public.

Justice Scalia praised the system of accountability for federal prosecutors in his dissent in a Supreme Court case about the Office of the
Independent Counsel.[23] Justice Scalia suggested that if the people are
dissatisfied with a federal prosecutor, they will (1) know that the prosecutor was appointed by the president, (2) vote the president out of
office, and (3) thereby effectively hold the prosecutor accountable. Even
if such direct links could be drawn, it is unlikely that the voting public
would oust a popular president because of the actions of a single federal
prosecutor. Of course, in the case of a second-term president, the the-
oretical possibility of this form of accountability does not exist.[24]

The prosecution of Marion Barry, former mayor of Washington,
D.C., in 1990, offers an illustration in a particularly stark context. The
mayor had long labored under a cloud of suspicion about drug use
and philandering. Jay Stephens, the U.S. attorney for the District of
Columbia at that time,[25] worked with federal law enforcement agents
to investigate the mayor's behavior. The investigation ultimately resulted in a sting operation in which a woman serving as a government
agent lured Barry to a hotel room on the promise of sexual favors. Law
enforcement officials videotaped him smoking crack cocaine and arrested him on the spot.[26] Television stations broadcast the videotape nationwide, and Stephens relied on it as a key piece of evidence in
Barry's prosecution for drug possession and related offenses.[27]

Jay Stephens received widespread criticism for his prosecution of
Mayor Barry.[28] Barry's popularity, especially among the poor and
working-class residents of the District of Columbia, did not diminish
even after his drug usage came to light.[29] Many members of the public
expressed the view that the prosecution constituted little more than a
political vendetta by a Republican prosecutor against a liberal mayor.
Attorney General Richard Thornburgh took no steps to stop or control
the prosecution, nor did Stephens suffer any reprisals, despite the widespread public outcry over the prosecution by Stephens's constituents.
As an appointed official, Stephens could not be voted out of office by
the electorate of the District of Columbia.[30]

Justice Scalia suggested that if a federal prosecutor "amass[es] many
more resources against a particular prominent individual . . . than the
gravity of the alleged offenses . . . seems to warrant, the unfairness will

come home to roost in the Oval Office."[31] This did not hold true in Mayor Barry's prosecution. George H. W. Bush was president during Barry's prosecution. Bush did lose his reelection bid, but no one attributed his 1992 defeat to the prosecution of Marion Barry.[32] The failure of President Bush and Attorney General Thornburgh to take any action against Jay Stephens suggests that concern about Bush's possible defeat did not serve as a sufficient check on Stephens's behavior.[33] Stephens was well aware that a significant percentage of his constituents opposed his prosecution of Barry; nonetheless, he pursued it zealously. Barry's prosecution received widespread national attention, and the local opposition to the prosecution undoubtedly was not shared by the majority of Americans; but even if it had been, it would not have been an issue in the presidential campaign. The actions of individual federal prosecutors simply are not viewed as matters of national concern in most cases.

In sum, the electoral system does not effectively hold federal or state and local prosecutors accountable to the constituents they serve. Unless the public is consistently informed of prosecutors' performance during their tenure in office, the electoral process will remain ineffective. Even if a method of informing the public were established, there is no guarantee that the electoral system would serve the accountability function effectively, given the low voter turnout for many public elections and the public's apparent lack of interest in the conduct of prosecutors, which will be discussed later in this chapter.[34] However, without this information, there is no possibility that the current system can succeed.

Accountability through Budgetary Restrictions

Theoretically, budgetary restraints serve as a mechanism of accountability for federal and state prosecutors. These prosecutors work within a prescribed budget and must allocate their resources accordingly. A prosecutor who spent over 50 percent of her budget investigating and prosecuting one individual would have limited resources available to prosecute other crimes. An AUSA undoubtedly would suffer reprisals from the U.S. attorney for that district, and the electorate would vote a state or local prosecutor out of office if she were unable to prosecute violent or otherwise serious crimes due to misallocation of her budget.

Numerous examples exist of federal prosecutors spending extra-ordinary sums of money investigating certain crimes or particular individuals without apparent limit or control.[35] The prosecution of former mayor Marion Barry provides one example. Much attention focused on the cost of the prosecution of a single individual on charges that many considered relatively trivial.[36] Estimates of the total cost of the investigation and prosecution ranged from $2 million to $50 million.[37] Even the low estimates seemed particularly extravagant in hindsight, since the jury acquitted Barry on all but one misdemeanor offense.[38] Yet the prosecutor was not accountable to the people of the District of Columbia for the allocation and management of his budget.[39] Other expensive prosecutions of single individuals for nonviolent offenses include the prosecutions of Representative Dan Rostenkowski, Governor Fife Symington, Congressman Joseph McDade, and John Delorean.[40] Each of these prosecutions involved massive expenditures that came to light because the defendants were public figures. The public would never become aware of similarly large allocations of resources in cases involving ordinary citizens unless the press uncovered and reported such information.

State and local prosecutors exercise similar power and discretion over the expenditure of their budgets, although most state and local prosecutors have greater budgetary constraints. Their financial resources do not compare to the deep pockets of federal prosecutors.[41] Like federal prosecutors, however, discretionary decisions to allocate extraordinary resources to particular cases are made in private and are subject only to a small possibility that the public may discover the decisions, disapprove, and respond in the electoral process.[42]

Jurisdiction and Time Limitations

Federal and state prosecutors do not serve indefinitely or without jurisdictional limitations. United States attorneys serve during the administration of the appointing president and may be removed when a new president is elected.[43] Each U.S. attorney prosecutes cases in her geographical district and may pursue only federal crimes. Elected state and local prosecutors operate within similar limitations. They are elected for a set term to prosecute violations of the state criminal code.[44]

In light of the broad scope of federal and state criminal laws,[45] the temporal and jurisdictional limitations on federal and local prosecutors serve to define rather than limit their power. They exercise vast discretion within these confines. Furthermore, these boundaries are irrelevant to the issue of accountability. Even though their power is limited to a defined area and period of time, there is no system in place that effectively holds prosecutors accountable to the people they serve.

THE EFFECT OF THE MEDIA
ON PROSECUTORIAL ACCOUNTABILITY

The existing mechanisms of accountability—the electoral system, budgetary restrictions, and time and jurisdiction limitations—fall far short of effectively controlling prosecutorial power. The difficult question is whether more effective systems of accountability actually would help to eliminate the arbitrary exercise of prosecutorial discretion. Even if there were systems in place to monitor unwarranted disparities and the public were made aware of them, would the public hold prosecutors accountable? The lack of outcry about even extreme cases of misconduct suggests that the public probably would not be outraged by other less stark injustices that play out in more subtle ways, like the race and class disparities that prosecutors may unintentionally cause. Many of the extreme examples of prosecutorial misconduct discussed in chapter 7 were made public, sometimes in widely distributed newspapers and other media outlets. However, there was little or no public response. The prosecutors who engaged in misconduct either continued to serve as prosecutors or advanced to other more prestigious or lucrative careers. These examples suggest that more transparency in prosecutor offices and a more informed electorate would not necessarily result in more accountability.

The Role of the News Media

Although prosecutorial misconduct is rarely revealed to the general public, on the occasions when it has been reported in newspapers and other media outlets, there has not been a significant response from the public, nor have the offending prosecutors suffered any reprisals.[46]

One reason may be that there has not been sufficient reporting of prosecutorial misconduct in the news media. More investigative reporting may be necessary to discover the many cases of prosecutorial misconduct that are rarely revealed to the public, and then there must be wide and frequent media coverage to assure that the public receives the information.

The American public receives most of its news through electronic media, especially television.[47] Newspaper subscriptions continue to decline as more and more people access internet news services and other electronic news sources, such as cable and radio programs.[48] Although Americans watch an average of thirty hours of television per week,[49] they only watch an average of sixty minutes of news programming each day.[50] In comparison, the average American who reads a newspaper does so only for about seventeen minutes per day.[51] These facts suggest that the most effective way to inform the public of prosecutorial misconduct is through the electronic media and a broad range of television programs.

The media has a great deal of control over what the public learns about our legal system. The overwhelming coverage of high-profile celebrity trials on news and other types of television and radio shows demonstrates how the media can flood the airways with information and influence the public's views about crime and criminal justice issues. The coverage of the O. J. Simpson and Michael Jackson trials provide stark examples.[52]

Members of the public who have had no personal experience with the criminal justice system may form their impressions of how the system works solely on the basis of what they see on television. Television programming about the legal system, even real trials that are televised, often serves to misinform the public, because many of the trials shown on television, particularly those of celebrity defendants, bear very little resemblance to how most trials are conducted in cases involving ordinary citizens. Thus, the constant saturation of the airwaves with stories about high-profile cases and the opinions of the pundits may in fact defeat legitimate goals, such as educating the public about how our criminal justice system really works. This is especially true when the information provided is not accurate or when choices are made to air sensational stories that serve no purpose other than the titillation of the viewing public.

The heavy influence of the media on public opinion and the media's excessive focus on crime may shed some light on why the public does not hold prosecutors more accountable for their behavior. A disproportionate number of news stories focus on crime—"if it bleeds, it leads." According to the Project for Excellence in Journalism, crime reports comprised 24 percent of local news programs from 1997 to 2002.[53] Reporting stories about crime is certainly an important responsibility of the news media. The public can play an important role in assisting law enforcement officials in the apprehension of individuals who commit crimes. In addition, the public has the right to know about criminal activity for a variety of reasons, including safety and prevention.

However, the overreporting of crime stories may create the impression that crime is more widespread than it is.[54] It may also generate unnecessary fear among the viewing public, and this fear may influence the extent to which the public requires prosecutors to perform their responsibilities ethically and responsibly. A viewing public that is led to believe that it is in constant danger of being harmed by criminals may be willing to look the other way if prosecutors engage in misconduct—even intentional misconduct—as long as they are successful in getting criminals off the street. If members of the public are so frightened by the possibility that they may not be safe that they are willing to overlook illegal behavior by prosecutors, then increased news reporting of misconduct will not convince them to hold prosecutors accountable for their misbehavior.

The Image of the Prosecutor in the Popular Media

Although many members of the public do not read the newspaper or watch news programs in large numbers, they do watch many hours of other television programs every day. Television shows about crime and lawyers are among the most popular, and prosecutor roles are featured in many of these shows.[55] One of the most popular shows is *Law and Order,* which focuses on the investigation and prosecution of criminal cases. The first half of the show features detectives who investigate crimes and arrest suspects, and the second half focuses on the prosecution of the case, including courtroom scenes. *Law and Order* is the longest running crime series and second longest running drama series in the history of television.[56] The show ranked fifth among drama series for the 2003–2004 season, with an average of 15.9 million viewers. Successful spinoffs from the series include *Law and Order: Special Victims Unit, Law and Order: Criminal Intent, Crime and Punishment, Law and Order: Trial by Jury,* and *Conviction.*[57]

Clearly, many members of the public receive knowledge of and form opinions about the prosecution function from images they receive in the popular media, especially fictionalized television shows. In light of its popularity and the sheer numbers of viewers who watch it, the *Law and Order* series alone undoubtedly informs many members of the public about prosecutors.[58] For some members of the viewing audience, these television shows provide their sole education about the prosecution function. Even those who watch news shows learn very little about what prosecutors do every day from news reports about crime.

Law and Order and other crime shows almost always portray prosecutors as heroes who put away the bad guys. This image of the prosecutor as the crime fighter who keeps the community safe is not inaccurate, but it is certainly incomplete. Television crime dramas rarely deal with issues like prosecutorial misconduct, race or class disparities, or the arbitrary exercise of prosecutorial discretion. Movies present a similar image of prosecutors.[59] With rare exceptions,[60] the dark side of prosecution is not the subject of movies about crime.

Even on the occasions when television shows depict prosecutors engaging in misconduct, or bending, if not breaking, the rules, their conduct is often portrayed as justifiable. For example, an occasional theme on *Law and Order* involves a younger, more idealistic prosecutor who will attempt to follow the law while a more experienced prosecutor focuses on getting a conviction. The younger prosecutor will suggest that they follow the rules, and the older prosecutor will respond with a speech about how he will do whatever he needs to do to put the guilty defendant behind bars, regardless of what the rules say.

An episode entitled "Misconception" demonstrates this theme. In this episode, a young couple plots to swindle a wealthy man by having the woman engage in an affair with him and then claim that her pregnancy is a result of the affair. When the blackmail fails, the couple hatches a plan in which the young man will attack the woman to make it appear that the wealthy gentleman tried to forcefully end the pregnancy. The couple then plans to sue him for civil damages. When the prosecutors uncover the deception, they are outraged and want to try the two for the murder of their unborn baby. Under New York law, however, a fetus cannot be murdered until it reaches twenty-four weeks. At the time of the attack, the woman was only twenty-two weeks pregnant, so there is legally no crime.[61]

Regardless of the fact that no crime was committed, the district attorney, Adam Schiff, and his chief assistant district attorney, Ben Stone, engage in a debate over the propriety of trying the couple for murder:

Schiff: You want the jury to ignore the evidence.

Stone: Chris and Amy want the jury to look at the law. I'll get the jury to look at Chris and Amy.

Schiff: The law's supposed to be a shield, not a sword. They're despicable, yes, but by the letter of the law, they're not guilty.

Stone: The legislature could never have conceived of anything like this. Wrong should not win by technicalities. You know that yourself.

Schiff: Get these bastards off the street.[62]

This quick exchange epitomizes espousal of the "persistent privileging of a private sense of justice over law when the two conflict."[63] Instead of highlighting the inappropriateness of the prosecutor's behavior, the show glorifies the prosecutor as the public's hero, even as he proposes to engage in misconduct.

These shows—especially episodes that acknowledge and implicitly justify prosecutorial misconduct—may unconsciously reinforce an acceptance of prosecutorial misconduct in the name of fighting crime. The combination of these images in fictionalized crime dramas, the dearth of news reporting and other public information about prosecutorial misconduct, and the overreporting of crime stories help to foster an atmosphere of permissiveness and indifference toward prosecutors who break the rules. These factors may also help to explain why the public's perception of the prosecution function is so one-sided and entrenched.

THE NEED FOR REFORM

For the most part, the media, the electorate, the judiciary, and the legislature have taken a "hands-off" approach towards the American prosecutor, most likely because of the nature of prosecutorial responsibilities. Prosecutors enforce the law against people accused of committing crimes—an unpopular group in a country with one of the most punitive approaches to crime in the world.[64] Because law enforcement is such a high priority in this country, there may be less interest in fairness in the prosecutorial process than in apprehending and punishing criminals at any cost. A more hopeful view of why prosecutors have not been held accountable is that so much of their conduct is private and protected from public scrutiny. This view would suggest that more thorough, accurate, and widespread reporting of the prosecution function, including misconduct, would result in more accountability.

The prosecution function is essential to the administration of justice. Although there may be disagreement on whether certain behaviors should be criminalized and the extent to which we use incarceration to punish criminal behaviors, most Americans agree that the prosecution of people who commit serious crimes is essential to a free and orderly society. However, it is important not only that those who perform this critical function do so in a manner that is legal and fair but also that they perform their duties and responsibilities in accordance with the highest ethical standards. Prosecutors should not seek to shield themselves from meaningful public accountability. Instead, they should acknowledge the breadth of their power and discretion and promote effective accountability in ways that are consistent with law enforcement goals.

The founders were right when they established accountability as a core constitutional value. And the electoral process can provide that accountability, but only if there is an engaged, fully informed electorate. An ideal system for the prosecution function would permit and encourage independent decision-making by a prosecutor who is regularly held accountable by an independent, fully informed electorate. The legislature, the legal profession, and the general public must implement significant reforms to assure the appropriate balance of independence and accountability. Chapter 10 will discuss specific proposals designed to control prosecutorial power and bring meaningful accountability to this important function of the justice system.

TEN

Prospects for Reform

Reform of the prosecution function is an essential component in any movement to eliminate unwarranted disparities and other injustices in our criminal justice system. However, prosecutorial reform promises to be a complicated undertaking for a variety of reasons. First, the need for reform is born of multiple, complex causes. The many state, local, and federal prosecutors perform their duties and responsibilities in a variety of ways. Most prosecutors are motivated by a desire to enforce the law in ways that will produce justice for the communities they serve. However, all too often, their well-intentioned prosecutorial decisions produce unintended, undesirable results, such as dissimilar treatment of similarly situated victims and defendants. Other prosecutors are motivated primarily by the desire to win and advance their careers. These prosecutors are more likely to do whatever it takes to secure convictions and thus are more likely to engage in prosecutorial misconduct, as discussed in chapter 7. Thus, the need for reform and the type of reform needed will vary from office to office.

Second, reform will be difficult because there is not widespread belief that it is necessary—either in the prosecution community or the public at large. Reform is most likely to be successful with the support, or at least the cooperation, of prosecutors and their constituents. However, prosecutors traditionally have resisted even modest efforts at reform.[1] The public, inundated by one-sided images of prosecutors in the news and popular media, and bereft of information about the most important functions that prosecutors perform, is far from viewing reform as an important priority. Thus, much education and advocacy is needed to secure the support of prosecutors and their constituents. Even if this support is secured, legislation may be necessary to ensure that needed reforms are implemented.

In light of the complexity and scope of the issues, no single strategy will achieve successful reform. As discussed in chapter 7, the legal remedies for prosecutorial misconduct have not been effective. Chapters 2–6 reveal that arbitrary, unsystematic decision-making without consideration of the possible disparities it may produce, exacerbated by unconscious race and class predilections, sometimes results in disparate treatment of similarly situated victims and defendants. There have been very few efforts to correct these injustices through prosecutorial reform. Thus, a multifaceted approach initiated from outside and inside of the prosecution community will likely produce the most successful results. Reform of the prosecution function should, at a minimum, seek to achieve two goals: (1) the elimination of the arbitrary exercise of prosecutorial discretion, and (2) the establishment of initiatives to strengthen the current mechanisms of prosecutorial accountability. This chapter will explore the possibilities.

EXTERNAL REFORM—THE RESPONSIBILITY
OF THE LEGAL PROFESSION

External reform of the prosecution function must include: (1) strengthening ethical rules and bar disciplinary proceedings and otherwise raising the standard of practice among prosecutors; (2) strengthening the electoral and appointment processes for prosecutors by increasing transparency in prosecution offices and educating the public about the prosecution function; and (3) passing legislation, when necessary, to ensure that essential components of reform efforts are realized.

Lawyers must take the lead in reforming the prosecution function. The support and cooperation of the public is necessary, but lawyers must assume the responsibility for generating that support and cooperation. If not the legal profession, then who? Only lawyers have the knowledge of and commitment to appropriate ethical behavior and the highest standard of performance within the profession. All lawyers, including prosecutors, are required to conduct themselves according to rules of professional conduct. Beyond the required ethical rules, the ABA has published advisory standards for the prosecution function. Few prosecutors affirmatively consult or attempt to abide by the ABA standards in their daily practice, and state bar disciplinary proceedings have not been effective in remedying prosecutorial misconduct.[2] Thus, the legal profession must take the lead in strengthening the disciplinary process and implementing reforms to assure that prosecutors follow the ABA standards and otherwise take steps to ensure that their discretionary decisions do not cause or perpetuate injustices in the system.

Reform efforts should be generated from the legal profession as a whole, through national, state, and local bar associations. Although criminal defense lawyers must play a vital role in the effort because of their knowledge of the issues, they are not in the best position to initiate reform efforts. Criminal defense lawyers would not be seen as credible because of perceived and actual bias against prosecutors. More important, they must maintain the delicate and sometimes conflicting balance of serving as both adversary and negotiator in their dealings with prosecutors as they continue to represent their clients. Thus, the entire profession must play a significant role in demanding reform and requiring the highest standards of practice from the prosecution community.

STRENGTHENING THE DISCIPLINARY PROCESS

National, state, and local bar associations should begin prosecutorial reform efforts by conducting in-depth investigations and evaluations of state disciplinary proceedings to determine (1) why they have not been effective in remedying prosecutorial misconduct, and (2) whether and what changes might make the process more effective. There are a number of reasons why this reform should take priority over others. First, the profession should seek to remedy intentional prosecutorial misconduct before tackling the unintentional prosecutorial practices that result in disparities and other injustices in the system. Behavior that is recognized by the courts as misconduct is a much easier target than the subtle, unconscious behavior that results in race and class disparities. Although some may believe that unconscious, unintentional practices are too difficult to correct or should not be the subject of reform because of the absence of bad faith, few would sanction prosecutors breaking established rules. Second, the harm caused by intentional prosecutorial misconduct is much more palpable than the dissimilar treatment of similarly situated people. Everyone understands the very real harm caused by a prosecutor who withholds exculpatory evidence that could free an innocent person from death row. Not everyone cares if one guilty criminal defendant serves more time than another similarly situated guilty defendant, primarily because of the unpopularity of people accused of crimes.

The second reason why strengthening the disciplinary process should be the top priority for reform is because the U.S. Supreme Court has identified this process as the appropriate remedy for prosecutorial misconduct.[3] As discussed in chapter 7, the Supreme Court provides no remedy for prosecutorial misconduct in cases involving harmless error, and it provides prosecutors immunity from civil lawsuits. The Court proposed that offending prosecutors be referred to state disciplinary authorities. However, an investigation by the Center for Public Integrity revealed only forty-four cases since 1970 in which prosecutors faced disciplinary proceedings for misconduct.[4] In the majority of the cases in which allegations of misconduct were sustained, prosecutors received punishment no more serious than a censure or a reprimand. The misconduct in these cases included discovery violations, using false or misleading evidence in the prosecution of cases, and threatening or harassing witnesses.

Since the remedy proposed by the Supreme Court for serious and unmistakable cases of intentional misconduct has proven ineffective, the legal profession must make this reform its highest priority. The Criminal Justice Section of the ABA should submit a resolution to the ABA's House of Delegates proposing that state and local bar associations evaluate their attorney disciplinary processes to determine whether they have been effective in remedying prosecutorial misconduct. The state and local bar associations should form task forces to conduct the evaluations. These task forces should first determine the number of complaints of prosecutorial misconduct that have occurred within a prescribed time frame and how they were resolved. They should then meet with members of the local trial court to determine the extent to which there have been claims of prosecutorial misconduct in the courts and whether members of the judiciary have referred offending prosecutors. Each jurisdiction may decide the extent to which it wishes to conduct an empirical study of the issue, but at a minimum, the task forces should do the type of data collection performed by the Center for Public Integrity. If it is determined that the disciplinary process has been underutilized for complaints of prosecutorial misconduct, each task force should determine the reasons for its underutilization and propose reforms to make it a more effective mechanism for remedying these claims.

The lack of transparency in prosecution offices is an overriding concern. If it is determined that there are far fewer complaints to the state disciplinary authorities than there are to the courts, the task forces may reasonably conclude that members of the bench and bar are failing to refer offending prosecutors. However, a low number of complaints in a particular jurisdiction—in the courts and with the state disciplinary authorities—may be interpreted in different ways. Low numbers may indicate that prosecutors in that jurisdiction rarely engage in prosecutorial misconduct. A dearth of complaints might also suggest that prosecutorial misconduct is not being discovered.[5] If the lack of transparency is preventing the discovery of prosecutorial misconduct, legislation may be required, as discussed below.

The ABA should also undertake a comprehensive study and review of the Model Rules of Professional Conduct with the specific goal of determining the extent to which these rules fail to address critical aspects of the prosecution function. As discussed in chapter 8, the current rules are silent on many of the most important prosecutorial duties and responsibilities. The ABA should determine the extent to which the rules might be amended or whether it would be more appropriate to draft a separate code of professional responsibility for prosecutors, as some scholars have suggested.[6]

STRENGTHENING THE ELECTORAL AND APPOINTMENTS PROCESSES

As discussed in chapter 9, the electoral process has not served as an effective mechanism for holding prosecutors accountable to their constituents. Low voter turnout is an overarching problem that affects all elected officials, including prosecutors. Voters need far more information than they are presently provided in order to elect their prosecutors and hold them accountable. First, they need a better general understanding of the prosecution function—what prosecutors do every day and how they perform their duties and responsibilities. Second, they need specific information about the prosecution offices in their communities—how the district attorney for their city or county

performs his or her responsibilities. Accordingly, reform should include (1) public information campaigns aimed at educating the public
about the prosecution function; (2) prosecution review boards to inform the public about how particular prosecution offices perform their
day to day duties and responsibilities; and (3) racial disparity studies that
reveal whether and the extent to which race-neutral prosecutorial
decision-making produces racially disparate results.

Public Information Campaigns

The organized bar should implement public information campaigns that
would provide information to the public about routine prosecution
duties and responsibilities. These campaigns would not provide information about specific cases or any other information that would hinder
law enforcement efforts. Instead, they would educate the public about
how prosecution offices function: their purpose, goals, duties, and responsibilities. For example, the campaigns would provide general information on the charging decision, the grand jury, and plea bargaining.
This information could be provided in brochures that would be available in courthouses and other public buildings. It might also be presented
in programs at town meetings and other public forums, as well as on
television and radio public service announcements and programs.

The implementation of public information campaigns would be
consistent with recent prosecution efforts to promote communication
with the public about prosecution programs. For example, community
prosecution offices have been implemented in many jurisdictions to
involve prosecutors with the communities they serve.[7] These offices
seek input from residents about their community goals and how
prosecutors might help to promote them. The public information
campaigns would complement this effort and both empower citizens
to hold prosecutors accountable and help promote confidence in the
criminal justice system.

Prosecution Review Boards

The organized bar should establish prosecution review boards. The
purpose of these boards would be to review complaints and conduct

random reviews of prosecution decisions to deter misconduct and arbitrary decision-making. These boards would differ in several ways from the proposed "Misconduct Review Board" included in an early draft of the CPA of 1998.[8] The misconduct review board, originally proposed but ultimately excluded from the final version of the CPA, would have reviewed the rulings of the attorney general on public complaints of misconduct. The proposal defined ten specific acts of misconduct[9] and permitted members of the public to file a complaint with the attorney general if they believed that any Justice Department attorney had engaged in the proscribed conduct. If the attorney general made no determination or imposed no penalty for the alleged misconduct, the person who filed the original complaint could resubmit it to the misconduct review board. If the board found misconduct, it could impose an appropriate penalty, including probation, demotion, dismissal, referral of ethical charges, loss of pension or other retirement benefits, suspension, or referral to a grand jury for possible criminal prosecution.[10]

The primary distinction of the prosecution review board would be the addition of a random review process. The board would not only review specific complaints brought to its attention by the public but also conduct random reviews of routine prosecution decisions. These random reviews could be conducted in a variety of ways. One method might involve the board's review of a selection of the closed files in a particular prosecution office and an examination of the file entries for each decision. The board would closely examine charging and plea bargaining decisions and look for compliance with the ABA's prosecution standards. These random examinations would encourage prosecutors to implement a practice of giving written reasons for their decisions. Board members would be permitted to interview prosecutors, victims, and witnesses to determine if the prosecutors met the established standards. Unlike state disciplinary proceedings, random review would not be dependent on the fortuitous discovery of practices or policies that are currently hidden from public view. It would permit affirmative investigations to discover bad practices, and its random nature would more likely deter arbitrary prosecution decisions.

The board would file a public report upon completion of the review. The report would not reveal any information about particular cases, but would report specific practices and policies that either violated or complied with the ABA Prosecution Function Standards.

The board might recommend disciplinary action against a particular prosecutor, refer specific prosecutors to state ethical boards, or simply recommend improvements. On the other hand, the board might file a report commending a prosecution office as a model in the promotion of the fair administration of justice. Public release of all reports would promote accountability.

Prosecution review boards might be established at the state, county, or local level. Members of the boards would be appointed by the governor, county executive, or mayor, depending on the board's jurisdiction. Board members should include attorney and nonattorney members, with an effort to include former prosecutors, who would assure balance and whose knowledge and expertise would be essential to the board's work.

Racial Disparity Studies

Much has been written documenting the racial disparities and race discrimination at every stage of the criminal process.[11] Given the inadequacy of current legal remedies to combat race discrimination in the criminal justice system,[12] the Court's affirmation of broad prosecutorial discretion,[13] and the high legal barriers erected to discourage selective prosecution claims,[14] other remedies must be constructed and implemented. As discussed in earlier chapters, prosecutors frequently make race-neutral charging and plea bargaining decisions that produce racial disparities. Fortunately, in light of their immense power and discretion, they are uniquely positioned and empowered to remedy these injustices most effectively and efficiently.

The elimination of race discrimination is totally consistent with the responsibility of the prosecutor to seek justice, not simply win convictions.[15] The duty to seek justice is not limited to the prosecutor's responsibilities in individual cases but also applies to the administration of justice in the criminal justice system as a whole. In fact, the prosecutor's duties include the oversight function of ensuring fairness and efficiency in the criminal justice system.[16] Those duties should include recognizing injustice in the system and initiating corrective measures.[17]

Not every disparity is evidence of discrimination. Since many legitimate factors affect prosecutorial decisions, it may be appropriate to treat victims and defendants differently, even in similar cases. A prerequisite to eliminating race discrimination in the criminal process is the determination of whether the dissimilar treatment of similarly situated people is based on race rather than some legitimate reason. Whether the treatment is intentional or purposeful should not matter— the goal should be elimination of harm.

Thus, the organized bar should first implement racial impact studies designed to reveal racially discriminatory treatment. Second, the bar should publish and widely disseminate these studies to the general public. The studies would compel prosecutors to acknowledge and focus on the important issue of racial disparity. These studies would assure that the issue is addressed by prosecutors in the electoral process and would provide additional information to the public about the extent to which the elimination of racial disparity is a priority in a particular prosecution office.

Racial impact studies would involve the collection of data on the race of the defendant and victim for each category of offense and the status of the case at each step of the prosecutorial process. For example, in each case involving an arrest for possession of cocaine, the prosecutor would document the race of the defendant, the defendant's criminal history, the initial charging decision, each plea offer made, accepted, or rejected, and the sentence advocated by the prosecutor. If relevant, the prosecutor should also document whether and how a decision was made to charge in federal versus state court and whether a departure from the sentencing guidelines was sought. The statistics would be collected for each type of offense so that an appropriate statistical analysis comparing the disposition of the cases of white and African American defendants and victims could be done. These studies not only would be helpful in determining whether defendants of color receive harsher treatment for the same criminal behavior but also, in cases involving victims, would demonstrate whether cases involving white victims were being prosecuted more vigorously than cases involving African American victims. The data would also indicate whether similarly situated defendants and victims of different races are treated the same at each step of the process.[18] Are defendants in cases involving white victims initially charged with the same offense as similarly situated defendants in cases involving black victims? Do they receive comparable plea offers? Do prosecutors advocate for the same dispositions at the sentencing hearings? The collection of this data would provide answers to these questions.

The data may help to reveal the extent to which whites are being arrested and presented for prosecution by law enforcement officers. If the majority of the cases in any particular category of offense involve African American defendants, the prosecutor should investigate further to determine whether African Americans comprise a majority of the population in that jurisdiction. If they do, the data would not necessarily indicate the selective detention and prosecution of African Americans. If African Americans do not comprise a majority of the population, further investigation would certainly be warranted, particularly if there is a considerable difference between the arrest rates and the African American population. The further investigation should attempt to determine whether African Americans commit the crime in question at greater rates than whites. In the absence of credible evidence that they do, the prosecutor should presume that no one particular race is inherently more likely to commit certain types of crimes.[19]

Significant conclusions could not be reached from the simple collection of data without the appropriate statistical analysis. The Baldus study used in *McCleskey v. Kemp* exemplifies the model statistical analysis of this type of data.[20] Widely acclaimed as one of the most thorough and statistically sound analyses of sentencing, the Baldus study examined thousands of murder cases over a seven-year period and took into account thirty-nine nonracial variables most likely to influence sentencing patterns in Georgia before reaching the conclusion that the race of the victim had a statistically significant correlation with the imposition of the death penalty.

Similar studies in prosecutors' offices would determine whether racial disparities exist in the prosecution of all types of cases and whether the disparities are statistically significant. A Baldus-type study that takes those factors into account would be essential to the credibility of the evaluation, because there are so many legitimate, nonracial factors that may be considered in prosecutorial decisions. This type of evaluation would indicate whether, and to what extent, disparate treatment of similarly situated victims and defendants is based on race.

The racial impact studies must be published and widely disseminated to produce the desired result. These studies would inform the public about the possible discriminatory effects of prosecution policies and practices. They would force a public debate about racial disparities and compel prosecutors to be truly accountable to their constituents. Prosecutors could do this either by establishing policies and practices to help eliminate the disparities or by explaining that there are legitimate, race-neutral reasons for such disparities. If the public was not satisfied with the results of the study, the efforts to eliminate the disparities, or the prosecutor's explanation for disparities, it could then remove the prosecutor from office through the electoral process. The public debate would also help the prosecutor to establish workable remedial policies and practices. Thus, public access to the studies would motivate prosecutors to correct inequities and help to make the electoral process a more meaningful check on unacceptable prosecutorial practices.

THE PROSECUTORIAL RESPONSE
AND THE NEED FOR LEGISLATION

Both of the proposals for reform made here—strengthening the disciplinary process and strengthening the electoral process—stand a much better chance of success with the cooperation and support of prosecutors. However, it is likely that a substantial number of prosecutors will oppose these reforms. Some will believe there is no need for reform, and that the current mechanisms of accountability are operating successfully. Others may believe that there is always room for improvement but disagree with the suggested strategies for reform— particularly the call for more transparency in prosecution offices. The extent to which prosecutors will support efforts for reform of the prosecution function will vary from office to office—depending on the prosecutor's views of how she should perform her duties and responsibilities.

Although all of the reform strategies would be easier to implement and more effective with the cooperation of prosecutors, two strategies—prosecution review boards and racial impact studies— could not be implemented without the full cooperation of prosecutors in the absence of enforcement legislation. Each of these strategies requires prosecutors to disclose information they would not otherwise be required to disclose by law. Prosecutors would undoubtedly resist these efforts for the same reasons they have resisted the discovery of their internal decisions in the past.

Criticisms of both strategies would undoubtedly include the Supreme Court's reasons for deferring to prosecutorial discretion in

Wayte v. United States: "Examining the basis of a prosecution delays the criminal proceeding, threatens to chill law enforcement by subjecting the prosecutor's motives and decision-making to outside inquiry, and may undermine prosecutorial effectiveness by revealing the Government's enforcement policy."[21] Prosecutors understandably also would be concerned about the time and resources necessary to implement these strategies. The prosecutor's primary function is law enforcement; any undertaking that substantially interferes with that responsibility would be subject to legitimate criticism.

In the case of racial impact studies, for example, if the collection of data were a tedious process that substantially interfered with the performance of important prosecutorial duties, most prosecutors would object to the studies. Prosecutors, however, could collect the relevant information in an efficient, nonintrusive manner. Prosecutorial offices could create forms with checklists on which the prosecutors could quickly and easily note the relevant information.[22] Most prosecutors routinely make written entries in case files whenever an action is taken in a particular case. These forms or checklists could be kept in the same case file and would involve no more time than the routine case file entries. The only difference would be the type of information and the format for its collection. The information also might be collected electronically in an equally efficient manner.

Time is not the only relevant factor. Few prosecutor offices would have the expertise or resources to perform the necessary statistical analysis of the collected data for racial impact studies. For that reason, the organized bar should help to secure these resources. One possible solution to the resource problem may be the volunteer efforts of local colleges and universities. Criminology and criminal justice departments may be willing to conduct such research and would provide a wealth of resources through the use of graduate students from various departments. The studies would provide a great public service as well as a rich academic experience for professors, scholars, and students. Use of university resources would also give the project the necessary objectivity that would be lacking if the prosecutors conducted it themselves.

Prosecutors may claim that the publication of review board reports and racial impact studies might chill law enforcement by subjecting the prosecutor's motives to outside inquiry. This argument suggests that prosecutors might be hesitant to prosecute certain cases if they believe that members of the public, criminal defendants, or victims will question their decisions. Thus, according to this argument, some criminal activity will not be prosecuted. However, the goal of the publication of the studies is not to chill appropriate and fair law enforcement but to totally eliminate unfair, discriminatory law enforcement. To the extent that law enforcement tactics or prosecutorial policies involve misconduct or discriminate on the basis of race, they should not merely be chilled— they should be entirely eliminated and replaced with tactics that enforce the law fairly and impartially. The reports and studies, and the knowl- edge that they will be published, should cause prosecutors to be more careful and meticulous in making decisions and should motivate pros- ecutors to follow ethical rules and assure that similarly situated victims and defendants are treated equitably.

The Supreme Court's concern that judicial interference with pros- ecutorial discretion would undermine prosecutorial effectiveness by revealing the government's enforcement policy would not apply to the publication of these reports or studies. The Supreme Court was con- cerned that if criminals were aware of how and under what circum- stances cases are prosecuted, they would adjust their behavior to avoid prosecution. For example, if it were common knowledge that a pros- ecution office had a policy of only prosecuting cases involving more than five grams of cocaine, dealers and users would distribute or possess quantities less than five grams. The publication of review board reports and racial impact studies would not generate this concern, because the studies would not reveal specific law enforcement policies unless they involved misconduct, in which case they should be exposed and elimi- nated. The information in these studies and reports would be limited to general demographic data.

In light of anticipated prosecutorial opposition, the organized bar might need to propose legislation to enforce these reforms. In addition to the prosecution review boards and racial impact studies, prosecu- tors might oppose other reform efforts as well. The state and local bar associations should meet with national prosecutor organizations such as the National District Attorneys Association to discuss and address their concerns and to seek their input and support. However, legis- lation ultimately may be required to assure that the reforms are im- plemented.

A MODEL REFORM EFFORT

In 2005, the Vera Institute of Justice[23] established its Prosecution and Racial Justice Project with the goal of helping prosecutors "manage the exercise of discretion within their offices in a manner that reduces the risk of racial disparity in the decision-making process."[24] The project's methodology is similar to that of the aforementioned racial impact studies, in that it involves the collection of data in prosecution offices to determine whether similarly situated defendants are treated differently at the charging and plea bargaining stages of the process in ways that reflect unconscious racial bias. This groundbreaking project was made possible in large part by the willingness of three chief prosecutors to grant Vera Institute staff broad access to their offices in order to track decision-making at key discretion points with the goal of identifying patterns of disparity. If such patterns are found, the chief prosecutors would then attempt to ascertain the cause or causes so that they may take corrective action where and when necessary.

These prosecutors—Peter Gilchrist of Charlotte, North Carolina, Paul Morrison of Johnson County, Kansas, and Michael McCann of Milwaukee, Wisconsin[25]—all enjoy an excellent reputation in the prosecution community and in their local jurisdictions. Other factors that made these prosecutors ideal candidates for the project included the location of their offices and the demographics of their communities. However, each of the prosecutors easily could have declined the offer to participate in the project. It is a time-consuming and invasive effort, and there are no obvious political benefits. Nonetheless, each prosecutor decided to accept the offer to participate because of his or her commitment to fairness and racial justice.

The Vera Institute staff began their work in Peter Gilchrist's office in Charlotte, North Carolina. The first challenge was to assure staff prosecutors and support staff that the purpose of the project was not to assign blame for racial disparities, but to assist them in their shared goal of enforcing the law effectively and fairly. A number of key factors assisted the Vera staff in building a relationship of trust with the prosecution staff. One of the most important ones was the leadership of the project director, Wayne McKenzie. McKenzie is an experienced prosecutor in the Kings County District Attorney's Office who took a leave of absence from his office to direct the Prosecution and Racial Justice Project at Vera. His leadership provided the project with the credibility and trust necessary to securing the support and buy-in of the prosecutors involved in the project and also will help to persuade other prosecutors to agree to similar projects in their offices. Another important factor that helped to secure support for the project was the fact that the data collection and management system that Vera would implement for the purpose of discovering possible bias also would be a very useful tool for prosecutors and other staff as they worked to manage their caseloads and measure general outcomes in their office.

The most important difference between the previously proposed racial impact studies and the Vera Institute's Prosecution and Racial Justice Project is in how the collected information will be used. A key component to the success of racial impact studies is the publication of the studies. The purpose of these studies would be not only to inform prosecutors of how unconscious bias may affect their decision-making but to inform the general public as well. However, the Vera Institute prosecutors agreed to participate in the project with the understanding that they would voluntarily address any findings of unconscious bias and make their own decisions about whether, and the extent to which, the findings of the project would be made public.

The Prosecution and Racial Justice Project will certainly, at a minimum, make some progress toward addressing unintended bias in the exercise of prosecutorial discretion in these three offices. If the project reveals bias, the prosecutors are committed to taking steps to address it. Solutions would vary, depending on how and at what stage of the process the bias occurs. The project's findings would advance the development of policies and practices to eliminate or reduce unwarranted disparities based on unconscious bias.

The main limitation of the project is its dependency on the voluntary efforts of the prosecutors themselves. Although these prosecutors are committed to eliminating bias in the decision-making process, they may or may not choose to reveal the project's findings to the general public. Nonetheless, the project has great potential for inspiring similar data collection projects in prosecution offices throughout the nation, with the encouragement and leadership of the prosecutors involved in the project. Their standing in the prosecution community provides them with the credibility to persuade other prosecutors to take similar voluntary action. They might also be instrumental in helping to establish policies and practices that the National District Attorneys

Association and other national prosecution organizations may endorse and promote to their membership.

The Vera Institute's Prosecution and Racial Justice Project will be completed in 2008. Whether or not the data collected in each office demonstrates evidence of unconscious bias, the project should inspire similar efforts in other prosecutors' offices if it proves beneficial to the offices involved. However, without the leadership of the project's chief prosecutors and/or the publication of the Project's findings, the full potential of the Project may not be realized.

CONCLUSION

Prosecutorial reform promises to be a long-term, complicated endeavor, in light of the complexity of the prosecution function and the vast differences in the exercise of discretion in prosecution offices across the nation. Of the many reform efforts suggested in this chapter, some may work in some jurisdictions but not in others. None of the proposals may be suitable in some locations, demonstrating the need for continued efforts to improve and develop the prosecution function. The most successful reform efforts will involve the cooperation of prosecutors, the organized bar, and the concerned public. All efforts should work toward assisting prosecutors in the fulfillment of the goal of "doing justice" for all.

NOTES

1. Prosecutorial Discretion

1. I was a staff attorney at the PDS for the District of Columbia from 1982 to 1988, deputy director from 1988 to 1991, and executive director from 1991 to 1994.

2. *Brady v. Maryland*, 373 U.S. 83 (1963).

3. *Id.* at 87 and n. 2.

4. *Id.* at 87.

5. *See* Angela J. Davis, *Prosecution and Race: The Power and Privilege of Discretion*, 67 FORDHAM L. REV. 13, 19 (1998) (arguing that prosecutorial discretion, "which is almost always exercised in private," renders the prosecutor the most powerful official in the criminal justice system); Bennett L. Gershman, *The New Prosecutor*, 53 U. PITT. L. REV. 393, 448 (1992) (describing the American prosecutor "as the most pervasive and dominant force in criminal justice"); *see also* James Vorenberg, *Decent Restraint of Prosecutorial Power*, 94 HARV. L. REV. 1521, 1555 (1981) (suggesting that the power held by the American prosecutor is inconsistent with due process standards); Daniel J. Freed, *Federal Sentencing in the Wake of Guidelines: Unacceptable Limits on the Discretion of Sentencers*, 101 YALE L. J. 1681, 1696 (1992) (positing that the federal sentencing guidelines enhance the power of American prosecutors by diminishing the power of the judiciary).

6. *See Atwater v. City of Lago Vista*, 532 U.S. 318, 322 (2001) (holding that an officer may make a warrantless arrest of an individual, even for very minor criminal offenses, without violating the Fourth Amendment upon the showing of probable cause); *see* I.C.A. § 321.485 (West 1997) (authorizing a peace officer to immediately arrest an individual for certain traffic offenses); D.C. CODE ANN. § 40-302 (1967) (rendering the operation of a motor vehicle after the revocation of an operator's permit an arrestable offense); TEX. TRAN. CODE ANN. § 545.413 (1999) (authorizing a peace officer to conduct a warrant-less arrest of an individual found in violation of state seatbelt laws).

7. *See* Andrew J. Taslitz, *Stories of Fourth Amendment Disrespect: From Elian to the Internment,* 70 FORDHAM L. REV. 2257, 2270 and n. 81 (2002) (stating that racial profiling violates the principles of a "jurisprudence of respect"); Tracy Maclin, *Race and the Fourth Amendment,* 51 VAND. L. REV. 333, 342 (1998) (stating that pretextual traffic stops on the basis of race should constitute a violation of the Fourth Amendment); Jeremiah Wagner, *Racial (De)Profiling: Modeling a Remedy for Racial Profiling After the School Segregation Cases,* 22 LAW & INEQ. J. 73, 95 (2004) (arguing that racial profiling is a form of segregation); William M. Carter, Jr., *A Thirteenth Amendment Framework for Combating Racial Profiling,* 39 HARV. C.R.-C.L. L. REV. 17, 26 (2004) (discussing psychologists' findings that racial profiling can inflict "serious emotional anguish").

8. *See, e.g.,* KRS § 15A.195; C.R.S. § 42-4-115; K.S.A. § 22-4604; TENN. CODE ANN. § 38-1-402, www.profilesinjustice.com.

9. Although the practice of racial profiling was widely condemned, after the bombing of the World Trade Center towers on September 11, 2001, the practice of racially profiling individuals who appeared to be of Middle Eastern descent was revived. *See* Charu A. Chandrasekhar, *Flying While Brown: Federal Civil Rights Remedies to Post 9/11 Airline Racial Profiling of South Asians,* 10 ASIAN L. J. 215, 215 (2003) (stating that perpetrators of racial profiling have increasingly targeted South Asians, Arabs, and those of Middle Eastern descent after the September 11, 2001, attacks); Marie A. Taylor, *Immigration Enforcement Post–September 11: Safeguarding the Civil rights of Middle Eastern–American and Immigrant Communities,* 17 GEO. IMMIGR. L. J. 63, 90 (2002) (arguing that the government has "implicitly condoned" the practice of racial profiling by "creating the impression that all persons of Arab or Middle Eastern descent are dangerous or potential terrorists"); *see also* Sharon L. Davies, *Reflections on the Criminal Justice System After September 11, 2001,* 1 OHIO ST. J. CRIM. L. 45, 45 (2003) (arguing that the amorphous ethnic characteristic of "Middle Eastern-ness" alone possesses no useful predictive power for separating innocents from potential terrorists"); David A. Harris, *New Approaches to Ensuring the Legitimacy of Police Conduct,* 22 ST. LOUIS U. PUB. L. REV. 73, 74 (2003) (criticizing the practice of racial profiling against individuals of Middle Eastern descent).

10. *See, e.g., General Electric Co. v. Joiner,* 522 U.S. 136 (1997); Raymond T. Elligett, Jr., & John M. Scheb, *Appellate Standards of Review—How Important Are They?* 70 FLA. B. J. 33 (1996).

11. *See* Jennifer Liberto, *Judge Won't Preside over Certain Cases,* ST. PETERSBURG TIMES, Sept. 27, 2003, www.sptimes.com (reporting on a recent decision to prevent County Judge Peyton Hyslop from presiding over first-appearance felony hearings in the wake of Hyslop's decision to lower the bail amount of a defendant charged with a violent offense who was subsequently arrested for another violent crime while free on bail).

12. Mandatory minimum sentencing laws and mandatory sentencing guidelines have been criticized widely for producing unfair results in particular cases. *See* John S. Martin, Jr., *Why Mandatory Minimums Make No Sense*, 18 NOTRE DAME J. L. ETHICS & PUB. POL'Y 311, 313 (2004) (positing that "the disparate application of mandatory minimum sentences in cases in which available data suggest that a mandatory minimum is applicable appears to be related to the race of the defendant, where whites are more likely than non-whites to be sentenced below the mandatory minimum standard."); *Testimony of Judge William W. Wilkins, Jr., Chairman United States Sentencing Commission*, 6 FED. SENT. R. 67 (1993) (stating that mandatory minimums "undercut certainty in sentencing"); Daniel J. Freed, *Federal Sentencing in the Wake of Guidelines: Unacceptable Limits on the Discretion of Sentencers*, 101 YALE L. J. 1681, 1702 (1992) (arguing that federal sentencing guidelines have failed to ensure uniformity in sentencing because of their complexity and rigidity). *See infra* chapter 6 for discussion of the federal sentencing guidelines.

13. *See* Robert S. Blanco, *Mixing Politics and Crime*, 59 FED. PROBATION 91 (1995) (discussing the case of Willie Horton, a Massachusetts man who commited a brutal murder while released on parole); *see also Doyle v. Elsea*, 658 F. 2d 5123 (7th Cir. 1981); *Kenner v. Martin*, 645 F. 2d 1080 (6th Cir. 1981).

14. *See, eg.*, 1995 N.Y. LAWS 3; 1998 N.Y. LAWS 1; MISS. CODE ANN. § 47-7-3; 61 P.S. § 331.19.

15. *See* Scott P. Johnson & Christopher E. Smith, *White House Scandals and the Presidential Pardon Power: Persistent Risks and Prospects for Reform*, 33 NEW ENG. L. REV. 907, 907 (1999) (criticizing President Ford's pardon of Richard Nixon because it was motivated by "partisan interests"); *The Fallout from Ford's Rush to Pardon*, TIME, Sept. 23, 1974, at 11 (discussing the consequences of Ford's decision to pardon Nixon); Charles Shanor & Marc Miller, *Pardon Us: Systematic Presidential Pardons*, 13 FED. SENT. R. 139, 143 (2000) (arguing that the "highly controversial pardons issued by President Clinton at the end of his presidency do a disservice to the pardon power with its solid constitutional foundations").

16. *See, e.g.*, Davis, *supra* note 5, at 17 (stating that prosecutorial discretion is a major cause of racial inequality in the criminal justice system); Vorenberg, *supra* note 5, at 1555 (stating that unchecked prosecutorial discretion as it exists today in the United States is inconsistent with due process standards); Robert L. Misner, *Recasting Prosecutorial Discretion*, 86 J. CRIM. L. & CRIMINOLOGY 717, 722 (1996) (proposing the implementation of restraints on the power of the prosecutor by tying prosecutorial discretion directly to the availability of prison resources); Gershman, *supra* note 5, at 394 (discussing the need to decrease the power of the prosecutor to restore equilibrium to the criminal justice system).

17. *See infra* chapter 7 for discussion of series on prosecutorial misconduct published in the *Chicago Tribune* and *Pittsburgh Post-Gazette*.

18. *See* discussion of *United States v. Armstrong* in *infra* chapter 6.

19. *See* discussion of mandatory minimum sentencing laws and sentencing guidelines in *infra* chapter 6.

20. *See* discussion in *infra* chapter 9.

21. *See* Sir Frederick Pollock & Frederic William Maitland, THE HISTORY OF ENGLISH LAW 476 (2d ed. 1923) ("To pursue the outlaw and knock him on the head as though he were a wild beast is the right and duty of every law abiding man.").

22. *Id.*

23. Mario M. Cuomo, *The Crime Victim in a System of Criminal Justice*, 8 ST. JOHN'S J. LEGAL COMMENT. 1, 4 (1992).

24. JOAN E. JACOBY, THE AMERICAN PROSECUTOR: A SEARCH OF IDENTITY 8 (1980).

25. *Id.*

26. *Id.*

27. *See id.* at 3–39 (discussing the origins and development of American prosecution); *cf.* POLICING & PROSECUTION IN BRITAIN, 1750–1850 (Douglas Hay & Francis Snyder eds., 1989) (containing essays debating the extent to which the system of private prosecutions served the wealthy over the poor). One justification for private prosecutions was that "[s]tate prosecutions were associated with autocratic regimes and abuses of power, while private prosecutions were seen as important safeguards of English freedom." Randall McGowen, *New Directions and Old Debates in the History of English Criminal Law*, 43 STAN. L. REV. 799, 799 (1991) (reviewing POLICING AND PROSECUTION IN BRITAIN, 1750–1850 (Douglas Hay & Francis Snyder eds., 1989)).

28. JACOBY, *supra* note 24, at 7.

29. *See generally* Juan Cardenas, *The Crime Victim in the Prosecutorial Process*, 9 HARV. J. L. & PUB. POL'Y 357, 359–66 (1986) (tracing the history of the conviction in the legal process).

30. JACOBY, *supra* note 24, at 9.

31. *Id.* at 8.

32. Police officers frequently initiate prosecutorial proceedings in simple criminal cases, often presenting the charges, examining witnesses, and addressing the magistrates. If the case is particularly complex, the police will hire a solicitor or barrister. The growing trend in modern England is public funding of solicitors' offices within police departments. Cardenas, *supra* note 29, at 363.

33. *Id.* at 366.

34. *Id.* at 367.

35. *Id.*

36. *Id.*

37. Cardenas, *supra* note 29, at 367–68.

38. *Id.* at 368–69.

39. JACOBY, *supra* note 24, at 18.

40. Cardenas, *supra* note 29, at 368.

41. *Id.* at 369.

42. *Id.* (noting that the attorney general only initiated prosecution in cases of special importance to the Crown).

43. The Dutch system of using a schout (a combination of a sheriff and a prosecutor) was adopted in the Dutch settlements of Connecticut, Delaware, Pennsylvania, New Jersey, and New York, while some southern colonies borrowed the Scottish practice of using a public prosecutor. *Id.* at 370–71; JACOBY, *supra* note 24, at 11–15; Abraham S. Goldstein, *Prosecution: History of the Public Prosecutor, in* ENCYCLOPEDIA OF CRIME AND JUSTICE 1286–87 (Sanford H. Kadish ed., 1983).

44. JACOBY, *supra* note 24, at 21.

45. *Id.*

46. JACOBY, *supra* note 24, at 22; Goldstein, *supra* note 43, at 1287.

47. Goldstein, *supra* note 43, at 1287 (reviewing the emergence of elected prosecutors in states).

48. *See* D.C. CODE ANN. § 23-101 (1998) (explaining that the District of Columbia is unique in its status as a city that is not part of any state government and has no local or state prosecutor. Thus, the U.S. attorney for the District of Columbia prosecutes local and federal crimes).

49. *See* Goldstein, *supra* note 43, at 1287 (describing the history and current state of elected prosecutors).

50. *Id.* at 1288 (illustrating lessons learned from the electoral process).

51. Judiciary Act of 1789, ch. 20, 1 Stat. 73, 92–93.

52. "And there shall . . . be appointed . . . a meet person learned in the law to act as attorney for the United States . . . who shall be sworn or affirmed to the faithful execution of his office, whose duty it shall be to prosecute [[cases, except in state supreme courts]." *Id.* at 92. The Act also described the role of the meet person assigned as attorney general, who shall "conduct all suits in the Supreme Court in which the United States shall be concerned, and to give his advice and opinion upon questions of law when required by the President of the United States, or when requested by the heads of any departments, touching any matters that may concern their departments, and shall receive such compensation for his services as shall by law be provided." *Id.* at 93.

53. *See* Lawrence Lessig & Cass R. Sunstein, *The President and the Administration*, 94 COLUM. L. REV. 1, 16 (1994) (discussing the framers' perception of the executive branch and arguing that they did not support a unitary, hierarchical executive).

54. *Id.* at 16–17 (describing the transition in supervisory roles accounting for prosecutorial oversight).

55. *See id.* at 17 n. 65 (citing LEONARD D. WHITE, THE JEFFERSONIANS: A STUDY IN ADMINISTRATIVE HISTORY, 1801–1829, 340 (1951)) (describing the overlapping oversight roles among three federal agencies).

56. *See id.* at 18–20 (detailing citizen-initiated prosecutions).

57. *See* JACOBY, *supra* note 24, at 30 (describing postwar crime and emergent state investigative roles).

58. *Id.* at 28 (quoting NATIONAL COMMISSION ON LAW OBSERVANCE AND ENFORCEMENT, REPORT ON PROSECUTION 11 (1931)).

59. *Id.* at 30.

60. *Id.* at 31.

61. JACOBY, *supra* note 24, at 31.

62. *Id.*

63. *Id.*

64. *Id.*

65. *See generally* James Vorenberg, *Decent Restraint of Prosecutorial Power*, 94 HARV. L. REV. 1521 (1981) (criticizing the acceptance of broad prosecutorial discretion and suggesting specific proposals for reform).

66. *See* Shelby A. Dickerson Moore, *Questioning the Autonomy of Prosecutorial Charging Decisions: Recognizing the Need to Exercise Discretion—Knowing There Will Be Consequences for Crossing the Line*, 60 LA. L. REV. 371, 377 (2000) (recognizing that prosecutorial discretion seeks to "alleviate the pressures of a criminal code that tends to make a crime of everything that people find objectionable"); Leslie C. Griffin, *The Prudent Prosecutor*, 14 GEO. J. LEGAL ETHICS 259, 263 (2001) (stating that prosecutorial discretion is necessary to prevent "legislative over-criminalization," as there are numerous criminal statutes that "should not be enforced at all."); Cynthia Kwei Yung Lee, *Prosecutorial Discretion, Substantial Assistance, and the Federal Sentencing Guidelines*, 42 UCLA L. REV. 105, 159 (1994) (positing that prosecutorial discretion responds to the problems of legislative overcriminalization).

67. Moore, *supra* note 66, at 378; Griffin, *supra* note 66, at 263; Lee, *supra* note 66, at 161, 165.

68. U.S. CONST. art. II § 3.

69. *Wayte v. United States*, 470 U.S. 598, 607 (1985).

70. *See, e.g.*, MD RULES, rule 16-812, MODEL RULES OF PROF'L CONDUCT R. 3.8 (detailing guidelines and responsibilities for prosecutors); W. VA. CODE § 7-4-1 (describing the duties and responsibilities of a prosecuting attorney).

71. *See, e.g., Law and Order* (NBC television show); *Law and Order: Criminal Intent* (NBC television show); *NYPD Blue* (ABC television show).

2. The Power to Charge

1. Interview with Michele Roberts, partner, Akin Gump Strauss Hauer & Feld LLP (Dec. 18, 1997).

2. Interview with Bernie Grimm via e-mail (November 21, 2006).

3. *County of Riverside v. McLaughlin,* 500 U.S. 44, 56–58 (1991). However, if the hearing has been unreasonably delayed, even if it occurs less than forty-eight hours after the defendant's arrest, there may still be a violation. *Id.*

4. *See infra* chapter 4 (discussing the relationship between prosecutors and crime victims).

5. According to the Supreme Court, the role of grand jury as finder of probable cause is one of the oldest charges given to the grand jury. *Branzburg v. Hayes,* 408 U.S. 665, 686–87 (1972). *See generally* CHARLES H. WHITEBREAD & CHRISTOPHER SLOBOGIN, CRIMINAL PROCEDURE § 23.05 (3d ed. 1993) (discussing more thoroughly the powers of the grand jury).

6. *Hurtado v. California,* 110 U.S. 516, 534–35 (1884).

7. Twenty-three states (Alabama, Alaska, Delaware, Florida, Kentucky, Louisiana, Maine, Massachusetts, Minnesota, Mississippi, Missouri, New Hampshire, New Jersey, New York, North Carolina, North Dakota, Ohio, Rhode Island, South Carolina, Tennessee, Texas, Virginia, and West Virginia) plus the District of Columbia require that indictments be used to charge certain crimes. These states tend to follow federal practice, requiring that indictments be used to charge serious crimes and allowing other charging instruments to be used to bring charges for minor felonies and misdemeanors. *See generally* Susan Brenner et al., *Federal Grand Jury: A Guide to Law and Practice,* www.udayton.edu (providing information on both federal and state grand juries).

8. "[P]robable cause is a flexible, common-sense standard. It merely requires that the facts available to the officer would 'warrant a man of reasonable caution in the belief'... that certain items may be contraband or stolen property or useful as evidence of a crime; it does not demand any showing that such a belief be correct or more likely true than false. A 'practical, non-technical' probability that incriminating evidence is involved is all that is required." *Texas v. Brown,* 460 U.S. 730, 742 (1983) (citations omitted).

9. *See United States v. Williams,* 504 U.S. 36–37 (1992) (holding that federal grand juries are not constitutionally required to disclose exculpatory information to grand juries). State courts are split on the issue of whether a prosecutor has the duty to present exculpatory evidence in the grand jury. States fall into one of three categories regarding this issue. Three states determined that prosecutors have a broad duty to disclose exculpatory evidence at the grand jury. Fourteen states determined that prosecutors have a limited duty to do so. The remaining thirty-three states impose no such duty. *See*

Sharon N. Humble, Annotation, *Duty of Prosecutor to Present Exculpatory Evidence to State Grand Jury*, 49 A. L. R. 5th 639 (1997) (detailing the states' stance on this issue); *Johnson v. Superior Court of San Joaquin County*, 124 Cal. Rptr. 32, 36, 539 P.2d 792, 796 (1979) (supporting the view that prosecutors have a broad duty to disclose all exculpatory evidence at the grand jury); *State v. Skjonsby*, 319 N.W.2d 764 (1982) (supporting the view that prosecutors have a limited duty to present exculpatory evidence to the grand jury but do not have a duty to present all evidence that may potentially or conceivably be exculpatory); *State v. Acquisto*, 463 A.2d 122, 123 (1983) (supporting the view that prosecutors do not have a duty to disclose exculpatory evidence at a grand jury proceeding and denying the appellant's motion alleging that failure to produce exculpatory evidence created a false indictment); *see also* William Glaberson, *New Trend Before Grand Juries: Meet the Accused*, N.Y. TIMES, June 20, 2004, at A1 (describing trend toward defendants testifying in the grand jury pursuant to New York law).

10. William J. Campbell, *Eliminate the Grand Jury*, 64 J. CRIM. L. & CRIMINOLOGY 174, 174 (1973) ("[T]oday, the grand jury is the total captive of the prosecutor, who, if he is candid, will concede that he can indict anybody, at any time, for almost anything, before any grand jury."), Frederick P. Hafetz & John M. Pellettieri, *Time to Reform the Grand Jury*, CHAMPION, Jan./Feb., at 12, 13 (1999). Furthermore, the courts are typically unwilling to punish prosecutors even if they abuse or misuse the grand jury procedures. Angela J. Davis, *The American Prosecutor: Independence, Power, and the Threat of Tyranny*, 86 IOWA L. REV. 393, 428–29 (2001).

11. *See, e.g.* Ric Simmons, *Re-Examining the Grand Jury: Is There Room for Democracy in the Criminal Justice System*, 82 B.U. L. REV. 1, 31 n. 136 (2002) *citing* U.S. Dep't of Justice, Compendium of Federal Justice Statistics 1990–1998 (showing that federal grand juries have an annual dismissal rate of less than 1%).

12. Most jurisdictions, like Michigan, limit the number of grand jury terms to return an indictment. MICH. COMP. LAWS ANN. § 767.26 (2000). However, some jurisdiction are more specific, such as Texas that gives 180 days to return an indictment, or New York, which only gives 45 days. TEX. CRIM. PROC. ANN. § 32.01 (2003); N.Y. CRIM. PROC. LAW § 190.80 (1993).

13. D.C. Sup. Ct. R. of Crim. Proc. 48(c).

14. Unless a court rules that it is otherwise admissible under the rules of evidence, hearsay (an out of court statement offered as proof) is not allowed at trial. Fed. R. Evid. 802. However, this preclusion doesn't apply to grand jury testimony. In fact, the Supreme Court has upheld grand jury indictments based entirely on hearsay evidence. *Costello v. United States*, 350 U.S. 359, 362–64 (1956).

15. STANDARDS FOR CRIMINAL JUSTICE: PROSECUTION FUNCTION § 3-3.9(a) (3d ed., 1993), www.abanet.org. This rule also instructs prosecutors not to bring charges that are not supported by enough *admissible* evidence to sustain a conviction, an instruction this prosecutor ignored. *Id.*

16. If I had referred the prosecutor to bar counsel, I would have become *persona non grata* to all of the prosecutors in that office, making it difficult for me to effectively negotiate with them in my representation of other clients. *See infra* chapter 7 (detailing the above issue further).

17. *See infra* chapter 3 (discussing in detail the plea bargaining process).

18. See Eric L. Muller, *The Hobgoblin of Little Minds? Our Foolish Law of Inconsistent Verdicts*, 111 HARV. L. REV. 771, 796–97 (1998) (noting that compromised verdicts are one reason for inconsistent verdicts); David F. Abele, Comment, *Jury Deliberations and the Lesser Included Offense Rule: Getting the Courts Back in Step*, 23 U.C. DAVIS L. REV. 375, 393–94 (1990) (arguing that compromised verdicts convict the innocent and fail to adequately punish the guilty because jurors disregard the presumption of innocence and the requirement of proving guilt beyond a reasonable doubt).

19. Merger is a complex common law criminal concept in which judges are prohibited from sentencing a defendant more than once for the same criminal act. According to the Supreme Court, merger is a corollary to the Fifth Amendment double jeopardy clause. *North Carolina v. Pearce,* 395 U.S. 711, 717–19 (1969), *rev'd on other grounds by* Alabama v. Smith, 490 U.S. 794 (1989). The states also apply the merger doctrine. See *generally* Mark E. Nolan, Comment, *Diverging Views on the Merger of Criminal Offenses: Colorado Has Veered off Course,* 66 U. COLO. L. REV. 523, 524–53 (1995) (discussing the merger doctrine as applied in Colorado), Jim Walden, *Criminal Law—Pennsylvania Purports to Abolish the Common Law Merger Doctrine,* 63 TEMP. L. REV. 385 (1990) (noting Pennsylvania's application of the merger doctrine), Joseph P. Bennett, Note, *The "Same Criminal Conduct" Exception of the Washington Sentencing Reform Act: Making the Punishment Fit the Crimes,* 65 WASH. L. REV. 397 (1990) (providing an explanation of the use of the merger doctrine in Washington).

20. *Nightline* (ABC News television show, Jan. 21, 2004).

21. *Id.*

22. *Id.* In fact, in an interview with *Nightline*, Ms. Tibitz claimed there was a general misperception about the charge in the jury room. The jury members thought it was a misdemeanor and that Marcus would go home after the trial. *Id.*

23. *Nightly News* (NBC television show, Jan. 21, 2004).

24. *Nightline* (ABC News television show, Jan. 21, 2004).

25. *Dixon v. State,* 596 S.E.2d 147, 149–51 (2004) (reversing the conviction of Marcus Dixon and holding that the legislature intended the

statutory rape and child molestation statutes to protect children from predators and that a statutory rape in which the defendant was no more than three years older than the victim could not be punished as felony aggravated child molestation).

26. *Id.* at 148. Georgia law classifies statutory rape as a misdemeanor when the victim is fourteen or fifteen years of age and the defendant is no more than three years older than the victim. OCGA § 16-6-3(b).

27. *District of Columbia v. Buckley,* 128 F.2d 17, 20–21 (1942) (recognizing the longstanding principle that a prosecutor may bring several charges arising out of the same act as a matter of public policy).

28. STANDARDS FOR CRIMINAL JUSTICE: PROSECUTION FUNCTION § 3-3.9(b), *supra* note 14 (illustrating several examples of appropriate factors to consider during the charging phase).

29. However, even if a prosecutor uses factors that are not legitimate, it remains almost impossible to challenge a prosecutor's decisions. For example, in *United States v. Chemical Foundation,* the Supreme Court found that "in the absence of clear evidence to the contrary, courts presume that [prosecutors] have properly discharged their official duties." 272 U.S. 1, 14–15 (1926) (citation omitted).

30. A Minneapolis study found that African Americans were stopped 152 percent more than expected and Latinos were stopped 63 percent more than expected. Minorities were also subjected to discretionary searches more often, even though discretionary searches of African Americans only produced contraband 11 percent of the time. Discretionary searches of Caucasian drivers produced contraband 24 percent of the time. Council on Crime and Justice & Institute on Race and Poverty, *Racial Profiling Study* (2003), www .crimeandjustice.org. *See also* Lisa Walter, Comment, *Eradicating Racial Stereotyping from Terry Stops: The Case for an Equal Protection Exclusionary Rule,* 71 U. COLO. L. REV. 255, 261 (2000) (referring to a Florida study showing that 70 percent of eleven hundred drivers stopped for traffic violations were either African American or Hispanic); Sean Hecker, *Race and Pretextual Traffic Stops: An Expanded Role for Civilian Review Boards,* 28 COLUM HUM. RTS. L. REV. 551, 562 n. 59 (1997) (citing an American Civil Liberties Union survey that found that while minorities make up only 21.8 percent of violators, they constitute 80.3 percent of those stopped and searched on Maryland portions of route I-95); *United States v. Leviner,* 31 F. Supp. 2d 23, 33-4 (D. Mass. 1998) (citing several studies that show African Americans are stopped and prosecuted more than other citizens); *id.* at 33 (reducing the sentence of an African American defendant, noting that African American motorists are stopped and prosecuted for traffic stops much more frequently than other citizens and suggesting that inflated arrest records lead to inequity in sentencing).

31. In *United States v. Armstrong,* the defendant presented evidence showing that, while there were as many Caucasian crack dealers and users as minority dealers and users, minorities were more likely to be prosecuted at the federal level and Caucasians prosecuted at the state level. 517 U.S. 456, 458–61 (1996). The federal level provides much harsher punishment for crack offenses than do state-level proceedings. The Supreme Court found that, even though prosecutorial discretion is subject to constitutional restraints, a defendant must provide "clear evidence" that a prosecutor has violated the Constitution. *Id.* at 465. Similarly in *McCleskey v. Kemp,* the defendant provided evidence showing that the death penalty was disproportionately sought and imposed against black defendants and those found guilty of killing whites. 481 U.S. 279, 286–87 (1987). While admitting that prosecutorial discretion could be used in a discriminatory manner, the Court required a showing of "exceptionally clear proof" before abuse of discretion can be found. *Id.* at 297, 311–12. *See also Ashe v. Swenson,* 397 U.S. 436, 452 (1970) (noting that prosecutorial discretion concerning the initiation and scope of a criminal prosecution is "virtually unreviewable").

32. An illegal arrest violates the Fourth Amendment of the U.S. Constitution. It's a well-settled principle that when evidence is obtained in violation of the Fourth Amendment search and seizure provisions, it will be suppressed and not available for use at trial. *Weeks v. United States,* 232 U.S. 383, 391–98 (1914). While *Weeks* only applied to federal searches, *Mapp v. Ohio* expanded the exclusionary rule to the states and state actors. Illegally obtained confessions are subject to the same analysis. The right to be protected from unreasonable interrogation is protected by the Fifth Amendment, and a violation results in the exclusion of that evidence from trial. Although prosecutors are not required to dismiss charges when evidence is suppressed, in most cases it is difficult to continue prosecution without the weapon, drugs, confession, or other crucial evidence. *Mapp v. Ohio,* 367 U.S. 643 (1961).

33. *See* NATE BLAKESLEE, TULIA: RACE, COCAINE, AND CORRUPTION IN A SMALL TEXAS TOWN (2005) for a complete discussion of the Tulia cases.

34. Terry McEachern accepted a two-year, fully probated suspension effective June 15, 2005. The bar association found that McEachern violated rules 3.03 (a) (1), (a) (2), and (a) (5), 3.04 (b), 3.09 (a) and (d), and 8.04 (a) (3) and (a) (4) by engaging in various practices involving dishonesty, fraud, deceit, and misrepresentation. The association concluded that McEachern made a false statement of a material fact to a tribunal, offered and used evidence that he knew to be false, counseled witnesses to give false testimony, prosecuted an offense without a showing of probable cause, and failed to timely disclose evidence to the defense that negated a showing of guilt. In addition to the suspension, McEachern was also ordered to pay $6,225 in fees. Disciplinary Actions, 68 Tex. B. J. 753, 758–79 (Sept. 2005).

35. *See infra* chapter 7 (noting the paucity of referrals of prosecutors to state disciplinary authorities).

3. Let's Make a Deal

1. Defendants plead guilty in approximately 95 percent of all cases. *See* Dep't of Justice, Bureau of Statistics, Felony Defendants in Large Urban Counties in 2000 28 (Dec. 2003), www.ojp.usdoj.gov/bjs/pub/pdf/fdluc00.pdf.

2. The defendant is entitled to a jury trial if the offense carries a penalty of more than six months. *See Bloom v. Illinois*, 391 U.S. 194 (1968).

3. Although some judges sentence the defendant at the time of the plea in minor misdemeanor cases, sentence is most often postponed so a presentence investigation can be conducted. *See, e.g.*, Mich. Comp. Laws Ann. § 769.1(1) (2000). These presentence reports investigate offense characteristics such as financial and emotional impact of the offense on the victim and offender characteristics such as age, marital status, education, propensity for violence, remorse, and past criminal records. *See, e.g.*, Okla. Stat. tit. 22 § 982 (2003).

4. Some prosecutors' offices have written guidelines or policies, but in most offices, the chief prosecutor does not require her staff to follow them in every case. Most offices do not have such guidelines. Robert L. Misner, *Recasting Prosecutorial Discretion*, 86 J. Crim L. & Criminology 717, 772 (1996) (noting that only about 12 percent of prosecutors' offices have written rules guiding plea bargaining and discussing the obstacles to reforming the plea bargain system).

5. The judge has the power to detain the defendant after he pleads guilty and before he is sentenced. *See, e.g.*, Tenn. Code Ann. § 40-35-116(b)–(c) (giving the judge authority to revoke bail upon a finding of guilty and if such a revocation is made, the defendant will be held in a secure facility).

6. For a general discussion of caseloads nationwide, their variations across geographical locations, and the negative impacts of large caseloads, *see* Jerold H. Israel, *Excessive Criminal Justice Caseloads: Challenging the Conventional Wisdom*, 48 Fla. L. Rev. 761 (1996); Ronald Wright & Marc Miller, *The Screening/Bargaining Tradeoff*, 55 Stan L. R. 29, 41 (2002) (noting that caseloads in recent history have increased due to institutional and doctrinal changes in the criminal justice system and noting the concurrent increase in the pressure to plea).

7. *See* chapter 4 *infra*, for a detailed discussion of the prosecutor's unique relationship with crime victims.

8. *See* Angela J. Davis, *Prosecution and Race: The Power and Privilege of Discretion,* 67 FORDHAM L. REV. 13 (1998); *see also infra* chapters 2, 5, and 6, for discussions of the effect of class and race on prosecutorial decisions.

9. *See infra* chapter 6, for a discussion of Attorney General Ashcroft's limitation of the federal prosecutor's plea bargaining power.

10. Fredrick Kunkle, *Maryland Seeks Return of Teen in Sex Case,* WASH. POST, July 1, 2003, at B5.

11. MD CODE, Criminal Law, § 3-305; MD CODE, Criminal Law, § 3-403; MD CODE, Criminal Law, § 1-202.

12. *Nineteen-Year-Old Potomac Man Sentenced for Role in Sex Assault on Escort Service Employee,* July 15, 2003, http://wjz.com.

13. In her motion to support the plea bargain, the state's attorney noted that she believed an adult record reflecting the seriousness of Andrew Klepper's crimes was sufficient punishment. In addition, she believed she had struck a fair balance between public justice—physically detaining Kleppar an additional eighteen months and keeping him out of the state for several years—and leniency: Klepper had a long history of mental illness and treatment that the prosecutor felt needed special accommodation.

14. Some legislatures have explicitly denounced the rehabilitation method of punishment. For example, the U.S. Senate cited the 1970s as the turning point from rehabilitation to incarceration and retribution. *See* S. REP. No. 98-225 at 40, n. 16 (1983), *reprinted in* 1984 U.S.C.C.A.N. 3182 (rejecting rehabilitation as an effective model of punishment and noting several studies the Senate relied on to reach that conclusion).

15. *Frontline: The Plea* (PBS television show, June 17, 2004), www.pbs.org.

16. *Id.*

17. *Id.*

18. *See e.g.,* N.C.G.S.A. § 14-210; I.C. § 18-5410; OKLA. STAT. ANN. Tit. 21 § 504; 13 V.S.A. § 2902.

19. 165 F.3d 1297 (10th Cir. 1999).

20. A majority of the circuit judges may order that an appeal or proceeding be heard or reheard by the court of appeals en banc when an en banc consideration is "necessary to secure or maintain uniformity of the court's decisions" or the proceeding involves a "question of exceptional importance." Fed. Cir. R. Rule 35, 28 U.S.C.A.

21. 165 F.3d 1297 (10th Cir. 1999).

22. *Id.* at 1309.

23. *Id.*

24. *See* Karen Lutjen, *Culpability and Sentencing Under Mandatory Minimums and the Federal Sentencing Guidelines: The Punishment No Longer Fits the Criminal,* 10 NOTRE DAME J. L. ETHICS & PUB. POL'Y 389, 399 (1996) (indicating that,

historically, mandatory minimums were set for drug offenses, violent crimes, and serious felonies).

25. *See* UNITED STATES SENTENCING COMMISSION, MANDATORY MINIMUM PENALTIES IN THE FEDERAL CRIMINAL JUSTICE SYSTEM 9 (1991) (showing that trends in the 1970s caused forty-nine states to implement mandatory minimum penalties by 1983).

26. Prosecutors are already required to provide exculpatory information to the defense. *See Brady v. Maryland*, 373 U.S. 83 (1963). However, they are not required to provide this information before a guilty plea. In addition, prosecutors regularly fail to provide this information, despite their obligation to do so. *See infra* chapter 7, for a full discussion of *Brady* violations.

4. Prosecutors and the Victims of Crime

1. "Society wins not only when the guilty are convicted but when criminal trials are fair; our system of the administration of justice suffers when any accused is treated unfairly. An inscription on the walls of the Department of Justice states the proposition candidly for the federal domain: 'The United States wins its point whenever justice is done its citizens in the courts.' " *Brady v. Maryland*, 373 U.S. 83, 87 & n. 2 (1963).

2. Interview with Lenese Herbert, former assistant U.S. attorney, U.S. Attorney's Office for the District of Columbia, Silver Spring, Maryland, Mar. 10, 2004.

3. *Id.*

4. Joan E. Jacoby, *The American Prosecutor in Historical Context*, PROSECUTOR, JOURNAL OF THE NATIONAL DISTRICT ATTORNEYS ASSOCIATION, MAY–JUNE 1997, 33, 38.

5. Peggy M. Tobolowsky, *Victim Participation in the Criminal Justice Process: Fifteen Years After the President's Task Force on Victims of Crime*, 25 N. ENG. J. ON CRIM. & CIV. CONFINEMENT 21, 22 (1999).

6. Walker A. Matthews III, *Proposed Victims' Rights Amendment: Ethical Considerations for the Prudent Prosecutor*, 11 GEO. J. LEGAL. ETHICS 735, 735 (1998).

7. Tobolowsky, *supra* note 5 at n. 168.

8. Susan Gegan & Nicholas Ernesto Rodriguez, *Victims' Roles in the Criminal Justice System: A Fallacy of Victim Empowerment*, 8 ST. JOHN'S J. LEGAL COMMENT. 225, n.115 (1992).

9. *See id.* at 246–48 (positing that constitutional amendments should be passed to afford the victim a more active role in the plea bargaining process).

10. Interview with Lenese Herbert, *supra* note 2.

11. D.C. ST § 22-404 (2001).

12. D.C. ST § 22-4514 (b)(2001).

13. The case was brought in 1984. At that time the domestic violence laws had not been reformed, and many jurisdictions frequently charged even serious assaults as misdemeanors for a variety of reasons, including lack of cooperation from victims.

14. My client was no longer living in their home. The judge had released him pending his trial and ordered him to stay away from the victim.

15. The purpose of the status hearing is to inform the judge whether there will be a guilty plea or if the case will go to trial. Guilty pleas are usually taken at the status hearing, but if there is going to be a trial, the judge confirms the trial date and addresses any pretrial matters the parties wish to resolve.

16. *See* Christine O'Connor, *Domestic Violence No-Contact Orders and the Autonomy Rights of Victims*, 40 B. C. L. REV. 937, 942–46 (1999); Cheryl Hanna, *No Right to Choose: Mandated Victim Participation in Domestic Violence Prosecutions*, 109 HARV. L. REV. 1849, 1863–65 (1996) (discussing the effect of these policies on the rights of women victims).

17. http://venus.soci.niu.edu/~archives/ABOLISH/rick-halperin/july03/0243.html.

18. *Id.*

19. Standards established by the National District Attorneys Association, the Department of Justice, and the American Bar Association include victims' interests among the factors that prosecutors should consider in their decision-making processes. National District Attorneys Association, *National Prosecution Standards*, § 43.6 (2nd ed., 1991), www.ndaa.org; Department of Justice, UNITED STATES ATTORNEYS' MANUAL, § 9-27.230 (1997), www.usdoj.gov/usao/eousa/foia_reading_room/usam/title9/27mcrm.htm#9-27.230; American Bar Association, *Standards for Criminal Justice: Prosecution Function* § 3-3.9(b) (3d ed., 1993), www.abanet.org.

20. A mistrial occurs when a trial is aborted after the jury is sworn. The judge must declare a mistrial and does so on the motion of either party. Mistrials may be declared when circumstances exist that "cast substantial doubt" on the overall fairness of the trial. *U.S. v. Matthews*, 13 M.J. 501, 515 (1982).

21. *District of Columbia Crime Rates 1960–2000*, www.disastercenter.com (noting the crime statistics for 1992).

22. Much attention was focused on the fact that JonBenet's mother had entered her in numerous child pageants, but this fact was discovered later, after the media began reporting the case.

5. Prosecutors and the Death Penalty

1. Death Penalty Information Center, *Innocence and the Death Penalty: The Increasing Danger of Executing the Innocent,* www.deathpenaltyinfo.org.

2. *See generally,* MICHAEL RADELET ET AL., IN SPITE OF INNNOCENCE (1992); SISTER HELEN PREJEAN, DEATH OF INNOCENCE (2005).

3. *Callins v. Collins,* 510 U.S. 1141, 1145 (1994), (Blackmun, J., dissenting).

4. In *Furman v. Georgia,* 408 U.S. 238 (1972), the Court held that the death penalty was unconstitutional as applied. Just four years later, in *Gregg v. Georgia,* 428 U.S. 153 (1976), the Court upheld the constitutionality of death penalty statutes that involve a bifurcated trial with the consideration of aggravating and mitigating factors. Similarly, the Supreme Court reversed itself in *Atkins v. Virginia,* 536 U.S. 304 (2002), and held that the execution of mentally retarded defendants violates the Eighth Amendment. This decision explicitly overruled the earlier decision of *Penry v. Lynaugh,* 492 U.S. 302 (1989). Finally, in *Roper v. Simmons,* 125 S. Ct. 1183 (2005), the Court held that the execution of defendants who were under the age of eighteen at the time of their crimes was unconstitutional, reversing their holding in *Stanford v. Kentucky,* 492 U.S. 361 (1989).

5. *See* Death Penalty Information Center, State by State Information, www.deathpenaltyinfo.org. New York and Kansas are included in the thirty-eight states with death penalty statutes, but in both of these states, the statutes were held unconstitutional. *See New York v. LeValle,* 817 N.E.2d 341 (2004) (holding that the New York statute's requirement that the court instruct the jury that if it failed to unanimously agree on either a death sentence or a sentence of life without parole, the court would sentence the defendant to life imprisonment with parole eligibility after serving minimum of twenty to twenty-five years created an impermissible risk of a coercive and thus arbitrary and unreliable sentence, in violation of the state constitution's due process clause). In April 2005, the New York legislature refused to reinstate a new death penalty law. *See also Kansas v. Marsh,* 102 P.3d 445 (2004) (holding Kansas death penalty statute unconstitutional because it required a finding of death when the jurors found the aggravating and mitigating factors to be equal). The U.S. Supreme Court reversed the Kansas Supreme Court, holding that the statute was constitutional. *Kansas v. Marsh* 126 S.Ct. 2516 (2006). At least two former governors—George Ryan of Illinois and Parris Glendenning of Maryland—declared moratoria on the death penalty during their administrations. *See, e.g., Maryland Death Penalty Moratorium,* CBS News, May 9, 2002, www.cbsnews.com. The Illinois legislature subsequently enacted a law to reform the application of the death penalty, and Ryan's successor, Governor Rob Blagoveich, announced that he would continue to support the

moratorium until the legislative reforms prove effective. In January 2003, Governor Glendenning's successor, Governor Robert Ehlrich, lifted Maryland's moratorium on the death penalty and authorized Maryland judges to sign death warrants.

6. The federal death penalty statute permits the death penalty for treason, espionage, and certain narcotics offenses. Pub. L. 103-322, title VI, § 60001–26, Sept. 13, 1994, 108 Stat. 1959 (codified at 18 U.S.C. 3591–98). The military also permits the death penalty for murder, rape, espionage, and desertion during a time of war. *See e.g.,* 10 U.S.C. § 906(a), 918, 885(c), and 920.

7. In 2003, China, Iran, the United States, and Vietnam were responsible for 84 percent of the known executions. Death Penalty Information Center, *The Death Penalty: An International Perspective,* www.deathpenalty info.org.

8. *See* Linda E. Carter & Ellen Kreitzberg, *Understanding Capital Punishment Law* 86 (2004) (explaining that the federal government and thirteen states have laws that permit the death penalty for offenses other than homicide, including treason, kidnapping, and the rape of a child).

9. *Woodson v. North Carolina,* 428 U.S. 280 (1976).

10. *But see* TEX. CRIM. PROC. CODE § 37.071 (Supp. 1976). The Texas statute does not include aggravating factors but instead limits capital murder to five specific types of killings.

11. MD. CODE ANN., Criminal Law § 2-303 (2003).

12. *See, e.g.,* James S. Liebman, *The Overproduction of Death,* 100 COLUM. L. REV. 2030, 2052 (2001) ("Since *Furman,* an average of about 300 of the approximately 21,000 homicides committed in the United States each year have resulted in a death sentence.") (footnote omitted); *see also* Leigh B. Bienen, *Criminal Law: The Proportionality Review of Capital Cases by State High Courts After Gregg: Only "The Appearance of Justice"?* 87 J. CRIM. L. & CRIMINOLOGY 130, n. 255 (1996) (noting statistics that show prosecutors in Maryland rarely seek the death penalty); Richard Perez-Pena, *The Death Penalty: When There's No Room for Error,* N.Y. TIMES, Feb. 13, 2000, sec. 4, at 3. (stating that prosecutors rarely seek the death penalty in Colorado).

13. *See* Department of Justice, U.S. ATTORNEYS' MANUAL, § 9–10.00, www.usdoj.gov/usao/eousa/foia_reading_room/usam/title9/10mcrm.htm.

14. *Id.; see infra* chapter 6 for discussion of the attorney general's control over this process.

15. Death Penalty Information Center, *Race of Death Row Inmates Executed Since 1976,* www.deathpenaltyinfo.org.

16. *Id.*

17. Death Penalty Information Center, Studies and Additional Sources, www.deathpenaltyinfo.org (citing John Blume, Theodore Eisenburg, &

Marton T. Wells, *Explaining Death Row's Population and Racial Composition*, JOURNAL OF EMPIRICAL LEGAL STUDIES (2004)).

18. UNITED STATES GENERAL ACCOUNTING OFFICE, DEATH PENALTY SENTENCING (1990).

19. Gennaro F. Vito & Thomas J. Keil, *Capital Sentencing in Kentucky: An Analysis of the Factors Influencing Decision Making in the Post-Gregg Period*, 79 J. CRIM. L. & CRIMINOLOGY 483, 502 (1988).

20. *See* Leigh B. Bienen et al., *The Reimposition of Capital Punishment in New Jersey: The Role of Prosecutorial Discretion*, 41 RUTGERS L. REV. 27 (1988); *see also The Futile Quest for Racial Neutrality in Capital Selection and the Eight Amendment Argument for Abolition Based on Unconscious Racial Discrimination*, 45 WM. & MARY L. REV. 2083 (2004), for a detailed discussion of studies that examine the influence of race in the implementation of the death penalty.

21. *McCleskey v. Kemp*, 481 U.S. 279, 286 (1987).

22. *Id.* at 286–87.

23. 481 U.S. 279 (1987).

24. *Id.* at 313, n. 37 (citing ABA Standards for Criminal Justice 3-3.8, 3-3.9 (2d ed. 1982)).

25. *Id.* at 333–34.

26. *Id.* at 357–58.

27. *See* Richard C. Dieter, *The Death Penalty in Black and White: Who Lives, Who Dies, Who Decides*, June 1998, www.deathpenaltyinfo.org (summarizing the findings of Professor Jeffrey Pokorak of St. Mary's University School of Law).

28. Jeffery J. Pokorak, *Probing the Capital Prosecutor's Prospective: Race of the Discretionary Actors*, 83 CORNELL L. REV. 1811, 1817 (1998) (suggesting the existence of unconscious bias in death penalty prosecutions).

29. Stephen Bright, *Discrimination, Death and Denial: The Tolerance of Racial Discrimination in Infliction of the Death Penalty*, 35 SANTA CLARA L. REV. 433, 453–54 (1995).

30. The law was passed by the legislature with the strong backing of Governor Pataki. The death penalty law was declared unconstitutional in 2004 by the highest New York state court. (*See supra* note 5.) In April 2005, the legislature refused to reinstate a new death penalty law. Marc Humbert, *N.Y. Legislators Kill Death Penalty Bill*, ASSOCIATED PRESS, April 12, 2005, http://news.yahoo.com.

31. MCKINNEY'S CONSOLIDATED LAWS OF NEW YORK, Correction Law Ch. 43, Art. 22-B, Refs & Annos (2003) (providing that the prosecutor has 120 days to notify a defendant if he intends to seek the death penalty).

32. In the Matter of Rafael Martinez et al., Appellants, v. George E. Pataki, et. al., Respondents *I*, 91 N.Y.2d 214, 691 N.E.2d 1002, 668 N.Y.S.2d 978 (1997), www.law.cornell.edu.

33. Harris's father is Jamaican, and her mother is Indian.

34. Press release, Kamala Harris, *Justice for Officer Espinoza,* Apr. 24, 2004, http://sf.indymedia.org.

35. Presidents of the San Francisco Bar Association, the Charles Houston Bar Association, La Raza Lawyers Association, and the Asian American Bar Association of the Greater Bay Area participated in a press conference at City Hall on April 28, 2004, to express the support of their organizations. *See* Adriel Hampton, *Lawyers' Associations Back Harris' Decision,* S.F. EXAMINER, Apr. 20, 2004, www.sfexaminer.com.

36. Jo Stanley, *Harris' No-Death-Penalty Stance Prompts Legislation,* SA-CRAMENTO OBSERVER, Apr. 27, 2004, www.sacobserver.com.

37. Dean E. Murphy, *Killing of Officer Stirs Death Penalty Debate,* N.Y. TIMES, June 12, 2003, at A7.

38. James S. Liebman, *The Overproduction of Death,* 100 COLUM. L. REV. 2030, 2078–81 (2000) (ultimately noting that "the more death sentences a local prosecutor can obtain, the more votes he will get").

39. U.S. GENERAL ACCOUNTING OFFICE, *supra* note 19; Richard Dieter, *The Death Penalty in Black and White: Who Lives, Who Dies, Who Decides,* Death Penalty Information Center, www.deathpenaltyinfo.org; Pennsylvania State Study, *Racial and Ethnic Disparities in the Imposition of the Death Penalty,* www.courts.state.pa.us/Index/supreme/BiasCmte/FinalReport.ch6.pdf; Maryland State Commission on Criminal Sentencing Policy, *Research on Death Penalty and Related Topics,* www.msccsp.org.

40. Raymond Paternoster and Robert Brame, *An Empirical Analysis of Maryland's Death Sentencing System with Respect to the Influence of Race and Legal Jurisdiction,* 36–37, http://www.newsdesk.umd.edu/pdf/exec.pdf.

41. *Id.* at 29.

42. Sarah Koenig, *Racial Factor Found in Md. Capital Cases; Those Who Kill Whites Are More Likely to Face Death Penalty, Study Says; "Systemic Disparities"; Jurisdiction Also Plays Big Role, Examination of State Statute Finds,* BALT. SUN, January 8, 2003, at B1.

43. *Id.*

6. Federal Prosecutors and the Power of the Attorney General

1. *See* Edwin Meese III, *The Dangerous Federalization of Crime,* HOOVER DIGEST (1999), www.hooverdigest.org (stating that state and local prosecutions constitute 95 percent of all prosecutions in the U.S.).

2. Of the federal criminal laws passed since the Civil War, approximately 40 percent have been passed since 1970. *See* James A. Strazzella, The

Federalization of Criminal Law, Task Force on Fed. of Crim. Law Rep. A.B.A. Crim Just. Sec. at 9–10, app. C (1998).

3. *See e.g.,* False Statement Offense Statute, 18 U.S.C. § 1001 (2004), *amended by* PL 109-248,120 Stat 587 (July 27, 2006) (mandating that any person who lies to a federal agent may be subject to prosecution, even if the lie is harmless and does not interfere with an investigation). Congress broadened this statute to include all false statements to federal officials, in order to protect the government from "deceptive tactics." Theo I. Ogune, *Judges and Statutory Construction: Judicial Zombism of Contextual Activism*, 30 U. BALT. L. F. 4, n. 154 (2000). The Federal Conspiracy Statute, 18 U.S.C. § 371, as interpreted by the federal courts, is also broad. *See* Lance Cole & Ross Nabatoff, *Prosecutorial Misuse of the Federal Conspiracy Statute in Election Law Cases*, 18 YALE L. & POL'Y REV. 225, 230 (2000) (positing that the statute is broad enough to encompass any conspiracy designed to impair or obstruct the lawful function of any branch of government).

4. Department of Justice, *Organizational Chart* (2004), www.usdoj.gov/ dojorg.

5. Although U.S. attorneys handle all litigation in which the United States is a party, including civil matters, this chapter will only discuss the federal prosecution of criminal cases.

6. 28 U.S.C. § 542 (2006).

7. JUDICIAL CONFERENCE OF THE U.S., REPORT OF THE FEDERAL COURTS STUDY COMMITTEE 106 (July 1, 1990).

8. Department of Justice, U.S. ATTORNEYS' MANUAL § 9-2.031 (2005), www.usdoj.gov/usao/eousa/foia_reading_room/usam/title9/2mcrm.htm# 9-2.031.

9. *Id.* § 9-27.220 (2005), www.usdoj.gov/usao/eousa/foia_reading_ room/usam/title9/27mcrm.htm#9-27.220.

10. *Id.* § 9-27.220 cmt. (2005), www.usdoj.gov/usao/eousa/foia_ reading_room/usam/title9/27mcrm.htm#9-27.220.

11. *Id.* § 1.1 (1997), www.usdoj.gov/usao/eousa/foia_reading_room/ usam/title1/1mdoj.htm.

12. Vicki Haddock, *The Jury Never Rests*, SAN FRAN. CHRON., June 1, 2003, www.sfgate.com.

13. Bob Egelko, *Five Years Sought for Pot Grower,* SAN FRAN. CHRON., May 29, 2003, www.sfgate.com.

14. Department of Justice, U.S. ATTORNEYS' MANUAL § 9-11.151 (2002), www.usdoj.gov/usao/eousa/foia_reading_room/usam/title9/11mcrm.htm#9-11.151.

15. *United States v. Washington*, 431 U.S. 181, 186, 190–191 (1977).

16. Department of Justice, U.S. ATTORNEYS' MANUAL § 9-11.151 (2002), www.usdoj.gov/usao/eousa/foia_reading_room/usam/title9/11mcrm.htm#9-11.151.

17. *See* Ellen S. Podgor, *Department of Justice Guidelines: Balancing "Discretionary Justice,"* 13 CORNELL J. L. & PUB. POL'Y 167, 170 (2004) (arguing for a heightened review by the judiciary, legislature, and executive when Department of Justice guidelines in the U.S. attorneys' manual are ignored).

18. Some suggest that President Ronald Reagan launched the modern War on Drugs during a speech he delivered at the Justice Department on October 14, 1982. *See* Leslie Maitland, *President Gives Plan to Combat Drug Network*, N.Y. TIMES, Oct. 15, 1982, at A1.

19. *See* written statement of Gerald B. Lefcourt, President, National Association of Criminal Defense Lawyers Before the House Appropriations Comm., Subcomm. Commerce, Justice and State, and the Judiciary, 104th Cong. (April 1, 1998), www.nacdl.org.

20. Patrick Walker, *The Disparity Between the Number of Grand Jury Sessions Convened and the Number of Defendants Indicted*, 87 JUDICATURE 178, 182 (2004).

21. *See generally* Eric E. Sterling, *The Sentencing Boomerang: Drug Prohibition Politics and Reform*, 40 VILLA. L. REV. 383, 408–12 (1995).

22. 21 U.S.C. § 844 (a) (West 2006) ("a person convicted under this subsection for the possession of a mixture or substance which contains cocaine base shall be imprisoned not less than 5 years and not more than 20 years").

23. Sterling, *supra* note 21, at 409.

24. *See* Harry Litman & Mark D. Greenberg, *Reporters' Draft for the Working Group on Federal-State Cooperation*, 46 HASTINGS L. J. 1319 (1995) (discussing criminal prosecution in the context of federalism); Geraldine Szott Moohr, *The Federal Interest in Criminal Law*, 47 SYRACUSE L. Rev. 1127, 1134–1135 (1997).

25. Department of Justice, U.S. ATTORNEYS' MANUAL § 9-27.220 (2002), www.usdoj.gov/usao/eousa/foia_reading_room/usam/title9/27mcrm.htm#9-27.110.

26. 517 U.S. 456, 459 (1996).

27. *See* Dan Weikel, *U.S. Defends Handling of Crack Cases Drugs: Prosecutors Deny Targeting Minorities. But Activists Demand to Know Why Whites Have Not Been Convicted*, L.A. TIMES, May 26, 1995, at 3; Gary Webb, *War on Drugs' Unequal Impact on U.S. Blacks*, SAN JOSE MERCURY NEWS, Aug. 20, 1996, at A1; Gary Webb, *Flawed Sentencing Blamed for Disparity*, SAN JOSE MERCURY NEWS, Aug. 20, 1996, at A11.

28. *See* 21 U.S.C. § 841(b)(1)(A)(iii) (West 2006) (requiring a sentence of ten years under federal law); CAL. HEALTH & SAFETY CODE § 11351–11351.5 (West 1991) (establishing two to five years penalty for distribution of cocaine under state law).

29. *United States v. Armstrong*, 517 U.S. at 459.

30. *See United States v. Armstrong,* 48 F.3d 1508, 1513–14 (9th Cir. 1995) (en banc), *rev'd,* 517 U.S. 456 (1996).

31. *United States v. Armstrong,* 517 U.S. at 469–470.

32. *Id.* at 465.

33. *Id.* at 464.

34. *See infra* chapter 5 (discussing in detail *McCleskey*).

35. Codified at 18 U.S.C. §§ 3141–3150 (1988).

36. 543 U.S. 220 (2005).

37. Mary Pat Flaherty & Joan Biskupic, *Justice by the Numbers: Despite Overhaul, Federal Sentencing Still Misfires,* WASH. POST, Oct. 6, 1996, at A1.

38. STEPHEN A. SALTZBURG & DANIEL J. CAPRA, AMERICAN CRIMINAL PROCEDURE, CASES AND COMMENTARIES 1476 (7th ed. 2004).

39. *Id.*

40. *Williams v. United States,* 503 U.S. 193 (1992).

41. *See* Charles J. Ogletree, Jr., *The Death of Discretion? Reflections on the Federal Sentencing Guidelines,* 101 HARV. L. REV. 1938 (1988) (criticizing the guidelines and considering ways to improve them); Steve Y. Koh, Note, *Reestablishing the Federal Judge's Role in Sentencing,* 101 YALE L. J. 1109, 1111 (1992) (suggesting that "the mathematical matrix improperly fosters judicial abdication of the duty of responsible and conscientious sentencing"); Orrin G. Hatch, *The Role of Congress in Sentencing: The United States Sentencing Commission, Mandatory Minimum Sentences, and the Search for a Certain and Effective Sentencing System,* 28 WAKE FOREST L. REV. 185 (1993) (examining whether the Guidelines meet Congress's goals); Jack B. Weinstein, *A Trial Judge's Second Impression of the Federal Sentencing Guidelines,* 66 S. CAL. L. REV. 357 (1993) (discussing his experience with the Guidelines); Kevin R. Reitz, *Sentencing Guideline Systems and Sentence Appeals: A Comparison of Federal and State Experiences,* 91 NW. U. L. REV. 1441 (1997) (discussing the appellate jurisdiction function with the new sentencing system); KATE STITH & JOSE CABRANES, FEAR OF JUDGING: SENTENCING GUIDELINES IN THE FEDERAL COURTS (1998) (showing that the present system has burdened the courts, dehumanized the sentencing process, and, by repressing judicial discretion, eroded the constitutional balance of powers); *Debate: Mandatory Minimums in Drug Sentencing,* 36 AM. CRIM. L. REV. 1279 (1999) (including a debate between Judge Stanley Sporkin and Congressman Asa Hutchinson).

42. *See* Judge Paul D. Borman, *Sentencing Law Symposium: The Federal Sentencing Guidelines,* 16 T.M. COOLEY L. REV. 1 (1999) (providing an explanation of the background and intricacies of the Sentencing Guidelines and stressing the need for a defense attorney at the sentencing hearing with the complicated procedures and application of the Guidelines).

43. Mary Pat Flaherty & Joan Biskupic, *Justice by the Numbers: Prosecutors Can Stack the Deck; Sentencing Powers Shift from Judges,* WASH. POST, Oct. 7, 1996, at A1.

44. United States Sentencing Commission, GUIDELINES MANUAL § 5K1.1 (2005).

45. Mary Pat Flaherty & Joan Biskupic, *Justice by the Numbers: Prosecutors and 5K: A Case of "Bad Faith"; How Florida Pilot's Plea Bargain Backfired,* WASH. POST, Oct. 7, 1996, at A12.

46. Ross Galin, *Above the Law: The Prosecutor's Duty to Seek Justice and the Performance of Substantial Assistance Agreements,* 68 FORDHAM L. REV. 1245, 1248 (2000).

47. Flaherty & Biskupic, *supra* note 45.

48. *Id.*

49. Mary Pat Flaherty & Joan Biskupic, *Rules Often Impose Toughest Penalties on Poor, Minorities; Justice Dept. Says the System Is Free of Bias,* WASH. POST, Oct. 9, 1996, at A1.

50. Named after its sponsor, Congressman Tom Feeney.

51. Pub. L. No. 108-21, 117 Stat. 650 (2003) (codified as amended in scattered sections of 18, 28, 42 and 47 U.S.C.). The PROTECT Act was widely known and supported for its child protection measures, such as the AMBER Alert System and anti–child pornography sections. As a result of the original bill's popularity, few in Congress could afford to speak out against the Feeney Amendment, and fewer still could afford to vote it down. As a result, the Feeney Amendment passed with little opposition. *See* Alan Vinegrad, *The New Federal Sentencing Law,* FED. SENTENCING REP. (June 2003), 2003 WL 22208841, at 5, 7 (noting the amendment received only fifteen minutes of debate in the House and none in the Senate, and the Protect Act was passed, over objections from legislators in both houses, 400 to 25 in the House and 98 to 0 in the Senate).

52. Protect Act, Pub. L. No. 108-21 § 401(k)(2)(B).

53. Edward Walsh & Dan Eggen, *Ashcroft Orders Tally of Lighter Sentences; Critics Say He Wants "Blacklist" of Judges,* WASH. POST, Aug. 7, 2003, at A1.

54. Laurie P. Cohen & Gary Fields, *Ashcroft Intensifies Campaign Against Soft Sentences by Judges,* WALL ST. J., Aug. 6, 2003, at A1 (showing that judicial intimidation through individualized reporting was a strong possibility because the Senate Judiciary Committee had already threatened to subpoena the sentencing records of district court judge James Rosenbaum of Minnesota).

55. See Chief Justice William H. Rehnquist, Remarks of the Chief Justice to the Federal Judges Association Board of Directors Meeting 2 (May 5, 2003), www.supremecourtus.gov/publicinfo/speeches/sp_05-05-03.html

(noting collection of individualized sentencing practices could lead to intimidation of judges in performing their judicial duties).

56. *See* Bruce Moyer, *New Sentencing Law Narrows Judicial Discretion*, FED.
LAW., May 2003, at 12 (predicting fewer downward departures due to judicial
chilling).

57. Ian Urbina, *In Angry Outbursts, New York's U.S. Judges Protest New
Sentencing Procedures*, N.Y. TIMES, Dec. 8, 2003, at A25.

58. *Id.*

59. *Id.*

60. *Id.*

61. *Id.*

62. *United States v. Mendoza*, No. 03-CR-730, 2004 WL 1191118, slip
op. at *6 (C.D. Cal. Jan. 12, 2004).

63. *Id.*

64. The United States Sentencing Commission has prepared a comprehensive summary of the major Supreme Court and circuit court cases concerning sentencing and the Guidelines. Also included are the existing conflicts
among the circuits. *See* www.ussc.gov/training/court.htm.

65. *See, e.g.*, *United States v. Koon*, 518 U.S. 81 (1996) (upholding defendants' downward departures and setting the standard of review as abuse of
discretion).

66. *See, e.g.*, *Mistretta v. United States*, 488 U.S. 361 (1989) (recognizing
the authority and upholding the constitutionality of the Sentencing Commission and the Guidelines); *Stinson v. United States*, 508 U.S. 36 (1993)
(holding that the commentary that explains the Guidelines is authoritative).

67. 543 U.S. 220 (2005).

68. *See e.g.*, *U.S. v. Wilson*, 350 F.Supp.2d 910, 928 (D. Utah 2005)
(stressing that heavy weight needs to be given to the guidelines even though
they became advisory); *U.S. v. Barkley*, 369 F.Supp.2d 1309, 1311 (N.D.
Okla. 2005) (finding that the sentencing should be consistent with *Booker*); *but
see U.S. v. Myers*, 353 F.Supp.2d 1026, 1029 (2005) ("This Court views
Booker as an invitation, not to unmoored decision making, but to the type of
careful analysis of the evidence that *should* be considered when depriving a
person of his or her liberty."). Scholars have argued that the *Booker* decision
has not resulted in a drastic change in federal sentencing. *See* James Carr, *Some
Thoughts on Sentencing Post-Booker*, 17 FED. SENT. R. 295, 2005 WL 2922210
at 4 (2005) (stating that since *Booker*, the rate of judicial departures from the
guidelines has been quite low).

69. *See* Paul McNulty, U.S. Attorney for the Dist. of Va., Speech at
University of Virginia Law School, *summarized at* www.law.virginia.edu ("If
the bad guys believe that they're better off going to a judge to get sentenced
rather than agreeing with the government to cooperate—getting certain

benefits for that under the sentencing guidelines as they have in the past—then our ability to get cooperation is going to go down substantially.").

70. *See infra* chapter 8 (discussing the Thornburgh Memo and prosecutorial ethics).

71. *See, e.g., United States v. Ferrara*, 847 F. Supp. 964, 969 (D.D.C. 1993), *aff'd*, 54 F.3d 825 (D.C. Cir. 1995) (stating that the memorandum does not constitute federal law); *United States v. Lopez*, 765 F. Supp 1433, 1446 (N.D. Cal. 1991), *vacated and remanded*, 989 F.2d 1032 (9th Cir. 1993), *superseded*, 4 F.3d 1455 (9th Cir. 1993) (stating that there are "profound flaws" in the policy that are not supported by case law); *United States v. Hammad*, 846 F.2d 854, 857–58 (2nd Cir. 1988) *aff'd on reh'g*, 902 F.2d 1062 (2nd Cir. 1990) (noting that ethical obligations apply to prosecutors).

72. *See* 28 C.F.R. § 77 (year).

73. 28 U.S.C. § 530B(a) (2004).

74. *See infra* chapters 7 and 8 (discussing these issues in depth).

75. "Operation Enduring Freedom" was launched against Afghanistan and its Taliban leaders in October of 2001. The Taliban officially fell on December 6, 2001, but American forces still remain. The United States officially began its war against Iraq on March 20, 2003, citing Iraqi links to Al Qaeda as one of the reasons for attack. These claims of links to Al Qaeda were later proven to be false. *See* Philippa Winkler, *The War Against Iraq: Whose Ends, Whose Means?* 9 NEXUS 163, 163 (2004) (stating that the war in Iraq was justified by "non-existent evidence" of links between Al Quaeda and the Ba'ath party in Iraq).

76. Uniting and Strengthening America by Providing Appropriate Tools Required to Intercept and Obstruct Terrorism Act of 2001 (USA Patriot Act), Pub. L. No. 107-56, 115 Stat. 272 (2001).

77. The ACLU has compiled the opinions of several conservative politicians, groups, and individuals on the Patriot Act, www.aclu.org.

78. Newt Gingrich, *The Policies of War: Refocus the Mission*, SFGATE.COM, Nov 11, 2003, www.sfgate.com.

79. Mimi Hall, *Armey: Justice "Out of Control,"* USATODAY.COM, Oct. 16, 2002, www.usatoday.com.

80. U.S. General Accounting Office, *Justice Department: Better Management Oversight and Internal Controls Needed to Ensure Accuracy of Terrorism-Related Statistics* 1, 13, 17–19 (2003), www.gao.gov/new.items/d03266.pdf.

81. Eric Lichtblau, *U.S. Uses Terror Law to Pursue Crimes from Drugs to Swindling*, N.Y. TIMES, Sept. 28, 2003, at A1.

82. William Walker, *603 Unidentified Detainees Still Held, U.S. Reveals*, TORONTO STAR, Nov. 28, 2001, at A16 (reporting that some of the detainees were believed to be "material witnesses" to the September 11 terrorist attacks).

83. Dan Eggen, *Deportee Sweep Will Start with Mideast Focus*, WASH. POST, Feb. 8, 2002, at A1 (citing Department of Justice intentions to compile absconder information into an antiterrorism database).

84. *Id.*

85. *Id.*

86. *Id.*

87. *See* David Cole, *Are Foreign Nationals Entitled to the Same Constitutional Rights as Citizens?* 25 T. JEFFERSON L. REV. 367, 386–87 (Spring 2003) (arguing that the right-privilege distinction does not justify denial of immigrants' rights); David Cole, *The New McCarthyism: Repeating History in the War on Terrorism*, 38 HARV. C.R.-C.L. L. REV. 1, 15 (Winter 2003) (critiquing the use of administrative processes as substitutes for criminal proceedings); David Cole, *Enemy Aliens*, 54 STAN. L. REV. 953, 974 (May 2002) (critiquing ethnic profiling for its overbreadth and ineffectiveness).

88. Attorney General John Ashcroft, Memorandum to All United States Attorneys, Department Policy Concerning Charging Criminal Offenses, Disposition of Charges, and Sentences (Sept. 22, 2003), www.crimelynx .com.

89. *Id.* (contending that sentence should not be dependent on the judge or prosecutor in a certain case).

90. *Ashcroft Plea-Bargain Order Is Potentially Disastrous*, NEWSDAY, Sept. 26, 2003, at A40 (noting that if even a fraction of previously plea bargained cases go to trial, the time demands, cost, and personnel needs for all facets of the criminal justice system will explode); *cf.* Gary Fields, *Order to Cut Plea Bargains Draws Ire*, WALL ST. J., Sept. 23, 2003, at A8 (showing that under a similar directive, issued by then–attorney general Richard Thornburgh, the percentage of defendants seeking trial increased).

91. It appears that Ashcroft's memorandum did not significantly curtail plea bargaining practices. According to one observer who supported the memorandum, "Attorney General John Ashcroft had the right idea when he attempted to curtail the all-too-common practice of filing more-serious charges against defendants simply to exert leverage to induce a plea to reduced charges. Unfortunately, prosecutors in the field either 'didn't get that memo' or simply disregarded it, because the practice continues unabated." Timothy Lynch, *Toward a Better Sentencing System*, THE RECORDER, 5 (January 28, 2005).

92. Stephanie Francis Cahill, *Snipers and Commerce: Dissenting Appeals Judges Cast Doubt on Prosecutions Using the Hobbs Act,* 89 A.B.A. J. 16 (2003).

93. Death Penalty Information Center, www.deathpenaltyinfo.org. Maryland's death penalty moratorium, implemented May 9, 2002 by then-governor Parris Glendening, ended when Robert Ehrilich took office in early 2003. Stephanie Hanes & Sarah Koenig, *Balt. Co. Judge Agrees to Execution of*

Oken, BALT. SUN, Jan. 22, 2003, at 1A, www.baltimoresun.com. In addition, Maryland did not have a record of implementing the death penalty on a regular basis. At the time of these arrests, there had not been an execution in Maryland since November 16, 1998.

94. Eunice Moscoso & Rebecca Carr, *Sniper Suspects to Be Tried in Virginia,* AUSTIN AMERICAN-STATESMAN, Nov. 8, 2002, at A16.

95. *Id.*

96. *Id.*

97. *See* Craig Haney & Richard Wiener, *Death Is Different,* 10 PSYCHOL. PUB. POL'Y & L. 373 (December 2004) (berating the attorney general for engaging in a "macabre version of forum shopping"). *See* Joan E. Schaffner, *Federal Circuit Choice of Law: Eerie Through the Looking Glass,* 81 IOWA L. REV. 1173, 1192 (1996) (noting that forum shopping is generally considered to be unethical). *See also* George D. Brown, *The Ideologies of Forum Shopping—Why Doesn't a Conservative Court Protect Defendants?* 71 N.C.L. REV. 649, 667 (1993) (indicating that one of the major dangers of forum shopping is unfairness to the defendant).

98. *See, e.g., "Shopping for Justice,"* INTELLIGENCER J., Nov. 8, 2002, at A8; Leslie T. Thornton, *"The Day Team Spirit Died,"* LEGAL TIMES, Nov. 18, 2002, at 70.

99. A AM. JUR. 2D *Constitutional Law* § 236 (West 2006).

7. Prosecutorial Misconduct

1. In the District of Columbia, adult criminal defendants (in both the federal and local District of Columbia courts) are prosecuted by the U.S. Attorney's Office.

2. *See* http://oag.dc.gov/occ/ (describing the attorney general's duties, which include prosecuting juvenile criminal cases). The corporation counsel's office is now known as the Office of the Attorney General.

3. *See e.g.,* JOSEPH F. LAWLESS, PROSECUTORIAL MISCONDUCT (2003); SCOTT CHRISTIANSON, INNOCENT: INSIDE WRONGFUL CONVICTION CASES (2004); BENNETT L. GERSHMAN, PROSECUTORIAL MISCONDUCT (1999); Casey P. McFaden, *Prosecutorial Misconduct,* 14 GEO. J. LEGAL ETHICS 1211 (2001) (addressing the ethical obligations of the prosecutor); Peter J. Henning, *Prosecutorial Misconduct and Constitutional Remedies,* 77 WASH. U. L. Q. 713 (1999) (discussing whether a prosecutor's misconduct violated defendants' rights and the existence of potential constitutional remedies); Rick A. Bierschbach, *One Bite at the Apple: Reversals of Convictions Tainted by Prosecutorial Misconduct and the Ban on Double Jeapordy,* 94 MICH. L. REV. 1346 (1996)

(arguing that the double jeopardy clause bars retrials under particular conditions when prosecutorial misconduct requires reversal of a conviction).

4. Steve Weinberg & Center for Public Integrity, *Breaking The Rules: Who Suffers When a Prosecutor Is Cited for Misconduct?* (2003), www.publicintegrity .org.

5. Editorial, *Policing Prosecutors,* ST. PETERSBURG TIMES, July 12, 2003, at 16A.

6. *See* Weinberg, *supra* note 4 (noting that there are countless other cases in which prosecutorial misconduct occurred but constituted harmless error).

7. *See generally, Chapman v. California,* 386 U.S. 18, 22 (1967) (adopting the harmless error rule and deciding that some constitutional errors are not significant or harmful and therefore do not require an automatic reversal of the conviction). The Court went on to state that, when determining whether the error was harmless, the question is whether the evidence might have contributed to the conviction. *Id.* at 23.

8. *See* Angela J. Davis, *The American Prosecutor: Independence, Power, and the Threat of Tyranny,* 86 IOWA L. REV. 393, 414–15 (2001).

9. *See, e.g., United States v. Armstrong,* 517 U.S. 456 (1996).

10. *See Rose v. Clark,* 478 U.S. 570, 580 (1986) (holding that the harmless error standard dictates that courts should not set aside convictions if the error was harmless beyond a reasonable doubt).

11. 318 U.S. 332, 340 (1943).

12. *Id.* at 341.

13. 411 U.S. 423, 435 (1973).

14. *Id.*

15. 461 U.S. 499, 506 (1983).

16. 424 U.S. 409, 424–25 (1976).

17. *Id.* at 430.

18. *See* Richard A. Rosen, *Disciplinary Sanctions Against Prosecutors for Brady Violations: A Paper Tiger,* 65 N.C. L. Rev. 693 (1987) (discussing how infrequently prosecutors are sanctioned for *Brady* violations).

19. Neil Gordon & Center for Public Integrity, *Misconduct and Punishment: State Disciplinary Authorities Investigate Prosecutors Accused of Misconduct* (2003), www.publicintegrity.org.

20. *Id.*

21. *See In re Doe,* 801 F. Supp. 478, 489 (D.N.M. 1992) (including the memorandum from Richard Thornburgh (June 8, 1989)).

22. *See infra* chapter 8 (discussing in more detail the Thornburgh Memo and the CPA).

23. *See* Department of Justice, Bureau of Statistics, *Felony Defendants in Large Urban Counties, 2000* 28 (Dec. 2003), www.ojp.usdoj.gov/bjs/pub/ pdf/fdluc00.pdf.

24. *See supra* note 20.

25. *See infra* chapter 8 (discussing prosecutorial ethics and the limitations of state disciplinary rules).

26. 373 U.S. 83 (1963).

27. 427 U.S. 97 (1976).

28. *Id.* at 107.

29. Ken Armstrong & Maurice Possley, *Verdict: Dishonor*, CHI. TRIB., January 10, 1999, www.chicagotribune.com.

30. *Id.*

31. *Id.*

32. *Id.*

33. *Id.*

34. *Id.*

35. *Id.*

36. *Id.*

37. *See* Bill Moushey, *Win at All Costs*, PITT. POST-GAZETTE, www.post-gazette.com.

38. *Id.*

39. *Id.*

40. Stephen Garvey, *Is It Wrong to Commute Death Row? Retribution, Atonement, and Mercy*, 82 N.C. L. REV. 1319, 1326 n. 27 (2004) (noting that 19 percent of the reversals of capital convictions or sentences in state court and 18 percent of those in federal court were due to prosecutorial failure to disclose exculpatory evidence or other forms of prosecutorial misconduct).

41. James S. Liebman, et al., *Capital Attrition: Error Rates in Capital Cases*, 78 TEX. L. REV. 1839, 1850 (2000) (citation omitted).

42. *See Banks v. Dretke*, 540 U.S. 668 (2004).

43. *Id.* at 704–6.

44. *Id.* at 674–75.

45. *Id.* at 677.

46. *Id.*

47. *Id.*

48. *Id.* at 678.

49. *Id.*

50. *Id.* at 682.

51. *Id.*

52. *Id.*

53. *Id.* at 683.

54. *Id.* at 685.

55. *Id.* at 685–86.

56. *Id.* at 685.

57. *Id.*

58. *Id.* at 684.
59. *Id.* at 685.
60. *Id.* at 686.
61. *Id.*
62. *Id.* at 686–87.
63. *Id.* at 689.
64. *Id.* at 691(citing *Strickler v. Greene,* 527 U.S. 263, 281–282 (1999)).
65. *Id.* at 696.
66. *See* Carissa Hessick, *Prosecutorial Subornation of Perjury: Is the Fair Justice Agency the Solution We Have Been Looking For?* 47 S.D. L. REV. 255, 256 (2002) (noting that public exposure of *Brady* violations has increased).
67. *See Shih Wei Su v. Filion,* 335 F.3d 119, 121, 130 (2d Cir. 2003) (affirming the conviction of Shih Wei Su, even though Judge Calabresi acknowledged that "the prosecution knowingly elicited false testimony from a crucial witness"). Judge Calabresi reasoned that the prejudice suffered by Shih Wei Su did not meet the legal standard that would require a dismissal. *Id.* at 129–30. *See* Editorial, *The Dedge Debacle,* FLORIDA TODAY, 2004 WLNR 16357164 (asserting that Wilton Dedge was wrongfully imprisoned for twenty-two years before he was finally exonerated by DNA evidence). Prosecutors allegedly suborned perjury when they knowingly encouraged the false testimony of a jailhouse snitch in order to win a conviction, and despite numerous appeals and retrials, no court ever reversed Mr. Dedge's conviction. *Id. See* Andrea Elliot, *City Gives $5 Million to Man Wrongly Imprisoned in Child's Rape,* N.Y. TIMES, December 16, 2003, www.talkleft.com (stating that Alberto Ramos spent seven years in prison for rape he did not commit, because the Bronx district attorney's office in New York withheld documents, including medical evidence, proving his innocence).
68. *See Gregg v. Georgia,* 428 U.S. 153, 188 (1976) (recognizing that the "penalty of death is different in kind from any other punishment imposed under our system of criminal justice"); *Ford v. Wainwright,* 477 U.S. 399, 411 (1986) (paying careful attention to the adequacy of capital proceedings generally as "a natural consequence of the knowledge that execution is the most irremediable and unfathomable of penalties; that death is different"); *Schiro v. Farley,* 510 U.S. 222, 238 (1994) (noting that the unique nature of capital sentencing procedures "derives from the fundamental principle that death is 'different' ").
69. *See Ring v. Arizona,* 536 U.S. 584, 606 (2002) (recognizing that states have developed complicated sentencing procedures in death cases because of constraints the Court has held the Eighth Amendment imposes); *see also Maynard v. Cartwright,* 486 U.S. 356, 362 (1988) ("Since *Furman,* our cases have insisted that the channeling and limiting of the sentencer's discretion in imposing the death penalty is a fundamental constitutional requirement for sufficiently minimizing the risk of wholly arbitrary and capricious action.");

Apprendi v. New Jersey, 530 U.S. 466, 522–523 (2000) (Thomas, J., concurring) (stating "In the area of capital punishment, unlike any other area, we have imposed special constraints on a legislature's ability to determine what facts shall lead to what punishment—we have restricted the legislature's ability to define crimes.").

70. In 1999, Steve Mills and Ken Armstrong, of the *Chicago Tribune,* conducted a multipart investigative series on the status of Illinois's death penalty. They examined over 285 capital cases since 1977. After conducting the study, Mills and Armstrong concluded: "Capital punishment in Illinois is a system so riddled with faulty evidence, unscrupulous trial tactics and legal incompetence that justice has been forsaken." Steve Mills & Ken Armstrong, *Death Row Justice Derailed,* CHIC. TRIB., Nov. 14, 1999, www.chicagotribune .com.

71. *See generally, Ring v. Arizona,* 536 U.S. 584, 585 (2002) (holding that the Sixth Amendment requires a jury, not a judge, to determine the presence or absence of aggravating factors in a capital sentencing proceeding); *Atkins v. Virginia,* 536 U.S. 304, 304 (2002) (determining that executing mentally retarded individuals violates the Eighth Amendment's ban on cruel and unusual punishment); *Roper v. Simmons,* 543 U.S. 551, 551 (2005) (holding that it is unconstitutional to execute persons who were under the age of eighteen at the time of their capital crimes).

72. *See* Adam Liptak & Ralph Blumenthal, *Death Sentences in Texas Cases Try Supreme Court's Patience,* N.Y. TIMES, Dec. 5, 2004, 2004 WLNR 13102712 (suggesting that the Supreme Court's Texas death penalty jurisprudence has been driven, in part, by its growing impatience with the U.S. Court of Appeals for the Fifth Circuit).

73. *Banks v. Dretke,* 540 U.S. 668, 692 n. 12 (2004).

74. Weinberg, *supra* note 4.

75. *Id.*

76. Ken Armstrong & Maurice Possley, *Verdict: Dishonor,* CHIC. TRIB., Jan. 10, 1999, at C1.

77. *Id.*

78. *Id.*

79. *Id.*

80. *Id.*

81. *E.g.,* CAL. PENAL CODE §127 (West 2006) (stating: "[E]very person who willfully procures another person to commit perjury is guilty of subornation of perjury, and is punishable in the same manner as he would be if personally guilty of the perjury so procured."); CAL. PENAL CODE § 126 (West 2006) (stating perjury is punishable by two, three, or four years in state prison, and thus, subornation of perjury is also punishable by two, three, or four years in state prison); MICH. COMP. LAWS. ANN. § 750.425 (West 2006) (stating

"[a]ny person who shall endeavor to incite or procure any person to commit the crime of perjury, though no perjury be committed, shall be guilty of a felony, punishable by imprisonment in the state prison not more than five years."); Va. Code Ann. § 18.2-436 (West 2006) (explaining that subornation of perjury occurs "if any person procure or induce another to commit perjury or to give false testimony under oath"); Va. Code. Ann. § 18.2-434 (West 2006) (defining subornation of perjury as a class 5 felony).

82. Ken Armstrong & Maurice Possley, *Prosecution on Trial in DuPage,* Chic. Trib., January 12, 1999, at N1.

83. *Id.*

84. *Id.*

85. *Id.*

86. *Id.*

87. *Id.*

88. Alden Long, *Illinois Prosecutors and Police Acquitted Despite Evidence They Framed Defendant,* June 16, 1999, www.wsws.org.

89. *See Law Enforcers Put on Trial,* www.angelfire.com.

90. *Id.*

91. The judge dismissed the claims against Armstrong, finding that he did not participate in the portion of the article that Thomas claimed to be libelous.

92. *See Jury Rules for Chicago Tribune in Prosecutor's Libel Case,* May 21, 2005, http://abclocal.go.com.

93. Telephone interview with staff attorney Sandra Levick of the PDS for the District of Columbia, July 17, 2006.

94. *See* Henri E. Cauvin, *Misconduct Probe Cuts Sentences in D.C. Case,* Wash. Post, December 24, 2004, at B1.

95. *See* Armstrong & Possley, *supra* note 76.

96. *See, e.g., Punish Prosecutors Who Cross the Line,* N.Y. L. J. 2 (January 27, 2004) (describing two citizens' frustration at the misconduct of prosecutors who contributed to the conviction of an innocent man).

97. *See Trial and Error,* Chi. Trib., wellengaged.com (listing *Tribune* reader responses to the *Chicago Tribune's* five-part series on prosecutorial misconduct on a bulletin board at the newspaper's website); *see* Davis, *supra* note 8 at 465 (citations omitted).

98. *See infra* chapter 10 (discussing how the legal profession might institute reform of the prosecution function).

8. Prosecutorial Ethics

1. *See* discussion *infra* chapter 7.

2. *Id.*

3. MONROE FREEDMAN & ABBE SMITH, UNDERSTANDING LAWYERS' ETHICS, 3rd Ed. 5 (2004).

4. MODEL RULES OF PROF'L CONDUCT, Comm'n on Evaluation of the Rules of Professional Conduct ("Ethics 2000") Chair's Intro., www.abanet .org.

5. *Id.*

6. www.abanet.org. http://www.abanet.org/cpr/mrpc/alpha_states.html.

7. *See, e.g.*, MODEL RULES OF PROF'L CONDUCT R. 1.5, 1.7, 1.8, 1.17, and 7.2, www.abanet.org.

8. *See, e.g.*, MODEL RULES OF PROF'L CONDUCT R. 3.3, 3.6, and 4.1, www.abanet.org.

9. Lon L. Fuller & John D. Randall, *Professional Responsibility: Report of the Joint Conference*, 44 A.B.A.J. 1159, 1218 (1958).

10. MODEL RULES OF PROF'L CONDUCT R. 3.8, www.abanet.org. The current rule is essentially the same as the original version. The Ethics 2000 Commission only recommended consolidating two of the sections of the original rule. The current section f is a consolidation of sections e and g of the previous rule.

11. *See* discussion *infra* chapter 7.

12. *See* FREEDMAN & SMITH, *supra* n. 3 at 314.

13. For example, former AUSA Julie Grahofsky stated that in close cases, she asked grand jurors not only whether they found probable cause but also whether they believed the case should go forward. Interview with Julie Grahofsky, former AUSA, at American University Washington College of Law, Washington, D.C., May 31, 2005.

14. National District Attorneys Association, *National Prosecution Standards*, Std. 43.3, 130 (2d. ed., 1991) www.ndaa-apri.org.

15. *Id.* at 131 cmt.

16. Irving Younger, *Memoir of a Prosecutor*, 62 COMMENTARY, 66 (Oct. 1976).

17. 373 U.S. 83 (1963).

18. *Id.* at 87.

19. *See* discussion *infra* chapter 7.

20. *See* discussion *infra* chapter 3 (discussing plea bargaining).

21. *See Kyles v. Whitley*, 514 U.S. 419, 437–38 (1995) (noting that the *Brady* rule encompasses evidence known only to police investigators, so the individual prosecutor has a duty to learn of any favorable evidence known to others acting on the government's behalf, including police). *But see U.S. v. Bagley*, 473 U.S. 667, 675 (1985) (holding that the prosecutor is not required to deliver his entire file to defense counsel but only to disclose evidence favorable to the accused that, if suppressed, would deprive the defendant of a fair trial).

22. "When the 'reliability of a given witness may well be determinative of guilt or innocence,' nondisclosure of evidence affecting credibility falls within this general rule." *Giglio v. United States*, 405 U.S. 150, 154 (1972) (citations omitted).

23. MODEL RULES OF PROF'L CONDUCT R. 3.8 cmt., www.abanet.org.

24. The current section f is a consolidation of sections e and g of the previous rule.

25. The original comment noted that rule 3.3(d) applied to grand jury proceedings. According to 3.3(d): "In an ex parte proceeding, a lawyer shall inform the tribunal of all material facts known to the lawyer that will enable the tribunal to make an informed decision, whether or not the facts are adverse." MODEL RULES OF PROF'L CONDUCT R. 3.3(d), www.abanet.org.

26. *See United States v. Williams*, 504 U.S. 36 (1992) (holding that the government is not constitutionally required to disclose exculpatory information to grand juries).

27. *See* American Bar Association, *Prosecution Function*, Standard 3-3.6(b), www.abanet.org.

28. Bruce A. Green, *Prosecutorial Ethics as Usual*, 2003 U. ILL. L. REV. 1573, 1582 (2003).

29. *Id.*

30. *Id.* at n. 49.

31. *Id.*

32. *Id.* at 1583.

33. *Id.* at 1584.

34. *Id.* at n. 54.

35. *Id.* at 1585.

36. *See* discussion in *infra* chapter 9.

37. 28 C.F.R. § 77.

38. *See* Rory K. Little, *Who Should Regulate the Ethics of Federal Prosecutors?* 65 FORDHAM L. REV. 355 (1996) for a discussion of the cases that led to the promulgation of the Thornburgh Memo and the subsequent federal regulations exempting prosecutors from the "no-contact" rule.

39. Richard L. Thornburgh, Memorandum to All Justice Department Litigators (June 8, 1989), *reprinted in In re Doe*, 801 F. Supp. 478, 489 (D.N.M. 1992).

40. *See e.g., In re Doe*, 801 F. Supp. 478, 480 (D.N.M. 1992).

41. *See e.g., Kolibash v. Committee on Legal Ethics*, 872 F.2d 571, 575 (4th Cir. 1989).

42. 28 U.S.C. § 530B(a)–(b) (2004).

43. 28 U.S.C. § 530B(a) (2004).

44. Under U.S. CONST. art. VI, cl. 2 (the supremacy clause), federal laws prevail when state and federal laws conflict. *See Edgar v. Mite Corp.* 457 U.S.

624, 631 (1982) (holding that "a state statute is void to the extent that it actually conflicts with a valid federal statute" and that "a conflict will be found where compliance with both federal and state regulations is a physical impossibility").

45. *See* Fred C. Zacharias & Bruce A. Green, *The Uniqueness of Federal Prosecutors,* 88 GEO. L. J. 207 (2000) for a thorough discussion of the CPA and its potential effects.

46. www.usdoj.gov/opr/

47. *See* Zacharias & Green, *supra* note 45, for a discussion of these differences.

48. State attorneys general do not typically supervise the county and local prosecutors of their states. In the majority of states, local prosecutors prosecute cases within the jurisdiction of the county, independent of the state attorney general. *See, e.g.,* IOWA CODE ANN. § 331.751 (West 1994); MINN. STAT. ANN. § 388.01 (West Supp.1995). In other states, local prosecutors prosecute crimes within the jurisdiction of a city. *See e.g.,* MD. ANN. CODE art. 10 § 34 (1957).

49. *See* Zacharias & Green, *supra* note 45 at 238 (suggesting that federal prosecutors may take their duty to "do justice" more seriously than state prosecutors, but recognizing that this generalization doesn't apply in all cases).

50. *See infra* chapter 7 (discussing case in which I filed a motion to dismiss an indictment for prosecutorial vindictiveness).

51. Fiscal Year 2003 Annual Report, U.S. Department of Justice, Office of Professional Responsibility www.usdoj.gov/opr/annualreport2003.htm. The OPR also opens an investigation in all cases in which judges "seriously criticize" a federal prosecutor, even if there is not a judicial finding of misconduct. Telephone interview with H. Marshall Jarrett, chief counsel and director of the OPR, July 14, 2006.

52. Interview with H. Marshall Jarrett, *supra* note 51.

53. Fiscal Year 2203 Annual Report, *supra* note 51, www.usdoj.gov/opr/annualreport2003.htm.

54. *Id.*

55. The OPR may continue an investigation after an attorney resigns. The deputy attorney general makes this decision on the basis of factors such as the seriousness of the allegation and how long the investigation has been pending. Telephone Interview with H. Marshall Jarrett, July 17, 2006.

56. The OPR will release some private information if the local bar office signs a confidentiality agreement. Offices that are required to report certain types of information to the public may not be permitted to sign these agreements.

57. In a case involving former AUSA Paul Howes (*see infra* chapter 7 for discussion of Howes's misconduct), Judge Collen Kollar-Kotelly of the U.S.

District Court for the District of Columbia ordered OPR to provide information it had redacted from its report. Telephone interview with Sandra Levick, PDS Appellate Training Director, July 17, 2006.

58. *Id.*

59. Green, *supra* note 28, at 1604.

60. *Id.*

9. Prosecutorial Accountability

1. "[T]he colonists transmuted the British system of mixed government based on social classes to a government in which three branches, the legislative, executive, and judicial, would check each other, regardless of the social class from which the officials were drawn." Abner S. Greene, *Checks and Balances in an Era of Presidential Lawmaking*, 61 U. Chi. L. Rev. 123, 139–40 (1994) (discussing the framers' overwhelming concern with either branch of government attaining power without sufficient checks).

2. The separation of powers is a means for "[a]mbition . . . to counteract ambition." The Federalist No. 51, at 356 (James Madison) (Howard M. Jones ed., 1961).

3. *See generally* William B. Gwyn, *The Indeterminacy of the Separation of Powers and the Federal Courts*, 57 Geo. Wash. L. Rev. 474, 484–94 (1989) (discussing federal courts' acceptance of criminal prosecution as part of the executive branch, but arguing that the framers did not intend prosecution to be an executive power); Rory K. Little, *Who Should Regulate the Ethics of Federal Prosecutors?* 65 Fordham L. Rev. 355, 379 (1996) ("Thus Congress has explicitly authorized the President to appoint, by and with the Senate's advice and consent, 'an Attorney General of the United States . . . [as] the head of the Department of Justice.' The department of Justice was established by Congress in 1870 as 'an executive department of the United States.'") (*citing* 28 U.S.C. §§ 501, 503 (1994)).

4. "Prosecution is not among the list of enumerated executive powers." Lawrence Lessig & Cass R. Sunstein, *The President and the Administration*, 94 Colum. L. Rev. 1, 70 (1994) (discussing the framers' perception of the executive branch and arguing that they did not support a unitary, hierarchical executive).

5. *Id.* at 94.

6. The Federalist No. 74 (Alexander Hamilton). *But see* Steven G. Calabresi & Kevin H. Rhodes, *The Structural Constitution: Unitary Executive, Plural Judiciary*, 105 Harv. L. Rev. 1153, 1166 (1992) (describing a theory of the unitary executive that allows the chief executive to maintain control through the power to veto the discretionary decisions of his subordinates).

The framers' support for a strong unitary executive must be viewed in light of the limited powers they gave to the executive. Greene, *supra* note 1, at 125 (discussing the framers' overwhelming concern with either branch of government attaining power without sufficient checks). Those limited powers are worlds apart from the modern prosecutor's broad powers and exercise of vast prosecutorial discretion unchecked by either the courts or the legislature.

7. *See* Juan Cardenas, *The Crime Victim in the Prosecutorial Process*, 9 HARV. J. L. & PUB. POL'Y 357 (1986) (describing police procedure in England); Harold J. Krent, *Executive Control over Criminal Law Enforcement: Some Lessons from History*, 38 AM. U. L. REV. 275, 280–81, 310 (1989) (also describing police procedure in England).

8. *See* John S. Baker, *State Police Powers and the Federalization of Local Crime*, 72 TEMP. L. REV. 673 (1999) (discussing how the founders would have been surprised to learn of the extensive and complex role the federal government has undertaken in the area of criminal law).

9. *But see* Krent, *supra* note 7 at 3117 (*citing* L. B. Schwarz, *Federal Criminal Jurisdiction and Prosecutorial Discretion*, 13 LAW & CONTEMP. PROBS. 64, 64–66 (1948), and arguing that the expansion of federal criminal laws calls for greater exercise of prosecutorial discretion).

10. *See infra* chapter 1 for a detailed discussion of the history of the American prosecutor. The framers clearly opposed unrestrained executive power, associating it with the tyrannical power of the king. *See* Lessig & Sunstein, *supra* note 4, at 13 (*citing* Gordon S. Wood, THE CREATION OF THE AMERICAN REPUBLIC, 1776–87, at 521 (1969) (discussing the hierarchy of the federal government)).

11. The Sentencing Reform Act of 1984, Pub. L. No. 98-473, 98 Stat. 2017–2034 (codified at 28 U.S.C. § 991 (1994)), established the federal sentencing guidelines. These guidelines eliminated judicial discretion at the sentencing stage, effectively causing the prosecutor's charging and plea bargaining decisions to be the determinants of the outcome in many criminal cases. Angela J. Davis, *Prosecution and Race: The Power and Privilege of Discretion*, 67 FORDHAM L. REV. 13, 23–24 (1998) (discussing prosecutors' vast discretion and power); *see also* Cynthia Kwei Yung Lee, *Prosecutorial Discretion, Substantial Assistance, and the Federal Sentencing Guidelines*, 42 UCLA L. REV. 105, 149 (1994) (discussing the immense discretion of prosecutors in determining whether a defendant will be sentenced to a mandatory minimum sentence under the guidelines). *But see* the discussion of *United States v. Booker*, 543 U.S. 220 (2005), *infra* chapter 6.

12. *But see* discussion of the Vera Institute's Prosecution and Racial Justice Project, *infra* chapter 10.

13. In Alaska, Hawaii, New Hampshire, New Jersey, and Wyoming, the governor appoints the attorney general. The legislature selects the attorney

general in Maine, and the state supreme court selects the attorney general in Tennessee. *See* Bill Isaeff, *Qualifications, Selection, and Term,* in STATE ATTORNEYS GENERAL: POWERS AND RESPONSIBILITIES 15 (Lynne M. Ross ed., 1990). The role of state attorneys general is determined by state constitutions, statutes, and case law. The state attorney general represents the state in civil and criminal matters and most focus on consumer protection, antitrust, child support enforcement, and related matters. State attorneys general also provide legal advice to governors and state agencies and some supervise local prosecutors. *See* Scott M. Matheson, Jr., *Constitutional Status and Role of the State Attorney General,* 6 U. FLA. J. L. & PUB. POL'Y 1, 3 (1993).

14. Robert L. Misner, *Recasting Prosecutorial Discretion,* 86 J. CRIM. L. & CRIMINOLOGY 717, 734 (1996).

15. Recent examples of district attorney and attorney general races featuring "tough on crime" campaign themes with little detail on office policies include Suffolk County, New York. *See* Rick Brand, *Democrats Bank on Anti-Catterson Theme,* NEWSDAY (Suffolk ed.), June 5, 1997, at A34; Jefferson Parish, La.: Drew Broach, *Jeff DA Candidates Spent Big, Owe Big,* TIMES-PICAYUNE, Jan. 16, 1997, at B1; Buffalo, N.Y.: Robert J. McCarthy, *In Presidential Year, Two House Races Hold Local Interest,* BUFFALO NEWS, Oct. 30, 1996, at 1F; Pennsylvania: Peter J. Shelly, *Fisher Exaggerates His Experience, Kohn Claims,* PITT. POST-GAZETTE, Oct. 26, 1996, at C1; Albuquerque, N.M.: Arley Sanchez, *DA Faces Ex-cop in Election,* ALBUQUERQUE J., Sept. 26, 1996, at 1; and Baton Rouge, La.: Angela Simoneaux, *DA Candidates for Crime Prevention,* BATON ROUGE ADVOCATE, Aug. 30, 1996, at 1B. Daniel C. Richman writes: "Many elections for chief prosecutor are not even contested. Those that are may be fought on whether a specific type of crime should be prosecuted, whether a murderer deserves execution, or on the loss of a high-profile case, as well as on an office's overall win-loss record. Individual referenda on the broad range of discretionary choices that every prosecutor makes are unlikely, indeed utterly impossible"; *Old Chief v. United States: Stipulating Away Prosecutorial Accountability?,* 83 VA. L. REV. 939, 963–64 (1997); *see also* Misner, *id.* at 772–73 (noting that barely 12 percent of prosecutors' offices have written guidelines, leaving the public with little basis for judging prosecutors' effectiveness).

16. See *infra* chapter 1 for a discussion of this model.

17. For example, one commentator noted: "The reality is that nearly all . . . decisions to prosecute or not to prosecute . . . and nearly all his reasons for decisions are carefully kept secret, so that review by the electorate is nonexistent except for the occasional case that happens to be publicized. The plain fact is that more than nine-tenths of local prosecutors' decisions are supervised or reviewed by no one." *See* KENNETH CULP DAVIS, DISCRETIONARY JUSTICE: A PRELIMINARY INQUIRY 190, 207–8 (1969); *see also* Donald

G. Gifford, *Meaningful Reform of Plea Bargaining: The Control of Prosecutorial Discretion*, 1983 U. ILL. L. REV. 37, 54 (discussing the public's lack of access to information about plea bargaining); Richman, *supra* note 15 at 963 (1997) ("[E]ven direct elections are not likely to prove an effective means of giving prosecutors guidance as to a community's enforcement priorities or of holding them accountable for the discretionary decisions that they have already made.").

18. *See* JOAN E. JACOBY, THE AMERICAN PROSECUTOR: A SEARCH OF IDENTITY 22 (1980); Abraham S. Goldstein, *Prosecution: History of the Public Prosecutor*, in 3 ENCYCLOPEDIA OF CRIME AND JUSTICE 1287 (Sanford H. Kadish ed., 1983).

19. 28 U.S.C. § 503 (1994).

20. *Id.* at § 541(a).

21. *Id.* at § 542(a).

22. *See* Bruce A. Green, *Policing Federal Prosecutors: Do Too Many Regulators Produce Too Little Enforcement?*, 8 ST. THOMAS L. REV. 69, 70 (1995) (noting that "evidence of prosecutorial misconduct, particularly in federal cases, may be difficult to obtain") (*citing* Joseph F. Lawless & Kenneth E. North, *Prosecutorial Misconduct*, TRIAL, Oct. 1984, at 28). *But see* Bill Moushey, *Out of Control Legal Rules Have Changed Allowing Federal Agents, Prosecutors to Bypass Basic Rights*, PITT. POST-GAZETTE, Nov. 22, 1998, at A1 (investigating federal agents and prosecutors who fabricated evidence).

23. *Morrison v. Olsen*, 487 U.S. 654, 732 (1988).

24. U.S. presidents may not serve more than two terms. U.S. CONST. amend. XXII, § 1.

25. Because the District of Columbia is not a state, local and federal crimes are prosecuted by the U.S. Attorney for the District of Columbia. D.C. CODE ANN. § 23-101 (1998).

26. Christopher Drew & Steve Daley, *Washington Mayor Arrested in Videotaped Cocaine Sting*, L.A. DAILY NEWS, Jan. 19, 1990, at N1, 1990 WL 5589890.

27. Barry was charged with fourteen counts of drug possession, conspiracy, and lying about drug activity to a grand jury. After a two-month trial, a federal jury convicted Barry of one count of cocaine possession, acquitted him of another count of possession, and deadlocked on the remaining twelve drug and perjury counts. Mike Folks & Matt Neufeld, *Mistrial: Jurors Falter on Twelve of Fourteen Counts*, WASH. TIMES, Aug. 11, 1990, at A1, LEXIS News Library.

28. *See, e.g.*, Barton Gellman, *For the U.S. Attorney, Life Goes On; Stephens Finds Himself Locally Loathed, Federally Respected*, WASH. POST, Aug. 14, 1990, at A7; Jill Nelson, *Backlash over Barry Case; Many Blacks Wrestling with Ambivalence*, WASH. POST, June 9, 1990, at A1; Tracy Thompson & Saundra

Torry, *Barry Arrest Tosses Stephens into the Perils of Politics; Public Interest, Need to Protect Case Clash*, WASH. POST, Jan. 26, 1990, at A1.

29. After he completed his prison term, Barry was elected to the city council in Washington, D.C., in 1992, elected mayor for a second term in 1994, and reelected to the city council in 2004. *See* www.dccouncil .washington.dc.us/BARRY/about/default.htm.

30. D.C. CODE ANN. § 23-101 (1998). The District of Columbia is unique in its status as a city that is not part of any state government and has no local or state prosecutor. Thus, the U.S. attorney for the District of Columbia prosecutes local and federal crimes. Had the case been prosecuted by a locally elected prosecutor, there might have been more responsiveness to the public disapproval.

31. *Morrison v. Olsen*, 487 U.S. 654, 729 (1988) (Scalia, J., dissenting).

32. *See* Tom Raum, *Bush, "Bill, You're Not Going to Win This," He Declares*, ARIZ. REPUBLIC, Nov. 3, 1992, at A1 (describing Bush's major campaign themes); David Shribman & Jill Abramson, *Winds of Change: Clinton Wins Handily as Democrats Reclaim Broad-Based Coalition*, WALL ST. J., Nov. 4, 1992, at A1 (noting former president George H. W. Bush's campaign themes of experience and honesty).

33. One can only speculate about whether the outcome would have been different with an unpopular prosecution in a jurisdiction other than the District of Columbia—where the residents always vote for the Democratic presidential candidate and have no voting representation in the U.S. Congress. *See generally* Jamin Raskin, *Is This America? The District of Columbia and the Right to Vote*, 34 HARV. C.R.-C.L. L. REV. 39 (1999) (arguing that District of Columbia residents have a constitutional right to voting representation in Congress).

34. *See* United States Elections Project, "Voter Turnout," http://elections .gmu.edu, for 2004 election turnout information. *See also* Fair Vote, Voting and Democracy Research Center, "Voter Turnout, www.fairvote.org, for election turnout information generally. In the 2004 general presidential election, the national average election turnout rate for the voting age population was 60.7 percent (projected). In the 2002 general presidential election, the national average turnout rate was 40 percent. In 2002, the voter turnout in West Virginia was 32 percent, whereas the turnout in South Dakota was 62 percent. The rate varied by state.

35. *See* Roscoe C. Howard, Jr., *Wearing a Bull's Eye: Observations on the Differences Between Prosecuting for a United States Attorney's Office and an Office of Independent Counsel*, 29 STETSON L. REV. 95, 141 (1999) (asserting that U.S. attorneys have significant discretion and often spend a disproportionate amount of time and money on cases involving celebrities or notorious conduct); Brett M. Kavanaugh, *The President and the Independent Counsel*, 86 GEO.

L.J. 2133, 2142 n. 27 (1998) (describing high-profile public corruption cases to which the Justice Department has devoted extraordinary resources).

36. Not everyone thought the charges were trivial. Tracy Thompson & Michael York, *U.S. Won't Seek Second Barry Trial, Stephens Says He'll Push for Tougher Sentence*, WASH. POST, Sept. 18, 1990, at A1. United States attorney Stephens noted that the jury "in rendering a guilty verdict on one count, has held Mr. Barry responsible for his criminal conduct. He must now accept responsibility for that criminal conduct." Gellman, *supra* note 28, at A7. Stephens went on to say that "Mr. Barry was held accountable for abusing the public trust as a public official." *Id. See also* Linda P. Campbell, *Marion Barry Gets Six Months on Drug Conviction*, CHI. TRIB., Oct. 27, 1990, at 1. Judge Penfield Jackson, in handing down Barry's sentence, noted that "his breach of public trust alone warrants an enhanced sentence" and that Barry's mayoral position was "of greatest significance" when he determined the severity of his sentence. *Id.*

37. Then–attorney general Richard Thornburgh refused to provide an estimated cost of the investigation. "I don't think we put a pricetag on justice," he said. Michael Isikoff, *Thornburgh Denies Justice Department Singles Out Black Officials for Prosecution*, WASH. POST, July 12, 1990, at A16. Other law enforcement officials estimate the cost at between $2 million and $3 million. *Id.* Barry claimed the cost was $50 million. Steve Twomey, *Barry's $50 Million Question; Mayor's Claim Would Make His Case the Costliest in Recent History*, WASH. POST, Aug. 7, 1990, at B1.

38. Barry was convicted of one misdemeanor charge of cocaine possession, found not guilty of a second charge of cocaine possession, and acquitted of all other charges, including the cocaine offense that was recorded on videotape. Mike Folks & Matt Neufeld, *Mistrial: Jurors Falter on Twelve of Fourteen Counts*, WASH. TIMES, Aug. 11, 1990, at A1.

39. The budgets for each U.S. attorney's office are allocated by the Department of Justice, whose budget is approved by the U.S. Congress. 28 U.S.C. § 548 (1994). Citizens of a particular U.S. attorney's district would ordinarily express disapproval of budgetary expenditures to their senators or other congressional representatives. Since citizens of the District of Columbia have no voting representation in Congress, one might speculate that the result may have been different in another jurisdiction. However, one is hard pressed to discover examples of citizens expressing disapproval of the budgetary allocations in a particular U.S. attorney's office.

40. *See* Kavanaugh, *supra* note 35, at 2142 n. 27 (noting examples of costly cases involving well-known figures).

41. *See* David L. Cook et al., *Criminal Caseload in U.S. District Courts: More Than Meets the Eye*, 44 AM. U. L. REV. 1579, 1594–95 (1995) (asserting that increasing federal budgets allow agencies to conduct more investigations and initiate an increasing number of prosecutions).

42. The public may or may not approve of such expenditures. The O. J. Simpson prosecution is one example of a local prosecutor devoting immense resources to one case. *See Pricey Proceedings: Tallying the Trial Tab,* 81 A.B.A. J. 34 (1995) (providing a breakdown of the costs in prosecuting the O. J. Simpson criminal trial, according to the Associated Press Human Resources Group, as the following: prosecutorial and investigative expense, $3.6 million; cost of food, security, and shelter for jury, $3 million; sheriff's department expenses, $2.7 million; superior and municipal court costs, $1.9 million; autopsies, $100,000). The public was undoubtedly aware of this fact due to the extraordinary national and international media coverage. It would be difficult to measure the public reaction to the prosecutor's allocation of resources to this case in light of the wide divergence of views about the case. *See generally* Katheryn K. Russell, THE COLOR OF CRIME 47–68 (1998).

43. With the approval of President Clinton, Janet Reno removed all ninety-three U.S. attorneys at the beginning of her tenure as attorney general. *See* Jerry Seper, *Reno Demands Resignations of U.S. Attorneys,* WASH. TIMES, Mar. 24, 1993, at A8 (noting that most of the nation's U.S. attorneys had been appointed by Presidents Reagan and Bush and that the call for their resignations was standard partisan politics); Michael York & Donald P. Baker, *Washington Area to Lose Two High Profile Prosecutors; All U.S. Attorneys Told to Tender Resignations,* WASH. POST, Mar. 24, 1993, at A1 (depicting the removal of the U.S. attorneys as routine for a new administration, while others claimed it could create turmoil within the U.S. attorneys' offices).

44. *See, e.g.,* CAL. CONST. art. V, § 11 (term of four years); MO. CONST. art. V, § 7 (four years); VA. CONST. art. V, § 15 (four years).

45. *See, e.g.,* Gerald G. Ashdown, *Federalism, Federalization, and the Politics of Crime,* 98 W. VA. L. REV. 789, 789–90 (1996) (discussing the history of criminal law and its federalization); Sara Sun Beale, *Too Many and Yet Too Few: New Principles to Define the Proper Limits for Federal Criminal Jurisdiction,* 46 HASTINGS L. J. 979, 981 n. 11 (1995) (acknowledging that only a small number of federal offenses existed prior to the Civil War); Kathleen F. Brickey, *Criminal Mischief: The Federalization of American Criminal Law,* 46 HASTINGS L. J. 1135, 1138 (1995) (discussing the history of criminal law); *see also* Sara Sun Beale, *Reporter's Draft for the Working Group on Principles to Use When Considering the Federalization of Criminal Law,* 46 HASTINGS L. J. 1277, 1278–82 (1995) (tracing the historical evolution and expansion of the federal criminal jurisdiction).

46. *See generally infra* chapter 7.

47. According to the Gallup Poll, 51 percent of Americans get their daily news from local television, 36 percent from national broadcast television, 39 percent from cable news, 27 percent from public television news, 17 percent from National Public Radio, 21 percent from radio talk shows, and 20 percent

from the internet; 44 percent get their daily news from local newspapers and 7 percent from national newspapers. *See* the Gallup Poll, December 2004. *Compare* with findings from the Pew Research Center that put American's daily newspaper readership at 42 percent and daily television news viewership at 40 percent; 29 percent regularly get news from online sources. *See* Pew Research Center, *Online News Audience More Diverse: News Audiences Increasingly Polarized*, June 8, 2004.

48. *See id.*

49. Findings of Neilson Media Research, as reported in *Tube Time Hits Record High*, VARIETY.COM, Sept. 29, 2005.

50. *See* Pew Research Center, *supra* note 47.

51. *Id.*

52. "The [Simpson] trial began on January 23rd 1995 and was televised throughout. More than 90 percent of the American television viewing audience claimed to have watched it and 142 million people listened on radio or watched television as the verdict was delivered. More than 2,000 reporters covered the trial and more than 80 books have been written about it." *See* BBC News, *Infamous Crimes*, at www.bbc.co.uk/crime/caseclosed/simpsoncase .shtml. In June 2005, there were 6,248 combined news segments about the Michael Jackson molestation trial on ABC, CBS, NBC, FOX, CNN, and MSNBC, compared to 126 segments about the genocide in Sudan. *See* American Access Project Fund, www.beawitness.org.

53. *See The State of the News Media 2004*, a report of the Project for Excellence in Journalism, March 15, 2004.

54. The time local television news devoted to crime-related stories increased from 22 percent to 27 percent between 1998 and 2002. *See Local TV News Project—1998* and *Local TV News Project—2002*, Project for Excellence in Journalism. During the same 1998–2002 time frame, reports of crimes nationwide decreased by nearly 4.8 percent. (In 1998, 12,475,634 crimes reported, compared to 11,877,218 in 2002.) *See* FBI UNIFORM CRIME REPORTS, 1998 and 2002.

55. For the week of November 7, 2005, six of the top ten television shows watched were crime-related dramas, as follows: ranked first, *CSI;* fourth, *Without a Trace;* tied for sixth, *CSI: Miami* and *CSI: NY;* ninth, *Cold Case;* and tenth, *NSCI. See* Nielsen Media Research.

56. *See Law and Order: About the Show*, www.nbc.com.

57. *See Law and Order, in* Wikipedia online encyclopedia, http://en .wikipedia.org.

58. *See* Naomi Mezey and Mark C. Niles, *Screening the Law: Ideology and Law in American Popular Culture*, 28 COLUM. J. L. & ARTS 91, 124 (2005) (demonstrating how *Law and Order*'s formula utilizes prosecutorial characters whose sense of justice regularly overcomes their personal and professional

flaws as they prosecute defendants whose culpability is never in doubt, regardless of whether they are ultimately convicted by the court. The formula placates the public by reinforcing a notion that justice is always clear-cut and the prosecutors will be the public's champion even when the courts will not).

59. Films such as *JKF*, *A Few Good Men*, *The Untouchables*, and *Helter Skelter* promote this view of the prosecutor.

60. In the movie *Crash*, a prosecutor, played by Brendan Fraser, is portrayed as someone primarily driven by political ambition. In one scene, he appears to prosecute someone for a murder on the basis of weak evidence in order to further his career.

61. *See* Dawn Keetley, *Law and Order, in* PRIME TIME LAW: FICTIONAL TELEVISION AS LEGAL NARRATIVE 42–44 (R. Jarvis & P.R. Joseph eds., 1998).

62. Quotation from "Misconception," *Law and Order,* episode 28, originally aired Tuesday, October 29, 1991, on NBC, as quoted, *id.* at 43.

63. *See* Keetley, *supra* note 61, at 42–43.

64. *See* Marc Mauer, RACE TO INCARCERATE, 19–22 (2d. ed. 2006) (describing the United States as the second leading country in the world in its rate of incarceration).

10. Prospects for Reform

1. The CPA, 28. U.S.C. § 530B (Supp. IV 1998), discussed in *infra* chapters 6 and 8, was widely opposed by federal prosecutors. *See* Allen Van Fleet, *How Government Lawyers Tilt The Ethical Playing Field*, 13 FALL ANTITRUST 13, 16 (1998) (discussing the opposition from the Justice Department and federal prosecutors to the CPA).

2. *See* discussion, *infra* chapter 7.

3. *Id.*

4. *Id.*

5. *Id.*

6. *See infra* chapter 8.

7. *See* Devin J. Doolan, Jr., *Community Prosecution: A Revolution in Crime Fighting*, 51 CATH. U. L. REV. 547, 551 (2002) (stating that prosecutor offices throughout the United States are rapidly embracing the community prosecution philosophy); Angela J. Davis, *The American Prosecutor: Independence, Power, and the Threat of Tyranny*, 86 IOWA L. REV. 393, 462 (2001) (discussing the recent use of community prosecution in order to involve prosecutors more fully within the communities they serve).

8. H.R. 3396, 105th Cong. (1998); Davis, *supra* note 7.

9. H.R. 3396, 105th Cong. (1998) § 201(a). The offenses include: (1) in the absence of probable cause seek the indictment of any person; (2) fail

promptly to reveal information that would exonerate a person under indictment; (3) intentionally mislead the court as to the guilt of any person; (4)
intentionally or knowingly misstate evidence; (5) intentionally or knowingly
alter evidence; (6) attempt to influence or color a witness' testimony; (7) act to
frustrate or impede a defendant's right to discovery; (8) offer or provide any
sexual activities to any government witness or potential witness; (9) leak or
otherwise improperly disseminate information to any person during an investigation; (10) engage in conduct that discredits the department. *Id.*

10. *Id.* § 201(b).

11. *See, e.g.,* David Cole, No EQUAL JUSTICE (1999); Marc Mauer, RACE
TO INCARCERATE (2d ed. 2006); *Developments in the Law—Race and the Criminal
Process,* 101 HARV. L. REV. 1475 (1988) (examining the problem of race
discrimination within the criminal justice system); Rebecca Marcus, *Racism in
Our Courts: The Underfunding of Public Defenders and Its Disproportionate Impact
upon Racial Minorities,* 22 HASTINGS CONST. L. Q. 219 (1994) (discussing the
disadvantages that racial minorities face in the criminal justice system due to
inadequate resources of public defender services); Mark D. Rosenbaum, *No
Equal Justice: Race and Class in the Criminal Justice System,* 98 MICH. L. REV.
1941 (2000) (discussing the "massive and flagrant abuses" of law enforcement
officers and their disparate effect on racial minorities); Milton Hume & Lance
Cassak, GOOD COP, BAD COP, RACIAL PROFILING AND COMPETING VIEWS OF
JUSTICE IN AMERICA (2003) (discussing the impact of the practice of profiling
on racial and ethnic minorities); RACIAL ISSUES IN CRIMINAL JUSTICE: THE
CASE OF AFRICAN AMERICANS (Marvin D. Free ed., 2003) (discussing the
enormous racial disparities in the criminal justice system).

12. Stephen B. Bright, *Discrimination, Death, and Denial: The Tolerance of
Racial Discrimination in Infliction of the Death Penalty,* 35 SANTA CLARA L. REV.
433, 438–39 (1995) (stating that federal and state courts have either failed to
provide adequate remedies for racial discrimination or set legal standards of
proof that are impossible to meet); Reenah L. Kim, *Legitimizing Community
Consent to Local Policing: The Need for Democratically Negotiated Community
Representation on Civilian Advisory Counsels,* 36 HARV. C.R.-C.L. L. REV. 461,
462 (2001) (stating that judicial intervention of racial discrimination in law
enforcement has not adequately addressed the "troubling consequences of
police discretion").

13. *See U.S. v. Armstrong,* 517 U.S. 456, 462 (1996) (holding that a
defendant must meet a high evidentiary burden suggesting a constitutional
violation based on selective prosecution in order for a judge to permit discovery on that issue); *McCleskey v. Kemp,* 481 U.S. 279, 297 (1987) (holding
that statistical evidence suggesting that the death penalty disproportionately
affected African Americans is not sufficient to demonstrate a discriminatory
purpose by the prosecuting attorney).

14. *Armstrong*, 517 U.S. at 462 (requiring a high evidentiary burden of proof for selective prosecution claims).

15. *See Berger v. United States*, 295 U.S. 78, 88 (1935); MODEL CODE OF PROF'L RESPONSIBILITY EC 7-13 ("The responsibility of a public prosecutor differs from that of the usual advocate; his duty is to seek justice, not merely to convict."); MODEL RULES OF PROF'L CONDUCT R. 3.8 cmt. (1983) (describing a prosecutor's responsibilities "to see that [a] defendant is accorded procedural justice and that guilt is decided upon the basis of sufficient evidence"); STANDARDS RELATING TO THE ADMIN. OF CRIMINAL JUSTICE Standard 3-1.2(c) (1992) ("The duty of the prosecutor is to seek justice, not merely to convict.").

16. Fred C. Zacharias, *Structuring the Ethics of Prosecutorial Trial Practice: Can Prosecutors Do Justice?*, 44 VAND. L. REV. 45, 57 (1991).

17. *See* MODEL CODE OF PROF'L RESPONSIBILITY EC 8-1; *see also.* EC 8-9 ("The advancement of our legal system is of vital importance in maintaining the rule of law and in facilitating orderly changes; therefore, lawyers should encourage, and should aid in making, needed changes and improvements."); MODEL RULES OF PROF'L CONDUCT pmbl. ("A lawyer should be mindful of deficiencies in the administration of justice"); STANDARDS RELATING TO THE ADMIN. OF CRIMINAL JUSTICE Standard 3-1.2(d) ("It is an important function of the prosecutor to seek to reform and improve the administration of criminal justice. When inadequacies or injustices in the substantive or procedural law come to the prosecutor's attention, he or she should stimulate efforts for remedial action.").

18. For purposes of the report, "similarly situated" defendants would have committed the same criminal act and have similar criminal histories. "Similarly situated" victims would have the same level of interest in prosecution and similar criminal histories. Other characteristics of either the defendant or the victim (wealth, education, jury appeal, etc.) should not be relevant to the prosecutor's calculus, as they would involve discriminatory treatment based on subjective, inappropriate criteria.

19. The prosecutor should not use conviction and sentencing rates as evidence of criminality, as the Supreme Court did in *Armstrong*. As Justice Stevens noted in his dissent in *Armstrong*, conviction and sentencing rates only reflect the number of individuals prosecuted and sentenced for certain crimes, not necessarily the number of individuals who committed these crimes. *Armstrong*, 517 U.S. at 482 (Stevens, J., dissenting).

20. *See* detailed discussion of the Baldus study, *infra* chapter 5.

21. 470 U.S. 598, 607 (1985).

22. *See* Charles W. Thomas & W. Anthony Fitch, *Prosecutorial Decision Making*, 13 AM. CRIM. L. REV. 507, 523–24 (1976) (advocating that prosecutors use forms and checklists to record the basis of their charging decisions).

23. The Vera Institute of Justice works closely with leaders in government and civil society to improve the services people rely on for safety and justice. Vera develops innovative, affordable programs that often grow into self-sustaining organizations, studies social problems and current responses, and provides practical advice and assistance to government officials in New York and around the world. www.vera.org.

24. Wayne McKenzie, *Briefing Memo for Advisory Board Meeting in Charlotte,* 1 (December 1, 2005).

25. Paul Morrison participated in the project until he was elected Attorney General in 2006. The Project is exploring alternatives to replace him. Michael McCann decided not to run for re-election in 2006 but will continue to work with the project along with his successor John Chisholm.

INDEX